# A CREATION-ORDER THEODICY

---

## *God and Gratuitous Evil*

---

### Bruce A. Little

**University Press of America,® Inc.**
Lanham · Boulder · New York · Toronto · Oxford

*To Nancy*
*my faithful and loving helpmate*
*to whom I owe much*

# Contents

*Contents*

# Preface

Maybe the most enduring and compelling argument against belief in the existence of the Christian God is the argument from evil. Although at one time many people were shielded from personally observing large scale horrific suffering that is not any longer the case. Distance and geographic location no longer serve as barriers to what we see and hear. It is difficult in the age of images and information to ignore the immense suffering around the world. Our different media screens confront us with images of starving children, horrific acts of terrorism and the destruction of natural disasters. On September 11, 2001 many watched the collapse of the Trade Towers in real time on their televisions, startling the viewer with horror and creating questions within. Viewing such enormous events of suffering creates not only angst, but a cry from within for some reasonable explanation. Often, in the midst of such events, it is common to call out to God, either to help or ask why He allowed it. Because the Church is the guardian of the knowledge of God, Christians are often the target of the "why" question. People usually do not raise questions regarding why there is some evil, but why is it that an all-knowing, all-powerful, all-loving God does not stop such horrific suffering as the Holocaust. Surely God could do that without sacrificing some greater good.

These questions surrounding suffering cannot be ignored by the Christian. Christians claim that the Christian Faith provides a worldview by which man can properly understand his world. It gives a framework for answering the tough questions of life. The Christian faith consists of a network of beliefs and forms a Christian worldview. This means that however the Christian answers the argument from evil, that answer must be consistent with other essential Christian beliefs. The Christian's task is not only to answer the argument from evil, but to do so in a way that avoids compromising other essential doctrines of the Christian Faith. And however one responds to this argument, he will soon find that it has implications for almost every major doctrine of the Christian faith.

Historically, the Church has answered the argument from evil with some form of a Greater-Good theodicy. This theodicy maintains that God is morally justified in permitting evil in this world because He only allows that evil from which he can bring about a greater good or prevent a worse evil. This means that there is no gratuitous evil, that all evil/suffering has a purpose designed by God. This position unnecessarily raises serious questions for the theist. Many attempts have been made recently to answer these questions by explaining evidentially how the good is obtained. But by all appearances these explanations have failed. I think this was made clear after September 11, 2001. The Church stuttered in responding to the cry for answers. Eventually, the world stopped asking. This was unfortunate for both the world and the Church. I will argue that the reason the answers were so weightless was because they were grounded in the Greater-Good theodicy which is flawed at its foundation.

The purpose of this book is twofold. The first is to give an historical context for understanding the importance and development of a theodicy. The second is to show the weaknesses of Greater-Good theodicies and to offer a theodicy that affirms both the providence of God and the existence of gratuitous evil. The proposed theodicy is named the Creation-Order theodicy because it is constructed upon an understanding the divine ordering as part of creation that was necessary for the infinite God to have a meaningful relationship with finite man. This ordering established how God would interact with His creation in general and man in particular. By this, God chose to limit the expression of some of His attributes in order to make it possible that man could function as a true moral being.

God's creation order takes into account the necessary arrangement that makes it possible for Him to have a meaningful relationship with finite man. This is a relationship where God's love is directed towards man and where man can freely respond to that love. This possibility is predicated upon the fact that man loving God is the highest function of mankind (Matt. 22:34-40). The Creation-Order theodicy affirms the providence of God in the affairs of men, yet allows for gratuitous evil but in such a way that it does not count against either the goodness and/or power of God. In doing so, this theodicy removes the burden of proof required by Greater-Good theodicies to demonstrate that the good *always* obtains—an almost impossible task. The Creation-Order theodicy maintains that it is not necessary to posit some good as moral justification for God's allowing certain evils occur. Rather it maintains that according to the creation order some evils occur because man has the power of moral choice. Bad choices result in bad consequences, however, they never threaten the counsels of God. God has not promised to stop all gratuitous evil (but His has assured the end), therefore there is no reason to build a theodicy on the assumption that He has.

Once gratuitous evil is acknowledged by the theist, the argument from evil is deprived of the strongest point.

This proposed theodicy owes much to other theologians and philosophers who have wrestled with the argument from evil. The fact remains that any advancement in the understanding of the argument from evil by today's theologians and philosophers owes much to those Christian scholars who have struggled with the problem in the past. With this debt in mind and full awareness of my own limitations the Creation-Order theodicy is offered as an alternative to the Greater-Good theodicy. If it is right, it is no longer incumbent upon the theist to try to demonstrate that good always comes from all evil/suffering.

Bruce Little
Wake Forest, North Carolina
May 2004

# Acknowledgments

I want to express my appreciation for those who have interacted with me on many of the complicated issues regarding the problem of evil. I want to thank L. Russ Bush for his guidance during my doctoral dissertation because a major portion of this book is based on my dissertation. I am also grateful for the students who have participated in the class on the problem of evil I have taught for three years at Southeastern Baptist Theological Seminary. Their questions and insights have helped crystallize some of my thinking on this subject. Finally, I would like to thank Anna Fishel for her editing expertise and Mark Walton for making sure the manuscript adhered to the proper form. While I am grateful for all the help I have received, I alone bear the responsibility for the content. Any mistakes or shortcomings are mine.

# Chapter 1

# Why Have A Theodicy?

On the clear autumn morning of September 11, 2001 America was abruptly confronted by the truth many had desperately endeavored to deny—that evil exists. Stunned by the enormity of the act and the uncertainty of its scope, America briefly acknowledged another unwanted truth—the existence of God. In a very small window of recent history, America acknowledged both the existence of evil and the existence of God. The first was undeniable and the second seemed indispensable, but how the two fit together once again raised the age old question: If God is all powerful and all good, how is it that evil of this magnitude could exist in a world created and maintained by God?

For a brief time the nation looked to religion for some explanation of how God fit into all of this mayhem in order that there might be a reasonable hope found in God. Unfortunately, what was heard was a mixture of appeals to mystery, charges of judgment, and promises of some greater good that would obtain because of it. In the end, the religious questions abated and a mantra expressing a secular hope swelled across the land. Disappointed by the religious confusion and theological ambiguity, America turned its hope to rebuilding through a united human effort thereby abandoning the inquiry about God and his relation to evil. It seemed reasonable that if the Church had no definitive answer to this question of evil, then it was quite possible that man was alone in the universe and belief in God was only a psychological pacifier for times of human angst but said nothing about the world in which man lives. It appeared that if one had to choose between acknowledging the reality of one or the other, evil would win and as a consequence the God question would either be dismissed or reserved only for personal religious talk.

Of course, this was not the first time the Christian community tried to defend God's existence against objections based on some horrific evil. One is reminded of the days of St. Augustine when Rome was invaded by the barbarians and Augustine attempted to harmonize the reality of the existence of evil and the claim for the existence of God. For Augustine, God allowed into this world only that evil from which

He could bring about a greater good or prevent a worse evil. This explanation, now known as the Greater-Good (G-G) theodicy,[1] became the working model by which most Christians thereafter would attempt a response to the argument from evil. The G-G theodicy, however, has not only proven to be unconvincing, it has in fact committed the theist to a very questionable position that unnecessarily requires him to prove more than is possible.

## A SYNOPSIS OF THE G-G THEODICY

The existence of evil (or suffering)[2] in a world created by the all-powerful, all-good, all-knowing God[3], *prima facie*, appears to present both logical and evidential contradictions. If the contradictions were real, they would seemingly make it impossible to reconcile the existence of evil with the existence of this all-powerful, all-good, all-knowing God, thus requiring the denial of one or the other, or perhaps some redefinition of either or both. Classical theism has viewed these two options as unacceptable. Historically, theism has attempted to offer some justificatory framework by which the existence of the all-knowing, all-powerful, all-good God is reconciled with the existence of evil. Most often, theodicies are constructed to answer the evidential argument from evil and not the logical argument.

Theists, at least since the time of Augustine, have most often responded to the evidential argument from evil by claiming that all evil in the world could be justified on grounds that God permits only that evil from which He can bring a greater good or prevent some greater evil. Such justificatory models have been referred to as G-G theodicies.[4] Furthermore, as Michael Peterson notes, the "Greater-Good Theodicy is, so to speak, the 'parent', and many particular theodicies are its 'offspring'."[5] Furthermore, he notes that some notion of the greater good is "integral to their [theists] search for a morally sufficient reason why God allows evil."[6]

G-G theodicies share certain basic tenets, while evidencing diversity with respect to the particulars. For example, they may differ in what should be understood as the good that obtains, or they may give different explanations as to *how* and *when* the good obtains. All of them, however, share two basic tenets that have made them highly susceptible to criticism. The first is that they deny the existence of gratuitous evil.[7] This necessarily flows from the initial assumption that all evil allowed by God is justified on the grounds that from it He brings forth a greater good. This assumption is necessitated by a particular application of God's sovereignty which maintains that everything in this life has a purpose precisely because God is sovereign. If any suffering could be determined as pointless (gratuitous), then God must not be sovereign and there would be some suffering from which a good did not obtain. Furthermore, if some good did not obtain, then the greater-good moral justification for God allowing the evil would collapse.

Clearly, at the heart of G-G theodicies lies the denial of gratuitous evil. Therefore, the theist, in order to maintain his G-G theodicy, must affirm that some greater good obtains in all cases and subsequently deny the existence of gratuitous evil in any case. In light of such a claim, however, suffering as encountered by those who experienced the Holocaust makes it difficult to argue that all the suffering, individually and collectively, serves a greater good. That is, making the claim that God was morally justified in allowing the horrific suffering because He would use the Holocaust to bring about a greater good creates a credibility problem for the theist. Such a claim is impossible to prove evidentially. In an attempt to protect God's character by denying gratuitous evil, it raises other serious questions about the character of the God who claims to be no respecter of persons.

Furthermore, in denying gratuitous evil the greater-good moral justificatory scheme also suggests that evil might be allowed because by it God prevents a worse evil. However, this creates at least two difficulties for the theist. First, it suggests that God is not omnipotent. If God were omnipotent, He would not be dependent on one evil in order to prevent a worse evil. This would make at least some evils necessary to the prevention of other evils. When applied to the Holocaust, for example, one would wonder just what the worse evil might be. The second difficulty with this position is that it is really meaningless. Once again, it is impossible to know whether such a claim is true or not. To know this evidentially would require the evil actually to occur and then be defeated. If it occurred, then it was not defeated. If it were permitted to obtain and then God changed what had happened to be as if it had not happened, then God would have the power to change the past. Even if that were possible—and I think it is not—then surely one who could change the past would be powerful enough to defeat a greater evil without using a lesser evil. Furthermore, the theist has no propositional statement in the Bible that affirms God uses lesser evils to prevent worse evils. Therefore, denying gratuitous evil, which is intended to protect the character of God (particularly his sovereignty) in the end, accomplishes just the opposite and raises serious questions for the G-G theodicy as a whole.

The second debatable tenet of G-G theodicies is a corollary of the first. If the good obtains in all cases, then on what basis is such a claimed offered? The theist, it seems, has two possible answers at this point. One would be to point to some propositional statement in the Bible that confirms the claim.[8] Unfortunately, for the proponents of G-G theodicies, no such statement exists. The other approach involves providing evidence from life that supports the claim. In fact, a review of the literature on this subject reveals that this is precisely what the theist attempts to do. He tries to support this basic assumption of his theodicy inductively. It is not to say that there may not be situations where one can point to some good obtaining from a particular evil. It is insufficient, however, for the theist to show that a good obtains from a particular evil, although this may be rather easy to do in some cases and most atheists would agree that in some cases this may be true. However, this would not establish that in *all* cases one would be justified in claiming the good obtained, and yet that is precisely what the G-G theodicy requires.

One must understand the enormity of the task before the theist, who wishes to prove his greater good scheme. Whereas he claims that *all* evil in this world is allowed by God for the purpose of bringing about a greater good, the theist must prove that it is so in *every* case. Unfortunately, there are many events of suffering where there is no confirming evidence that any greater good or some good obtained. The theist at this point claims that God did bring about a good but that it is not visible to human perception. It is reasonable to assume that on certain occasions this might be the case. That is, the human observer, being limited in knowledge and awareness, simply fails to see the good that obtained. If the theist only had to appeal to this argument on rare occasions, then it might very well be allowed. Regrettably (for the theist), it is more often than not the case, especially where the suffering is either of gargantuan proportions, such as the Holocaust, or when it involves innocents such as children.[9] The fact is that the empirical evidence that the good always obtains is scarce at best and suspect at worse, and yet it forms a major plank in the G-G theodicy.

In order for the theist to raise the G-G theodicy to a more defensible posture, he must show that in *most* cases the good obtains, especially in situations where the human suffering appears so odious to the moral sensibilities of humanity. In fact, here they should be able to demonstrate the good obtains in all such cases. Yet, it is precisely such episodes of human experience that the theist must confess that he cannot produce the evidence that would support his claim that the good always obtains. Furthermore, in the absence of the preponderance of evidence, typically the theist moves to a deductive argument—God is sovereign, therefore the good *must* obtain. But this is an inferential argument and, in order for it to have some compelling power, it must have sufficient indisputable warrant on which the conclusion is made from the evidence. It will be argued in the following pages that the warrant is lacking and so the conclusion fails. This does not mean that the work of theodicy should be abandoned, only that the theist must find more convincing grounds on which to answer the argument from evil.

## THE OCCASION FOR THE ARGUMENT

It is not the existence of evil in and of itself, but the fact that evil exists in a world created by the all-good, all-powerful Christian God that creates the moral dilemma for the theist. According to C. S. Lewis, the claim that God exists "creates rather than solves the problem of pain, for pain would be no problem unless, side by side with our daily experience of this painful world, we had received what we think a good assurance that ultimate reality is righteous and loving."[10] Or as Vladimir Lossky writes, "Evil as a problem thus stems necessarily from Christianity."[11] Furthermore, it is not that there is *some* evil in the world that gives rise to the argument from evil, but that there is so much suffering. So often the human experience painfully reminds us that suffering tends to be unequally distributed as well as the fact that often it is the innocent and the righteous who suffer. That innocent children suffer was precisely the point made by Fyodor Dostoevsky in *The Brothers Karamazov* and Albert Camus in *The Plague*. One also finds the perplexing phenomena of the righteous suffering in the Bible in the book of *Job*. In light of such confounding phenomena, the theist has more often than not felt compelled to develop a theodicy to explain how God is morally justified in permitting the continuance of such suffering in the world of which He is both creator and sustainer. In so many cases, such horrific suffering has all the appearance of being without purpose or gratuitous.

David Basinger points out that, in fact, gratuitous evil seems to be the most difficult issue within the evidential argument from evil.[12] Peterson writes with agreement, "The evidential argument from gratuitous evil is now widely considered the most formidable objection to theistic belief."[13] The primary reason gratuitous evil is so formidable that most theodicies claim all evil obtains some greater good and this seems difficult to understand when some of the horrific evils are considered.

As already noted, many theists simply deny that gratuitous evil exists by contending that certain evils only 'appear' to be gratuitous. This position flows from the assumption that God is all-knowing, all-good and all-powerful, and that his sovereign providence insures that everything that happens in his creation has its purpose (called meticulous providence). The question that remains, however, is whether classical theism as a whole necessarily requires the theist to deny gratuitous evil in order to preserve God's ontological integrity. In the pages that follow it will be argued that it is neither theologically aberrant nor philosophically inconsistent to claim gratuitous evil exists while affirming that God is all-knowing, all-good all-powerful, and sovereign.

## THE NATURE OF THE ARGUMENT

The argument from evil has been cast in at least two forms or versions. Peterson identifies these as, "(t)he problems of consistency and gratuity."[14] There are those who think that the problem of consistency, which is a logical problem,[15] has recently been put to rest by Alvin Plantinga.[16] Even if this is so, Plantinga agrees that it still leaves the problem of gratuity unresolved. He acknowledges that "an *a posteriori* argument from evil may be given. The atheologian might hold, for example, that we actually find certain kinds of evil that no good state of affairs, no matter how impressive, could possibly outweigh—severe, protracted, and involuntary human pain for example."[17] In the end, however, Plantinga concludes that the most the evidential argument does for the atheologian is that it "provides *him* with a decisive reason for believing that God does not exist; but he could hardly claim that the *theist* is involved in any difficulty here."[18] While Plantinga's point is well taken, it is still important to demonstrate that the theist is not just rational in his belief in God's existence, but to that the argument from evil does not count against the belief that God exists. Even if Plantinga's point is correct, there are still important evidential questions that require an answer from the theist.

This leads to the second version of the argument from evil, which is the one that Peterson identifies as the problem of gratuity. It is also known as the evidential argument or the probability argument. This version argues that in light of the kind and extent of suffering in this world, it is more likely that God does not exist than He does exist. The question is whether or not the evil that appears gratuitous is, in fact, gratuitous. And if it is gratuitous, then does that count conclusively against God's power and goodness? As Edward Madden and Peter Hare suggest, "The really interesting problem of evil is whether the apparent gratuity can be explained away by more ingenious measures or whether the gratuity is real and hence detrimental to religious belief."[19] The assumption of the G-G theodicies is that if gratuitous evil exists, it would seriously challenge the claim that an all-good, all-powerful, all-knowing, sovereign God exists. So, the adherents of the G-G theodicy claim gratuitous evil does not exist because it cannot exist for, if it exists, then God is neither all-powerful nor sovereign over His creation.

A general survey of suffering experienced by mankind, however, seems to indicate a contrary conclusion, not that God is not sovereign but that gratuitous evil exists. The weight of the evidence for gratuitous evil is such that it escapes the principle of indifference. A general principle of life is that what seems to be usually is, unless there is strong and sufficient independent evidence to the contrary. Given this, at least from an evidential point of view, it seems reasonable to identify much suffering in this life for what it appears to be—namely pointless. At this juncture, the theist is confronted with a choice. Either the theist must deny what seems obvious and claim that gratuitous evil is only in appearance, not in reality, or he must find a way to reconcile the existence of gratuitous evil with the providence of God. The latter alternative appears to offer the greatest promise for the theist. Without something on this order, evil will continue as a strong defeater for any claim that God exists. This would, however, require the theist to abandon the G-G theodicy, which would arguably place the theist in a stronger defensive position. Stronger because it can be argued that the G-G theodicy inadvertently strengthens the atheist's position.

Unquestionably, the strength of the evidential argument from evil has been abetted by the theist's greater good response. By grounding the argument in the assumption that God is morally justified in permitting evil in this world because from it He brings a greater good, places the onus squarely on the theist. Even if the theist does not initiate the response on evidential grounds, he opens himself up to at least being expected to give some supporting evidence. It is predictable that the atheist would ask to see the good that obtained as the G-G theodicy implies that it can be verified evidentially. After all, if God is at work bringing good from the all too obvious evil, surely the good ought to be equally visible. The fact is, it is not. In the absence of such compelling evidence, it seems that the atheist's objection maintains its force. This, however, does not mean that a person should give up his belief that God exists, nor his personal commitment to God, as he may have other reasons that counterbalance the evidence from evil. As is so often the case, the problem does not lie in the facts but rather in the explanatory system crafted to interpret the facts.

In addition to the concerns already raised, there are theological implications associated with the G-G theodicy. For example, is the good a necessary good (that is, necessary to the plan of God) or only an incidental good? If it is a necessary good, can that good be obtained apart from the evil from which it comes? If the good is necessary and logically bound to the evil, then it logically follows that the antecedent evil is also necessary. This raises questions of God's relationship to and dependence on evil for certain goods in this world. That is, does God need evil to accomplish some good? And if more good makes a better world, then does it logically follow that more evil is actually better, as in each case the good outweighs the evil making a net gain of good? Furthermore, how should one understand the purpose of the Incarnation—did Jesus really come to destroy evil? Or consider the question of social justice. If evil is necessary to the good, should Christians attempt to stop evil? If certain evils are stopped, would that mean that certain goods would never obtain? These are only a few of the questions that must be—and will be—considered in judging the theological implications of G-G theodicies and, hence, their theological integrity as well as their practical sufficiency.

In addition, there is a question regarding the basic principle under-girding G-G theodicies. Although adherents to the G-G theodicies strenuously argue to the contrary, it seems hard to avoid the conclusion that such theodicies make the consequent the justification of the antecedent (what is referred to as the end justifying the means). To suggest, however, that God allows moral evil (the antecedent) because it brings about some good (the consequent) means either one of two things: (1) God is not able to bring about the good without the evil; or (2) God has planned evil in order to bring about the good. Either way, it seems that the character of God is compromised. If (1), then there is something that God cannot do, namely bring about some (not all) good without using evil, and if (2), then the goodness of God is questioned as it makes evil necessarily planned by God. It must be added, however, that there is no denial here that it is possible for God to use *some* evil to bring about a good, but that is quite different from suggesting that *all* evil brings about a good. Further, it could be argued (and will be) that in many cases where a good obtains, it is in spite of, not because of, the evil in a mediate sense.

## CLARIFICATION OF TERMS

It is important to understand what is and is not being discussed in these pages and how certain terms or concepts are being used. Although there may not be universal agreement with the definitions given, the purpose here is to acquaint the reader with the definitions of words/concepts as used in this book. At the very least, this should minimize confusion even if it does not produce universal agreement. From this, one can more easily determine (for those who will critique this position) whether the argument itself or the definitions used in the argument present the point of controversy.

## Free will

This term carries baggage that proves unnecessarily confusing and requires too many qualifications in order to convey its exact meaning. Therefore, the term/phrase of choice here will be "power of moral choice" as it expresses what has been commonly understood by "free will", but without the possible confusion. To affirm that the will is free is difficult to defend, if used in the sense of indeterminism. In the phrase power of moral choice; the word power signals that man has been given the ability (authority) to make authentic choices from the options permitted within his circumstances. In that way his choices may be limited, but not the authority itself. There are times when he may not actually be able choose because of overpowering circumstances or his choices may be limited, yet he still has the ability itself to choose.

The term "moral," limits the notion of choice to moral beings, such as man, which also entails the notion of judgment as Gottfried Leibniz suggested. This excludes animals, which do seem to have some power of choice, but not *moral* choice, that is, there is no evidence that animals make moral judgments. The word "choice" implies two things; in order for choice to be authentic there must be at least two possibilities that are equal in possibility, but not necessarily in desirability or workability. For example, one may require more energy or sacrifice. Furthermore, there must be corollary consequences for each choice. When taken as a whole, "power of moral choice" affirms that God has given man true ability to choose from two or more possibilities where man can refrain from one and choose the other, authentic possibilities from which to choose which require moral judgment. From each choice certain consequences follow. The consequences may vary, may be direct or indirect, immediate or delayed, and may affect the individual as well as others, but consequences do follow.

## Good

The concept of good has two definitions. One can speak of good in the intrinsic sense. For example, when one says that God is good, the meaning is that whatever else God is, the quality of goodness is always present in his character. Furthermore, even though God's ways are not our ways (Is. 55:8), his view of what is good may not always be clearly understood by man, but it is never contrary to good as revealed in God's word. As Lewis writes, "If God's moral judgment differs from ours so that our 'black' may be His 'white,' we can mean nothing by calling Him good; for to say 'God is good,' while asserting that His goodness is wholly other than ours, is really only to say 'God is we know not what.' And an utterly unknown quality in God cannot give us moral grounds for loving and obeying Him."[20] Therefore, the fact that "God's ways are not our ways" is not justification for using the term good equivocally. This is often a reply heard when someone asks what good obtained from some evil and the reply is that we do not always understand what is good as God does.

The other definition involves good in the sense of something being favorable in a relative sense. That is, S is a favorable state of affairs from the perspective of X; however, from the perspective of Y, it could be an unfavorable state of affairs. For example, it is good for John that he arrived at the store in time to purchase the last Skill Saw on sale. However, it is not good for Paul that John arrived when he did because he also needed the Skill Saw. In this case, good is not something intrinsic to the act. It would not be good from both the perspective of X and Y. However, this is an example of good being a relative evaluative term entirely, in that a certain happening appears favorable to or consistent with an individual's particular desires or needs.

When good is used as a state of affairs issuing out of some 'evil' state of affairs, it may refer to the general state of affairs or some relative good for an individual. However, it cannot mean good in some intrinsic sense. In fact, most often as explained by G-G theodicies, the good is of the relative kind. That is, if the evil happens to an individual, the good is what comes to that individual (or to those whom the individual loves) as a result of God using the evil—a good that could not have come to pass without the antecedent evil. Such a distinction is necessary when discussing G-G theodicies as one can see from the following two statements. It is good (intrinsic sense) not to murder innocent people. On September 11, 2002, several thousand people were murdered in the Trade Tower attack, at least some of whom were innocent, but good (relative sense) came from the event. Surely, the word good is not being used in the same way in both statements. Therefore, when good is used in the G-G theodicies it is good in the relative sense, which seems to have serious ethical implications.

## Evil

Defining evil proves a somewhat difficult task. Everybody seems to know when they have encountered evil, but defining it requires a little more thought, so as not to be so narrow that something fails to be included or to be so broad that everything is included. The attempt here is not so much to define in a particular way but to clarify how the word is used in this context.

Several areas need clarification. First, sin and evil are not being used interchangeably, although it is rather common to do so in theological discussions. Instead, evil is employed to identify that activity (mental or physical) flowing from the fallen*ness* of this world that causes suffering. Therefore, evil and suffering are used interchangeably. The idea of evil includes moral evil—sin; natural evil—famines and the like; and physical evil—disease and the like. Suffering refers to that which stands in opposition to pleasure. While all suffering flows from sin, not all suffering is sin. For example, when one suffers under the discipline of God for an act(s) of disobedience, the suffering caused by God for this reason (Heb. 12: 7–11) would not be sin.

Second, the question addressed in this book is not primarily about *how* evil entered the world. It is generally agreed among theists that giving man the power of moral choice (a good thing) opened the possibility (not the necessity) of sin entering into the world and hence evil (Rom. 12). The more debatable issue centers on the intensity and kind of suffering that is often unequally distributed and continues in a creation over which an all-good, all-powerful, all-knowing God allegedly and providentially presides. It is reasoned that if God is the omnipotent, omniscient one, then at least He could stop the most horrific of evils, if He were truly the omnibenevolent one.

Third, one must avoid arguing from *what* God might do with evil or *how* He might use evil to *why* God allows evil. These are different questions. While the consideration of what God might do with evil (or in spite of evil) legitimately commends itself to the Christian community, it is not the proper way to get to the *why* question. One should not attempt to answer the *why* question from its answer to the *what/how* question. That would be arguing from the ends to justify (not explain) the means. It is one thing to discuss what God might do in spite of evil, but one should not reason backwards and explain the causal notion of evil in terms of its beneficent consequent (if there is such).

The error of such reasoning can be made clear in the following scenario. A Christian girl suffers sexual abuse from her father (the evil). As a result, she has great compassion for other young girls who suffer the same humiliation and abuse. As an adult she goes into social work and helps many young girls (the good). It would seem to be a stretch to argue that God allowed the evil because of the good. The good only continues if other young girls are sexually abused because they are the ones she helps. In order for the good to obtain, other continuing evil is necessary. There is no argument that God may have brought some good to others through the suffering of another; however, it seems theologically convoluted to argue from the *how/what* God might use/do with evil to *why* God allowed the evil.

## Omnipotence

God is Himself and not His opposite. God cannot violate His own nature, and thus He cannot do the logically impossible. The law of non-contradiction does not stand above or apart from God but rather issues from the essence of God. This law expresses something of the true nature of ultimate reality—a thing is what it is and not something else. Therefore, to say that the law of non-contradiction binds God is not to imply that there is something greater than God to which God is a servant. It simply means that the perfection of God's reality is of such a quality that He is not capable of doing that which entails a logical contradiction of Himself. To do so would result in some violence to the harmony of His own essence or, in fact, be destructive to it. As Lewis correctly observes,

> . . . meaningless combinations of words do not suddenly acquire meaning simply because we prefix to them the two other words, "God can." It remains true that all *things* are possible with God: the intrinsic impossibilities are not things but nonentities. It is no more possible for God than for the weakest of His creatures to carry out both of two mutually exclusive alternatives; not because His power meets an obstacle, but because nonsense remains nonsense even when we talk about God.[21]

Therefore, the problem of evil cannot be answered by arguing in any way that God does the logically impossible. Nor can God be charged with being less than omnipotent on grounds that He cannot act contrary to the law of non-contradiction. It would be like saying that God is not omnipotent because He cannot lie or make a rock so heavy He cannot lift it. It must be pointed out, on the other hand, that God is not bound to do something just because it is logically possible for him to do it.

## Omniscience

The knowledge of God is understood to be without limits within the range of what is logically possible for God to know. This means that God's knowledge is not limited by scope or kind, only by quality. God cannot know that which is counter to the facts of actuality or potentiality. For example, God cannot know that a being is a boy and a non-boy at the same time, same place, and in the same way. God's knowledge does, however, encompass the true actual as well as the true potential. The difference is that the true actual is the event itself actualized, while the true potential deals only with what might be whether or not it is ever actualized. God's omniscience includes middle knowledge in which God knows all true counterfactuals.

God can know at $t_1$ that at $t_2$ $A$ failed to accomplish $P$. God cannot know, however, at $t_1$ that at $t_2$ $A$ accomplished $P$, if in fact, $A$ did not accomplish $P$ at $t_2$. It does seem, however, that God could know at $t_1$ what would happen, if at $t_2$ $A$ would have accomplished $P$ and what would be the state of affairs if $A$ would have failed to accomplish $P$. For example, God could know that if $A$ accomplished $P$, $A$ would then become a millionaire even though $A$ did not accomplish $P$. After $A$ has failed to accomplish $P$, however, it is not possible for God to know that $A$ is a millionaire (that is in relation to accomplishing $P$).

God knows all potential choices and the consequences of all actual choices. God's working among men in this world, however, is on the basis of actual choices, not potential choices. Whereas one can only know what is true, God knows all true propositions. Therefore, God knows $X$ because it is true and not necessarily because He determined it.

Furthermore, if God knows all things, that means that He must know things He has not determined. If God can only know that which He has determined, either all things are determined or there are some things that God does not know (at least prior to their happening). If all things are determined, then the power of moral choice is non-authentic and the foundation of all theodicies since Augustine is destroyed. If, however, God does not know all things, then He is not omniscient. The only lack of knowledge that would not count against God's omniscience would be knowledge that is logically impossible for God to know.

But what kind of knowledge might this be? Some have suggested that it is the knowledge associated with the future choices of his moral agents.[22] This, however, seems hard to maintain logically. For example, are there examples where God claims to know some future choices of His moral agents? Consider the case of the people mentioned in Revelation 11:10, where in speaking of a future event, God proclaims He knows what these people will choose to do after killing the two witnesses—they will "rejoice over them, make merry, and send gifts to one another." Clearly, these are independent future choices of moral beings. If God can know in one case the future choices of His moral agents, then there are no logical grounds on which to argue such knowledge is logically impossible for God to know. Since God knows such knowledge, it must be logically possible. So, it appears that God can know things He has not determined, which means that all His knowledge is not causal. Therefore, the view of omniscience here is that God knows all things (events/happenings mental and overt) at which point they were logically knowable. That is, God could not know that He *had* created a world before the world was created (contingent knowledge), although He could always *know* (natural knowledge) that He would create a world.

Also, God knows all essential Truth or what might be called natural knowledge or necessary knowledge. By this it is affirmed that God knows all that is true concerning Truth itself in the absolute sense and in this sense God never acquires knowledge. Such knowledge is not knowledge about what happens, this is knowledge in its essential state by which all other propositions and formation of all authentic propositions are judged.

## Belief/Believe and God

The word *belief* is commonly called into service and often serves multiple meanings that are distinguished only by the context, and then, only if one is listening carefully. For example, the two statements: "I believe I am right, but you should ask John" and "I believe that God exists" use the word believe, but in two different senses. In the first sentence the word is used to raise the possibility being wrong, while the second sentence is a firm affirmation of confidence. A concern develops, not so much because of the fluidity of the term but with the connotation associated with the word. When the word believe is used in a philosophical/theological context, people often immediately assume (without warrant) that someone is affirming something of a personal religious nature. The word, however, even when speaking of God, does not necessarily speak of something religious. For example, while a person might say that he believes God exists, he may have no intention of conveying any religious connotation or association with that statement. He might affirm he believes *that* God exists without being overtly religious in any sense. It can also be said that one believes *in* the God that exists. The first sentence makes a statement about the way a person understands reality,[23] and the second confesses a personal commitment to God and is clearly a religious statement. Of course, the second statement would reasonably be made only by one who also affirmed the first. Further, it should be pointed out that the second affirmation says nothing substantively about the existence of God. It is possible for God not to exist and for people to still make some religious commitment to the idea that God does exist. Therefore, religious affirmations by themselves contribute little to the larger question of God's existence, as religious testimony often affirms notions contrary to reality. This leaves the reality issue (as opposed to religious issue) as the question of first order—does God exist? Therefore, to say I believe that God exists is to say something first and foremost about reality and not something about my personal religious commitments.

## THE FORMATION OF THE EVIDENTIAL ARGUMENT FROM EVIL

Theistic proposals for solving the problem of evil are often made in response to objections raised by proponents of atheism. In order to determine the adequacy of a theistic response, it will be helpful to review some of the most significant objections to theism as formed by noted atheologians. Edward Madden and Peter Hare have broadly denied that there is any satisfactory theistic response to the argument from evil. John L. Mackie[24] has developed an especially forceful logical version of the argument from evil. William Rowe[25] crafts an evidential argument that appears to be a very damaging argument against the G-G theodicy. A look at these arguments will provide a philosophical backdrop for developing and understanding a later critique of G-G theodicies.

### Edward Madden and Peter Hare

Madden and Hare provide a helpful introduction since they reject all theistic and quasi-theistic explanations for the problem of evil, including Process solutions.[26] They frame the problem as follows: "If God is unlimited in power and goodness, why is there so much *prima facie* gratuitous evil in the world?"[27] In particular, it is the problem of what appears to be gratuitous evil that they consider as the Achilles heel of the theist's position. Although they admit that some evil appears to result in some good, they point out that "much evil resists simple explanation; it is *prima facie* gratuitous."[28]

Interestingly, these authors argue that the logical problem is no problem at all for the theist, since they are sure the theist can easily rebut the objection that the existence of evil and the existence of an almighty God in some way, when conjoined, form a formally inconsistent statement. As they point out, "To rebut the alleged self-contradiction he [the theist] only has to show that there is some *possible* explanation of evil, whether it takes the form of saying that some higher good may be served or that any creation may entail the existence of some evil."[29] In fact, they suggest that to state the problem as entailing a formal inconsistency really "begs the main question at issue."[30]

What Madden and Hare claim they are looking for is a version of theism that maintains "a personal God who is a relevant object of worship, one who insures that good will eventually prevail, and one who is compatible with the Judaeo-Christian tradition."[31] While they agree that it is logically possible that a successful theodicy someday might be constructed, they suggest that "there is not only no evidence for the likelihood of such success but that the repeated failures, the recurrence and clustering criticisms, the permutations of basic moves which have been found wanting, and the slight variations of old favorites count heavily against the likelihood of what no one denies is always a possibility."[32] They do, however, believe that the free-will theodicy offers the most promise of all theodicies, but they conclude that it too has been unsuccessful in solving the riddle of God and evil. In the end, they are convinced that gratuitous evil presents the theist with an insurmountable problem for his belief system.

## John L. Mackie

John Mackie's widely quoted article *Evil and Omnipotence* serves as a useful example of how the logical atheistic objection is framed. Mackie claims that Christian theists face a problem of logical consistency with their claim that the all-good, all-powerful, all-knowing God exists coupled with their affirmation of the existence of evil. Mackie claims this makes theism logically inconsistent. If it is logically inconsistent, then it cannot be true. Mackie's concern is the logical version of the problem of evil. Whereas his objections to theism have implications for the evidential version of the argument from evil, it is included here. He deals with the matter of free will, which is common to both the logical and evidential version of the problem of evil. As Madden and Hare point out, "Theists of all shades and varieties rely upon some version of the free-will solution as the most fundamental approach to the problem of moral evil."[33]

Mackie maintains that an all-good and all-powerful God would not allow evil in his world and, since evil exists, it must logically follow that God does not exist. He is clear that this is a philosophical problem and "not a scientific problem that might be solved by further observations, or a practical problem that might be solved by a decision or an action."[34] Mackie is not saying that no one has offered any proposed solutions, only that the solutions often present the theist with *"other* problems to face."[35]

For example, Mackie believes theists use the term omnipotence but then subtly restrict it, which would entail a logical fallacy (equivocation). He charges others with forwarding the notion that evil is only an illusion. He maintains that others define evil as "merely the privation of good, that evil in a positive sense, evil that would really be opposed to good, does not exist."[36] All of this, Mackie protests, disallows the theists' explanations because they fail either by logical inconsistency or logical fallacy: "In all cases the fallacy has the general form suggested above: in order to solve the problem one (or perhaps more) of its constituent propositions is given up, but in such a way that it appears to have been retained, and can therefore be asserted without qualification in other contexts."[37] Mackie concludes that all theodicies either explicitly or implicitly entail some form of fallacy (either formal or informal).

To further make his point, Mackie looks at the G-G theodicy by focusing on its assumption (as he understands it) that "evil is necessary as a counterpart to good, that if there were no evil there could be no good either."[38] He agrees that this would solve the problem of the existence of evil but that it entails a qualification of God's omnipotence, namely that there must be some things God cannot do (such as create good without also creating evil). He argues this would be a limitation on God's omnipotence. Mackie then acknowledges that some theists might argue that omnipotence does not include logically impossible tasks. He continues that one is no better off with that proposition either because, if God is bound to the laws of logic then He is circumscribed by something either beyond or above Himself and therefore not limitless. Either way, Mackie thinks that the theist has qualified omnipotence (which is not omnipotence).[39]

He looks at another possible approach for theists in which they could claim God voluntarily binds Himself. He concludes this, after considering that possibility that it is "impossible to hold that an omnipotent God *binds himself* by causal or logical laws."[40] If God is circumscribed by laws of logic, then He is not omnipotent and the definition of omnipotence no longer means all-powerful. Mackie points out that what at first appears to be a solution ultimately fails on grounds of simple logic. If the laws of logic are violated, then the response is non-rational, which is no defense at all.[41]

Mackie continues his case by pointing out that appealing to free will as an explanation for the presence of evil in God's creation suffers a similar defeat. He thinks, however, that this may be the "most important proposed solution of the problem of evil"[42] in that it makes man, not God, responsible for evil. Mackie acknowledges that even though free will "would lead to some important evils, it must be argued that it is better on the whole that men should act freely, and sometimes err, than that they should be innocent automata, acting rightly in a wholly determined way."[43] As good as this sounds it fails, because, in his thinking, this would make the idea of freedom of the will incoherent.

His argument is that if God gave man free will and man exercised it some of the time to do good, then "there cannot be a logical impossibility in his freely choosing the good on every occasion."[44] Therefore, God cannot be both the all-powerful God and all-good God, if He does not avail Himself of the option for creating man in such a way that he would always choose good. Certainly that would be best, and a good God would always do His best. Since it is logically possible, God can do it (which is one definition of divine omnipotence). Therefore, if God could do—but did not do—what is best, then He is not all-good and if it was a logical possibility, and He did not do it, then He is not omnipotent. As Plantinga observes, "Mackie agrees with Leibniz that God, if omnipotent, could have created just any world he pleased and would have created the best world he could. But while Leibniz draws the conclusion that *this* world must the best possible, Mackie concludes instead that there is no omnipotent, wholly good God."[45] Either way, Mackie thinks he has soundly defeated the logical possibility of defending God's existence against the reality of evil. For Mackie, the existence of evil creates a logical impossibility for the theist.

As John Feinberg points out, "Mackie believed the traditional problem of evil deals a devastating blow to all theistic positions committed to God's omnipotence and benevolence and evil's existence."[46] Some, however, think that Alvin Plantinga in his Free Will Defense has offered a satisfactory rebuttal to Mackie's challenge to the logical version of the argument from evil. In fact, William Alston makes that point precisely when he says "it is now acknowledged on (almost) all sides that the logical argument is bankrupt, but the inductive argument is still very much alive and kicking."[47] While others may not be so sure of Plantinga's success, in either case, the evidential argument from evil remains unsatisfactorily answered.

## William Rowe

William Rowe presents his objection to theism by focusing on the inductive approach to the evidential problem of evil, arguing that theism lacks plausibility in light of evil. Rowe, who refers to himself as a friendly atheist, centers his evidential argument on the reality of gratuitous evil. He argues:

The latest formulation I have given of the evidential problem of evil goes something like this. (E 1 is the case of a fawn trapped in a forest fire and undergoing several days of terrible agony before dying. E 2 is the case of the rape, beating, and murder by strangulation of a five-year-old girl).

P: No good we know of justifies an omnipotent, omniscient, perfectly good being in permitting E 1 and E 2;

therefore,

Q: No good at all justifies an omnipotent, omniscient, perfectly good being in permitting E 1 and E 2,

therefore,

not-G: there is no omnipotent, omniscient, perfectly good being.[48]

Rowe begins by pointing out what he is and is not saying. Concerning P he asks, "What counts as a 'good that we know of?' I do not mean to limit us to goods that we know to have occurred. Nor do I mean to limit us to those goods and goods that we know will occur in the future."[49] Bound up in the notion of 'goods' is anything past, present or future, even something like God rewarding someone in His kingdom. The only stipulation that Rowe places on the good is that in order for it to count as a good, it must be actual. He also suggests that the non-existence of God would be sufficient reason for affirming P as true.

What Rowe does not allow into the discussion is what he calls background information $k$. There can be no evidence outside the reality of evil to tip the scales, such as the enormous amount of evil (this would support the atheist position) or order in the universe (this would support the theist position—this would include theistic arguments). That is, $k$ by itself can neither make "God's existence nor his nonexistence more likely than not."[50] Conversely, if P appears to be true and, consequently, "lowers the probability of God's existence, it is open to the theist to reply that the addition to $k$ of other information concerning the occurrences of ordinary and mystical religious experiences restores the balance or even tips the scales in favor of theism."[51] What Rowe says is that it is possible that a person "might have stronger evidence for the existence of God than is provided by the problem of evil for the nonexistence of God."[52] This, however, would be personal or existential evidence that only has weight for the individual and has no influence in the discussion of the public debate on the problem of evil.

With this in place, Rowe develops his inductive argument concluding that there is no sufficient reason to believe that there is any good knowable to man that would justify God permitting E 1 and E 2. This is, of course, as long as the definition of God remains as the all-good, all-knowing and all-powerful God. His point follows that even if one accepts the good of E 2 to be Sue's enjoyment of the presence of God forever, an all-good, all-powerful God would find a better way to accomplish that good. He even answers a response that suggests that God allowed Sue to die because, had she lived, she would have hardened her heart against the Lord and been shut out of His presence forever. Rowe quickly, and correctly, points out that this runs counter to the notion of free will, which is a foundational plank of the theist's position on the presence of evil in the world. He concludes that "given our common knowledge of the evils and goods in our world and our reasons for believing that P is true, it is *irrational* to believe in theism unless we possess or discover strong evidence in its behalf. I conclude, therefore, that the evidential argument from evil is alive and well."[53]

Rowe's argument seems to raise some serious questions for those who are committed to the premise of G-G theodicies. Although Alston thinks that Rowe's formulation of the problem "is the most careful and perspicuous,"[54] he is sure that the theist's position will prevail. While Alston thinks maybe he has answered Rowe's question sufficiently, just in case all are not convinced, he comforts himself with a common retreat:

Even if we were fully entitled to dismiss all the alleged reasons for permitting suffering that have been suggested, we would still have to consider whether there are further possibilities that are undreamt of in our theodicies. Why should we suppose that the theodicies thus far excogitated, however brilliant and learned their authors, exhaust the field?[55]

In fact, Alston thinks this is a very convincing position for he says the skeptic would still "face the insurmountable task of showing herself to be justified in supposing that there are no other possibilities for sufficient divine reasons. That point by itself would be decisive."[56] In other words, even if the theist's response has not answered all the questions at this point, it does not mean that fuller and more satisfying answers may not be forth coming in the future. Therefore, the theist should not be concerned that all the objections have not been answered.

While it is true that in time a more satisfying theistic response to the argument for evil may be developed, it seems unwise for the theist to take comfort in that position. After all, if the G-G theodicy is theologically legitimate, then it should be able to answer the questions now. What this reveals is that the G-G theodicy is an inadequate framework from which to construct a response to the evidential argument from evil. Alston is right on one point, namely that the G-G theodicy does not answer all the questions. This being true, it signals the need not for more answers from exhausted G-G theodicies but rather a new paradigm altogether.

## UNDERSTANDING THE CHALLENGE OF A NEW THEODICY

Theists currently involved in the work of theodicy generally agree that the argument from evil has yet to receive a sufficient answer, and understandably so as it is a most difficult task. Richard Swinburne suggests that "in the West in our modern world, most theists need a theodicy. Without a theodicy, evil counts against [our belief in and understanding of] the existence of God."[57] Swinburne suggests that evil weighs against theism as a consistent system, unless the theist has a theodicy. Furthermore, the complexity of developing a satisfactory theodicy is highlighted by Swinburne's own confession. He points out that even though he had addressed the subject earlier[58] he admits "that theodicy is a considerably more difficult enterprise than I represented it there."[59] Millard Erickson also suggests that theodicy has not yet finished its work. In his discussion on the importance of the doctrine of God, he says, "The problem of evil, of course, is a major and, indeed, perhaps the largest, problem for any theism."[60] Erickson suggests that the coming theological debates will include discussions of the problem of evil which he thinks may very well be the greatest problem for theists.

The appearance of several recent books[61] dealing with subject of theodicy indicate that the argument from evil has not yet been put to rest. The fact that the issue continues to receive serious attention by theologians and philosophers alike indicates that a convincing and comprehensive theodicy has yet to be developed.[62] And while much has been done in developing convincing arguments for God's existence, responses to the argument from evil have not fared as well. Some might argue that this is to be expected for the ways of God in this matter are a mystery, hidden from the eyes of the mortal. While there is no disagreement that there are matters belonging to God alone, in light of biblical record and human experience this is not one of those matters.

It is the human experience that begs for some answer, some meaningful clarification. More Christians than one would acknowledge they are dissatisfied with the standard fare on the argument from evil whether it relates to their personal lives, ministering to others, or to understanding suffering in general. Most Christians, however, resist complaining publicly less their faith be questioned. Although some become bitter towards God in the midst of their suffering, most simply experience a reduced confidence in God. While the majority will continue to believe in God, they sense disappointment because they searched in vain to find the good from suffering experienced either by themselves or one they love. Consequently, it must be clear that the demand for a more satisfactory theodicy goes beyond a philosophical quest, and it is more than just satisfying one's curiosity, it is about answering the silent (or muffled) request from the hearts of multitudes of Christians. It is the painful cry of the heart, "Where's the good?" The echoing reply of the preacher, "It is there, you just cannot see it" fails to heal the soul deep down.

When evaluating the importance of a theodicy, one must understand that a theodicy serves at least two important functions. One is to answer the objections brought by the atheist who thinks that evil is a defeater of any claim for belief in God. Most, when thinking about theodicy, think of it only in these terms. There remains, however, another important function of a theodicy, namely, to serve as a platform from which the Christian understands his own encounters with suffering. Those who would suggest that theodicy is a poor use of one's time and energy should understand that without a theodicy, comforting those who suffer has no enduring foundation. Effective Christian ministering to those who are suffering requires proper understanding of the relationship of suffering to God. As Peterson claims, "Thus, it is quite legitimate for theists to try to formulate some reasonable understanding of evil for themselves, and whatever understanding they obtain moves them in the direction of theodicy."[63] Furthermore, it is essential that any theodicy not only answer the particular problem of evil, but at the same time be consistent with all other Christian truth claims concerning creation and God's character. Consequently, it is necessary within a Christian theistic world view to develop a theodicy as part of the Christian belief system.

It logically follows that, if God works within the space-time context (which now contains evil), to avoid providing an explanation for the existence of evil in God's creation seems to leave a part of the space-time reality outside the Christian worldview. Such a position would have serious implications for the reality of miracles and other acts of God, such as the incarnation and resurrection of Jesus the Christ. Trinitarian theism most often affirms miracles (God working in the space-time context), which deal (directly or indirectly) with the problem of evil. Furthermore, much of the biblical text either explicitly or tacitly deals with evil. To suggest that there is no explanation for why God allowed evil in this world and while He continues to permit much horrific evil is to say that much of what happens in space-time is unexplainable.[64] Logically, another possibility would be to conclude that God does not work in the space-time context.[65] In either case, what would be left is a God that looks very much like a Deistic God not the Trinitarian God of the Bible. The theme of God dealing with evil runs throughout the Bible; therefore, it seems reasonable to assume there is sufficient information on which a theodicy can be constructed. Furthermore, as Peterson points out, most theists have not considered a theodicy impossible. He writes:

> Rather, they [theists] conceive of the project of theodicy as drawing out the implications of one's theological position from evil. After all, religious believers commonly accept that the doctrines and teaching of their faith have implications for all sorts of important matters— moral and spiritual virtues, the meaning of redemption, the purpose of human life, and so forth. So, it would be odd indeed to think that religious beliefs have no implications whatsoever for understanding something so important as evil in the world.[66]

If one avoids an attempt to explain why God allows evil, that choice will have implications for understanding miracles as well as an overall depreciation of the Christian view of history. It is assumed that a theodicy is necessary to a Christian theistic world view.

Furthermore, the problem of evil, as discussed by contemporary scholars, is both tacitly and explicitly bound up in the renewed discussion over the nature of God. That is not to say that the discussion of evil has been responsible for the renewed interest in the nature of God, only that it is related to the discussion on the problem of evil. Presently, issues such as the impassibility of God, the eternality of God, the omniscience of God, and the omnipotence of God are often being reviewed in light of the problem of evil.[67] Whereas these issues shape one's view of the nature/attributes of God and His relationship to His creation, they obviously have significance for the way in which evil is understood in terms of its continued existence in a world created by an all-good, all-knowing, all-powerful God.

Logically, if evil exists as a reality in this world and this is God's creation, then there must be some explanation for its continued existence—an explanation that is compatible with God's being and His creative choices. God does not ask mankind to believe that which stands in contradiction to His character, nor does He hide His working among men. To deny the possibility of a theodicy is to leave much of the biblical material outside an understandable Christian worldview. Yet, suffering is precisely the point at which questions are most frequently asked concerning the Christian theistic worldview.

Historically, the Christian community as a whole answers the problem of evil by appealing to some form of a G-G theodicy. As Peterson points out, "Most theodicies therefore follow the strategy of specifying either greater goods that are gained or worse evils that are averted by God's permitting evil."[68] As such, most theodicies have a common theme running through them, namely that *"God (who is omnipotent, omniscient, and wholly good) would design the universe such that evil is necessary to a greater good.* Theists have typically taken a *greater-good approach* as integral to their search for a morally sufficient reason for why God allows evil."[69] The Evangelical[70] consensus seems to be that, while no one theodicy has yet achieved the status of being a final and fully satisfactory explanation of all evil, it seems that theodicy is possible and necessary.

Importantly, any theodicy that shows the promise of answering questions from the evidential argument from evil, must deal with gratuitous evil as more than appearance. The fact remains that gratuitous evil remains as the most serious challenge to theism. David Basinger points out that, "One of the challenges facing any theist is the tremendous amount of seemingly unnecessary evil in the world."[71] Madden and Hare argue, "The crucial problem of evil . . . is not why the world is not perfect if there is a God but rather, since some evil obviously serves good ends, why there is, nevertheless, *prima facie* gratuitous evil remaining."[72] By admitting that gratuitous evil is not contrary to the traditional view of God, a major plank of the argument from evil is removed. As Ronald Nash has observed, if gratuitous evil could be shown not to count against God, then there would "seem to be good reasons to conclude that the stalemate is over and that the probabilities favor theism."[73] This is the challenge for the theist and a reasonable as well as an achievable goal for the theist.

## NOTES

1. Robert Adams "Theodicy" in *The Cambridge Dictionary of Philosophy* (1995), notes that the term 'theodicy' is "from Greek *theos,* 'God' and *dikē,* 'justice'. Michael Peterson, *God and Evil* (Boulder, CO: Westview Press,

1998), 85 explains that it is "as John Milton says, an attempt to 'justify the ways of God to man.'" The term itself appears to be first used by Gottfried Wilhelm Leibniz (1646–1716).

2. The terms 'evil' and 'suffering' will be used interchangeably. The word 'evil' is not being used in a strict theological sense, but rather in the sense that whatever is named evil is something that causes suffering and that all suffering is in some way related to evil, but not necessarily evil itself. For example, suffering is sometimes caused by God's judgment, but one would not call that moral evil even though it does mean suffering. Nonetheless, it is related to evil, namely the evil of immorality.

3. From this point forward, the term 'God' or 'theism' is used to speak of God in a  restricted way that includes the idea that God is omnipotent, omniscient, eternal, and omni-benevolent or a belief in the existence of such a Trinitarian God who acts in space and time.

4. The idea of the 'greater good' can be understood in at least two ways. The first is a greater good with reference to the state of affairs before evil came into existence. In this case, the greater good is measured against what was prior to evil, which makes the conditions prior to evil a 'greater good' than the evil that came about as a result of the good state of affairs. This good state of affairs is most often described as the fact that man was given the power of moral choice (commonly referred to as free will). The second way to understand the term is where 'greater good' is in reference to the evil; that is, what happens is in some way better than the evil state of affairs out of which it comes. This helpful distinction was made by William Hasker who credits William Rowe for calling the two notions to his attention. See William Hasker, "The Necessity of Gratuitous Evil," *Faith and Philosophy* 9 (Jan 1992): 40.

5. Michael Peterson, *God and Evil* (Boulder, CO: Westview Press, 1998), 89.

6. Ibid., 103.

7. Gratuitous evil is evil which causes unnecessary or pointless suffering. That is, it is evil that appears so excessive (both in terms of extent and/or intensity) that it seems inexplicable in terms of any greater good particularly when the one suffering is innocent, such as a child burning to death. Gratuitous evil is evil that not only *appears* pointless, but is in *reality* pointless.

8. I realize that immediately some will think of Romans 8:28 and understandably so. The most that one can get from this text (and it may be more than the text actually yields which will be discussed later) is that the good obtains for the Christian only. Therefore, it cannot be applied universally to all suffering and, would not support a theodicy.

9. When I speak of children being innocent, I am not suggesting they are not corrupted from birth. I am not using the word in its theological sense, but rather in a sense of personal moral culpability for personal actions.

10. C. S Lewis, *The Problem of Pain* (New York: Macmillan, 1962; reprint, New York: Simon & Schuster, 1996), 12–13 (page citations are to the reprint edition).

11. Vladimir Lossky, *Orthodox Theology: An Introduction*, trans. Ian and Ihita Kesarcodi-Watson, (Crestwood, NY: St. Vladimir's Seminary Press, 1989), 79.

12. David Basinger, *The Case For Freewill Theism* (Downers Grove: InterVarsity Press, 1996), 83.

13. Peterson, *God and Evil*, 85.

14. Michael Peterson, "God and Evil: Problems of Consistency and Gratuity," *Journal of Value Inquiry* 13 (1979): 305.

15. Eleonore Stump, "Knowledge, Freedom, and the Problem of Evil," in *The Problem of Evil*, ed. Michael L. Peterson (Notre Dame: University of Notre Dame Press, 1992), 317–18, notes that "the free-will defense successfully rebuts the claim that the presence of evil in the world is logically incompatible with God's existence. But many people, theists as well as atheists, feel that the free-will defense leaves some of the most important questions about evil unanswered. If there is a God, the *nature* and *quantity* of evil in the world still remains a puzzle; and even if they do not support a conclusive argument, they still provide strong evidence against the probability of God."

16. Alvin Plantinga addressed the logical problem of evil in: *God, Freedom, and Evil* (Grand Rapids: William B. Eerdmans Publishing Co., 1974); *God and Other Minds* (Ithaca, NY: Cornell University Press, 1990), 115–83; and "The Free Will Defense," in *Philosophy of Religion*, ed. Melville Y. Stewart (Sudbury, MA: Jones and Bartlett Publishers, 1996), 369–398.

17. Plantinga, God and Other Minds, 128.

18. Ibid., 130.

19. Edward Madden and Peter Hare, *Evil and the Concept of God* (Springfield, IL: Charles C. Thomas Publisher, 1968), 3.

20. Lewis, The Problem of Pain, 33.

21. Lewis, The Problem of Pain, 25.

22. This would be those who subscribe to the openness view of God, which claims that God does not know the future choices of His moral agents.

23. This does not mean that the person lives as if God exists, only that he thinks it is more likely that God exists than that He does not exist.

24. John L. Mackie, "Evil and Omnipotence" in *Philosophy of Religion,* ed. Melville Stewart (Sudbury, MA: Jones and Bartley, 1996).

25. William Rowe, "The Evidential Argument from Evil: A Second Look," in *The Evidential Argument From Evil*, ed. Daniel Howard-Snyder (Bloomington: Indiana University Press, 1996).

26. Madden and Hare, *Evil and the Concept of God*, 12. Madden and Hare note, "The thesis of this book is that neither theism nor quasi-theism is able to make sense of the facts of evil and that this incompetence constitutes a good reason for rejecting each one of them."

27. Ibid., 3.

28. Ibid.

29. Ibid., 5.

30. Ibid.

31. Ibid., 10.

32. Ibid., 14.

33. Ibid., 74.

34. Mackie, "Evil and Omnipotence," 333.

35. Ibid., 334.

36. Ibid.

37. Ibid., 335.

38. Ibid., 336.

39. One might correctly argue that the laws of logic do not stand above God, but flow from and are essential to His nature. This still does not remove the substance of Mackie's argument. It would seem that this is not really a matter of it being logically impossible for God to create good without evil, but rather it is an ontological issue. Therefore, one would need to demonstrate that there is something about God's character that requires Him to use evil to bring about good.

40. Mackie, "Evil and Omnipotence," 334.

41. Some existentialists might argue that non-rational explanations for theistic claims are a plus for theism. However, theists of this persuasion are not interested in building a defense for Christianity in the sense that encourages theists to develop a theodicy. Søren Kierkegaard and Friedrich Schleiermacher would perhaps be examples of those who would advance this position.

42. Mackie, "Evil and Omnipotence," 340.

43. Ibid.

44. Ibid., 341.

45. Alvin Plantinga, "God, Evil, and the Metaphysics of Freedom," in *The Problem of Evil*, eds. Marilyn McCord Adams and Robert Merrihew Adams (Oxford: Oxford University Press, 1996), 87.

46. John Feinberg, *The Many Faces of Evil*, 2nd ed. (Grand Rapids: Zondervan Publishing House, 1994), 13.

47. William Alston, "The Inductive Argument from Evil and the Human Condition," in *The Evidential Argument from Evil*, ed. Daniel Howard-Snyder (Bloomington: Indiana University Press, 1996), 97.

48. Rowe, "The Evidential Argument from Evil: A Second Look," 262-63.

49. Ibid., 264.

50. Ibid., 265.

51. Ibid., 266.

52. Ibid.

53. Ibid., 282.

54. Alston, "The Inductive Argument from Evil," 98.

55. Ibid., 119.

56. Ibid.

57. Richard Swinburne, *Providence and the Problem of Evil* (Oxford: Clarendon Press, 1998), x.

58. See Richard Swinburne, *The Existence of God*, rev. ed. (Oxford: Clarendon Press, 1991), 200-224.

59. Swinburne, *Providence and the Problem of Evil*, x.

60. Millard Erickson, *God, the Father Almighty* (Grand Rapids: Baker Book House, 1998), 288.

61. Some of the recent books on evil include: Gregory A. Boyd, *Satan and the Problem of Evil* (Downers Grove: InterVarsity Press, 2001); William L. Rowe, ed., *God and the Problem of Evil* (Malden, MA: Blackwell Publishers, Inc., 2001); David O'Conner, *God and Inscrutable Evil* (New York: Rowman & Littlefield Publishers, 1998); Michael Peterson, *God and Evil* (Boulder, CO: Westview Press, 1998); Richard Swinburne, *Providence and the Problem of Evil* (Oxford: Clarendon Press, 1998); Daniel Howard-Snyder, ed., *The Evidential Argument from Evil* (Bloomington: Indiana University Press, 1996); Hans Schwarz, *Evil: A Historical and Theological Perspective,* trans. Mark Worthing (Minneapolis: Fortress Press, 1995); R. Douglas Geivett, *Evil and The Evidence for God* (Philadelphia: Temple University Press, 1993); Michael Peterson, *The Problem of Evil: Selected Readings* (Notre Dame: University of Notre Dame Press, 1992); John Hick, *Evil and the God of Love,* rev. ed. (San Francisco: Harper & Row, 1978).

62. It is important to say at this juncture that I am not suggesting the theodicy offered in this book is necessarily convincing or comprehensive, rather it is an attempt to shift the paradigm for a new approach to answering the argument from evil.

63. Peterson, *God and Evil*, 87.

64. Some may be satisfied with a position that simply confesses much of life as a mystery, but it is not a consistent position. The premise of biblical faith is that God has revealed Himself and His ways to mankind. The claim is not that we have exhaustive knowledge, but that we have sufficient knowledge. Thus, to take refuge in unexplainability is to presume that divine revelation is insufficient at a critical point in establishing the biblical worldview.

65. This too is possible but inconsistent with well-established doctrines such as the doctrine of creation itself. If God created the world, the world cannot be inconsistent with God's character. If time and space are created by God, then clearly they are not contrary to God as revealed in the incarnation.

66. Peterson, *God and Evil*, 86.

67. Examples of this are found in: Millard Erickson, *God the Father Almighty* (Grand Rapids: Baker Book House, 1998); Michael Peterson, *God and Evil* (Boulder, CO: Westview Press, 1998); David Basinger, *The Case for Freewill Theism* (Downers Grove: InterVarsity Press, 1996); Clark Pinnock and others, *The Openness of God* (Downers Grove: InterVarsity Press, 1994).

68. Ibid., 88.

69. Ibid., 103.

70. The term 'evangelical' is used to identify the contemporary Christian theological position that emphasizes the importance of personal religious commitments and affirms the historic doctrines of orthodox Christianity. These include: the Trinitarian nature of God, the deity and virgin birth of Jesus Christ, salvation by grace alone through faith in the substitutionary death of Christ, His

resurrection, the personal return of Christ at the end of the age, and the infallibility of Scripture.

71. Basinger, *The Case For Freewill Theism,* 83.

72. Madden and Hare, *Evil and the Concept of God*, 49.

73. Ronald Nash, *Faith and Reason* (Grand Rapids: Zondervan Publishing House, 1988), 221.

# Chapter 2

# The Historical Context of Greater-Good Theodicies

This chapter reviews three varieties of the G-G theodicy as developed by Augustine of Hippo, Thomas Aquinas, and Gottfried Leibniz. Each one affirms that God exists and develops some form of a greater-good explanation for why evil continues to exist in God's created order. The three share certain common ideas regarding the problem of evil and, as R. Douglas Geivett concludes, even the theodicy of Leibniz shares in "the tradition established by his precursors Augustine and Aquinas."[1] One important commonality is the belief that there are positive arguments for God's existence. As Geivett notes, each one agrees on the "important role of traditional arguments for the existence of God."[2] In fact, Aquinas developed his Five Ways in the context of considering the argument from evil. If evil is an argument against God's existence, he reasoned, then it is wise to determine if there is any evidence for God's existence. In each theodicy considered, there is a general commitment to an understanding of God as the one who is omnipotent, omniscient and omnibenevolent.

## AUGUSTINE

In attempting to absolve God of any culpability for evil in the world and to explain its presence in God's created order, Augustine of Hippo (A.D. 354–430) developed an explanation for the existence of evil based on the actuality of human free will. His defense recognized the actuality of human free will (as man was in the garden before the fall), a tradition continued by both Aquinas and Leibniz. Augustine began his discussion with the conviction that God exists and that a right understanding of the issues of life and death must be predicated upon and interpreted by this truth. For Augustine, a right view of God required that "we believe Him [God] to be almighty, utterly unchangeable, the creator of all things that are good, though Himself more excellent than they, the utterly just ruler of all He has created, self-sufficient and therefore without any assistance from any other being in the act of creation. It follows from this that He created all out of nothing."[3]Augustine then moved to the moral question of the problem of evil, which focused on the evidential version of the problem.

## Suffering and God's Justice

Augustine first distinguishes between God doing evil and God's justice resulting in just suffering of the evil doer. He writes:

> If you know or believe God is good—and it would be wrong to think otherwise—He does not do evil. Again, if we admit God is just—and it would be wicked also to deny this—He both rewards the good and punishes the bad. Now these punishments are evils to those who suffer them. Consequently, if no one is punished unjustly—as we must necessarily believe, since we believe everything is ruled by God's providence—God is certainly not the cause of the first kind of evil, but He is the cause of the second kind."[4]

God's punishment of the wicked is just as it is right that God should reward the good and punish the evil. From the standpoint of God's justice, men will suffer as a consequence of their evil deeds as this is what "his [God's] justice requires, and, since it is a function of his justice, the performance of the punishment cannot be evil."[5]

In this sense God is responsible for the suffering of the wicked since their suffering is their just punishment. The punishment was not to perfect the soul but rather was the just and sovereign act of God and, for Augustine, punishment followed the wicked into eternity. As Jaroslav Pelikan says, for Augustine "(t)he basis of predestination was not human merit, but divine grace; and even in the case of those who were predestined to damnation, the will of God was good and just, for they received the damnation which they—and the saved as well—deserved."[6] For Augustine, this means that some suffering—that which flows from the justice of God on disobedience—cannot rightfully be labeled evil.

## The Will And Evil

Concerning the source of evil, Augustine argues that the evil results from an inappropriate act of the human will. God, however, had not given the will for that purpose, however, it made wrong choices a possibility. Adam was created in grace, but that grace "did not include a confirmed perseverance in good, but the choice between good and evil was left to the decision of his free will."[7] The will was free "so they [Adam and Eve] may act for or against the divine will."[8] Unfortunately man's will turned away from God, not because God determined it to be so, but because man chose the lesser good. The will was free to choose, which meant that God bore no responsibility for the resulting evil, as the will itself was good. As Augustine explains, just "because sin occurs through free will, we must not suppose that God gave man free will for the purpose of sinning. It is a sufficient reason why it ought to be given, that man cannot live rightly without it."[9] Geivett points out that by "living rightly", Augustine means "leading a righteous life. Such a life is one that is morally praiseworthy or commendable."[10] Living for God was to be a choice and it was God's intent that man should choose the good. Louis Berkhof notes that Augustine taught that had man "proved obedient, he would have been confirmed in holiness. From the state of *posse non peccare et mori* (the ability not to sin and die) he would have passed to the state of the *non posse peccare et mori* (the inability to sin and die). But he sinned, and consequently entered the state of the *non posse non peccare et mori* (the inability not to sin and die)."[11] The act of the will to choose to disobey did not flow from some evil in the will itself, rather it was the improper exercise of the will. The will could not be evil as it came from God and whatever comes from God is good, for God alone is good. Free will, that which was necessary for man to be man, was one of those good things because it came from God.

Evil, therefore, was not God's choice for man. Evil resulted when man, through the exercise of his free will (good), turned "away from the unchangeable good (the virtues), and towards changeable good (bodily beauty). Since this turning from one to the other is free and unforced, the pain which follows as a punishment is fitting and just."[12] So any suffering in the world is the just consequence of free choice. Adam and Eve freely turned from that which is good and unchangeable to that which is changeable, thus bringing a just punishment upon all, punishment that has brought suffering into the world.

According to Augustine, goods could be put into three categories. He writes:

> Virtues, then, by which we live rightly, are great goods, but all kinds of bodily beauty, without which we can live rightly, are the least goods. The powers of the soul, without which we cannot live rightly, are the middle goods. No one uses the virtues wrongly, but anyone can use the other goods, middle and the least, wrongly as well as rightly.[13]

The will belongs to the middle good and as such is good in and of itself, but has the power to turn to either the unchanging good or the changing good. The will, unfortunately, turned away from the unchanging good to the changing good. This "turning away" for Augustine anticipates, as Robert O'Connell points out, "(t)hat the consequences flow inexorably from the very nature of the soul's own evil act. Turn away 'perversely' from union with the Highest reality, and by its very nature the turn must be a turn toward lesser realities; it can have no other terminus except the 'diminishment' and 'privation' of being which Augustine equates with 'corruption,' evil."[14] God's grace, however, can overcome the influence of this vitiated will if man will look to this grace.

According to Augustine, it is not that God gave man good things and bad things from which to choose, but goods of different categories (higher goods and lower goods). Everything that man was given from which to choose could be classified as a good. God did not give man bad things from which to choose because all that was had been created by God. Whereas evil as no essence of its own, it can not exist as an independent entity. Evil is in the will turning from the unchangeable good to the changeable good. Augustine writes:

> The will, then if it clings to the unchangeable good which is common to all, obtains the principal and important human goods, though the will itself is a middle good. But the will sins, if it turns away from the unchangeable good which is common to all, and turns towards private good, whether outside or below it. . . . Evil is the turning of the will away from the unchangeable good, and towards changeable good. Since this turning from one to the other is free and unforced, the pain which follows as a punishment is fitting and just.[15]

This choice changed man, not substantively, but surely accidentally as man became corrupted, but not non-human. Augustine points out that now man finds something within himself that gives impetus to evil—the will has been corrupted (vitiated). In this way, each bears his own culpability for not turning to the One who alone can help—for not turning to the unchangeable Good. According to Etienne Gilson, for Augustine man to be man requires he have a will and it must be

> a will that is personal and free; and since the will itself is an intermediate good, it remains free to turn towards the supreme good and to possess it in happiness, or to turn away from it to enjoy itself and lower things, which act constitutes moral evil and sin. Tuning away from the Sovereign Good, turning to secondary goods: these are, in brief, the two free acts which decide our eternal happiness or misery.[16]

Arguing that the corruption came through a wrong turning of the will, and affirming that the will is good, requires an explanation of the cause responsible for the will's turning wrongly. That is, why did or what caused the will to turn from the unchangeable to the changeable? Did the will move by its own power in that direction? If so, then of course, God would be responsible for sin, since He made the will with the inclination to turn from the unchangeable to the changeable. As Augustine notes, if "the will which were given, of its very nature moves as it does, it cannot help turning in this direction. There cannot be any fault, if nature and necessity compel it."[17] Therefore, Augustine maintains that the will is culpable for its own turning. He notes:

> So what need is there to ask the source of that movement by which the will turns from the unchangeable good to the changeable good? We agree that it belongs only to the soul, and is voluntary and therefore culpable; and the whole value of teaching in this matter consists in its power to make us censure and check this movement, and turn our wills away from temporal things below us to enjoyment of the everlasting good.[18]

The power of the will, Augustine argues, resides in the soul and could not come from a natural inclination of the will. The will comes from God and only good comes from God. Plainly, he argues that one cannot go further than this: "Perverted will, then, is the cause of all evil."[19] As Gilson points out, for Augustine "the only honest answer that can be made to this question is that we do not know anything about it."[20] It is enough to know that God is not the cause of the will turning wrongly.

This, however, presents another concern, namely, if this was the way things would turn out, why did God give man free will in the first place? Augustine responds by pointing out that:

> Man himself is something good in so far as he is man, for he can live rightly when he so wills. Obviously, if this is true, the question you [Euodius] propose is solved. If man is something good and cannot do right except when he so wishes, he ought to have free will, without which he could not do right. Because sin occurs through free will, we must not suppose that God gave man free will for the purpose of sinning. It is a sufficient reason why it ought to be given, that man cannot live rightly without it.[21]

Free will is necessary for man to be man (a moral being). The only way man can do right is if he has the power of will to choose to do right. Man simply can not *do* right without free will. It is necessary to human*ness*. Augustine elaborates on this point:

> You [Euodius] said you thought free choice of will ought not to have been given, because by it we sin. Against your view I argued that we could not act rightly except by this free choice of will, and I claimed that God had given it rather for this purpose. You replied that free

will ought to have been given us in the same way that justice has been given, for we can only use justice for its right purpose. This reply of yours forced us into that complicated discussion in which I tried to prove to you that good things, great and small, only come from God. This could not have been shown so clearly, unless we first refuted the wicked opinion of the fool who said in his heart, *There is no God.* . . . These two propositions, that God exists and that all good things come from Him, we already held with firm faith, but we have examined them so carefully that the third point also becomes most clear, that free will is to be counted among good things.[22]

Augustine's further point is that free will is good because it comes from God, so why should not God give to man that which is good? In fact, that is what one would require of a good God. Just because man might use it for evil is no reason why God should initially withhold the good from man. Furthermore, Augustine argues that it is God's goodness that led Him to create man with free will, for it is better to be a moral being than a non-moral being:

Such is the generosity of God's goodness that He has not refrained from creating even that creature which He foreknew would not only sin, but remain in the will to sin. As a runaway horse is better than a stone which does not run away because it lacks self-movement and sense perception, so the creature is more excellent which sins by free will than that which does not sin only because it has no free will.[23]

The truth is, Augustine argues, God's giving man free will must be considered as one of the crowning acts of the gracious and good God. This, he maintains, was a good act of God even though it led to terrible consequences for man when he misused his free will to choose the least goods. Yet, if God knew that the will of man would turn in the wrong direction, then there was the question of the relationship between God's knowledge of what happened and His causing what happened.

This is the question of whether or not God's foreknowledge caused man to sin. The argument is that if God foreknew that man would sin, and since God only knows all true things, man was determined to sin. This supposedly follows logically from the position that God cannot know any non-true state of affairs, so if He knows something will be, then it must be and cannot be otherwise. Augustine responds that this would not be the case. He reasons that if a person foreknew that another will sin, this does not mean that the foreknowledge causes the sin. Augustine concludes: "Your foreknowledge would not be the cause of his sin, though undoubtedly he would sin; otherwise you would not foreknow that this would happen. Therefore, these two are not contradictory, your foreknowledge and someone else's free act. So too God compels no one to sin, though He foresees those who will sin by their own will."[24]

Furthermore, he argues:

> Hence we do not deny that God has foreknowledge of all future events, and yet that we will what we will. Since He has foreknowledge of our will, that will must exist, of which He has foreknowledge. It will be a will, because He has foreknowledge of a will. Nor could it be a will, if it were not in our power. So He has foreknowledge also of our power over it. My power is not taken away by His foreknowledge, but I shall have it all the more certainly because He whose foreknowledge is not mistaken has foreknown that I shall have it.[25]

God's knowledge of the fact that man would sin and that man in actuality did sin was not a causal relationship. Man's will, Augustine argues, operated independently of God's foreknowledge, but not outside the scope of His foreknowledge, thus avoiding the idea that God caused man's will to turn in the direction it did. As Robert Brown points out, Augustine holds to the "compatibility of human free will (on an indeterminist account) with divine omniscience."[26] Augustine denies that God's knowledge of man's turning away from Him was causal knowledge.

According to Augustine, the reality of the will is found in the fact that the will has its power because God knows it to be the case and God only knows true things. If the will does not have the power to choose, then God cannot know that it has the power to choose, and yet God does know it had the power to choose. Therefore, God could not have determined that man would sin, as that would contradict what God knew, namely that man has the power to choose. What God knows is not necessarily dependent on what He determines. If will is to be will, then it must be free to exercise that for which it was created, namely to exercise its power of which God also foreknew. By the will, man can choose certain types of goods—goods that change and goods that do not change and this will is real.

## Gratuitous Evil

Augustine's application of his foundational view of God denies the possibility of gratuitous evil—all evil has a purpose because God is omnibenevolent and sovereign. He notes, "In relation to the whole, to the ordered connection of all creation in space and time, no one whatever can be created without a purpose. Not even the leaf of a tree is created without a purpose."[27] God not only created all things for a purpose, but also because of His omnibenevolence and His providence, one can be assured that God will bring good from the evil He permits in His world as a result of the fall. God will not allow evil to override His good purposes for His creation, even though man unwisely uses his will against God. According to Hick, Augustine teaches that "God mysteriously overrules the malicious deeds of the wicked (and, when necessary, the well-intentioned but ill-judged efforts of the virtuous) and eventually brings good out of evil, and indeed brings an eternal and therefore infinite good out of a temporal and therefore finite evil, which is a thought of great promise for Christian theodicy."[28]

For Augustine, even the suffering of children has redemptive value, for "God does good in correcting adults when their children whom they love suffer pain and death."[29] If children suffer, however, no good accrues to them, at least not in Augustine's scheme. The good is that parents become better parents. But this leaves open the question of whether a better parent is a sufficient good in order to justify the horrible suffering of an innocent. In other words, what determines what good can be classified as greater in relation to any evil? Richard Middleton's reminder is that "whereas Augustine's explicit position in *De Libero Arbitrio* is that the world is no worse for all the evil in it, due to God's providence (technically, that all evil is 'counterbalanced' by good), by the time we get to his later *Enchiridion* Augustine boldly claims that 'God judged it *better* to bring good out of evil than not to permit any evil to exist'."[30] As Geivett points out, Augustine's theodicy argues that even though evil is not necessary, because the all-good God, Creator of all but Himself "both can and will bring ultimate good out of the evil."[31] Norman Geisler and Winfried Corduan note that Augustine believes that everything God created is good and therefore, "God is able to use the evil of the parts for the greater good of the whole according to his own good purposes."[32]

Augustine maintains that the all-powerful God can work in space and time turning the evil that comes about by man's free will in order to bring about a greater good. In this theodicy, no evil is pointless. If God can not bring good out of the evil, then in His providence, this evil state of affairs would not exist. Further, God can bring good out of any amount of evil, great or small. Clearly, God is not responsible for evil because it comes by man's misuse of something good (free will), and yet, in God's providence He brings good from the evil.

**Animal Suffering**

In response to why animals suffer, Augustine argues:

Neither willingly nor with indifference, but reluctantly and with struggle, it meets bodily suffering, and is distressed by the collapse of its unity and soundness. Only the pain of beasts makes us realize (sic) the striving for unity in the lower living creatures. If we did not realize (sic) this, we should not be sufficiently reminded that everything is constituted by that supreme, sublime, and ineffable unity of the Creator.[33]

Animal suffering teaches us that something is out of joint. Unity is what is desired but is not evident. Where does this unity come from, but from the trinitarian creator God. In other words, everything has a purpose and gratuitous evil does not exist even in animal suffering according to Augustine. The good, according to Augustine, is in giving man free choice and when that is used wrongly, God in His providence brings good out of the evil. This includes animal suffering and even the suffering of children. In this way, the greater good is seen both in God's good choice in the way and what He creates as well as His providential action in creation.

## Summary

Augustine began his discussion with the conviction that God was all-good and all-powerful and then asked the question: "I should like you to tell me: is God the cause of evil?"[34] He did not argue that evil was the necessary path by which God did something better in creation. Evil resulted from the turning of the will, which was good in and of itself. Because God is good, He ultimately turns all evil for good, for all things in God's providence have a purpose. Evil is a privation. It is not something in and of itself. It is a lack. As Berkhof observes, "Augustine does not regard sin as something positive, but as a negation or privation. It is not a substantial evil added to man, but a *privatio boni*, a privation of the good."[35] Augustine understood evil, not as something that was a created substance, but a lack in the good substance as created by God. That is, evil was an accidental and not a substantive aspect of creation.

Augustine's discussion of evil turns not on what he gathers from the evidence, but rather from his theological commitments. His argument is deductive. It is Augustine's view of the providence and goodness of God and not the preponderance of the evidence that led him to the notion that in the end the good obtains. Evil is the result of the will turning against the highest Good and, since it was good (even necessary) that man have the power of choice, God is not culpable for evil. In His grace and providence He brings good out of evil. So the greater good is seen in both truths, namely that it is a greater good that man have free will than that he not have free will, and that God is able to bring a greater good from the evil caused by man's free will. This is the foundation for all G-G theodicies. As Middleton observes, "Augustine's *strategy* in constructing a theodicy has become standard in Western, and especially Christian, intellectual history."[36] This includes both the notions of the greater good of free will as well as God bringing good out of evil, which necessarily entails a denial of the existence of gratuitous evil.

## THOMAS AQUINAS

Thomas Aquinas (1225–1274) addresses the subject of evil in connection with his proofs for God's existence. He argues, as does Augustine, that a discussion about evil can only be understood correctly if viewed in light of the evidence that God does exist—a fact Aquinas argues could be "demonstrated from those of His effects which are known to us."[37] That is, although evil apparently argues against the all-powerful, all-good God's existence, the evidence from the world in which man lives provides evidence to the contrary. Therefore, it is proper to begin with the evidence for God before considering the evidence against God. Even so, Aquinas confesses that the existence of evil makes it seem as though "God does not exist."[38] In the words of Geivett, "He [Aquinas] understood well that evil had been proposed as a serious objection to the existence of God, for in the *Summa theologiae* the problem of evil first appears under the heading 'Whether God Exists?'"[39] Therefore, although the evidence for the existence of God is compelling, Aquinas still thinks it necessary to respond to those who argue from the presence of evil to the non-existence of God.

### God's Omnipotence and Goodness

Aquinas builds on the Augustinian notion of God's omnipotence and goodness and concludes that God will only allow evil if He can bring good from it. Aquinas points out:

> As Augustine says (*Enchridion* xi): 'Since God is the highest good, He would not allow any evil to exist in His works, unless His omnipotence and goodness were such as to bring good even out of evil.' This is part of the infinite goodness of God, that He should allow evil to exist, and out of it produce good.[40]

God, in His providence and goodness will and because of His nature, must bring good out of the evil, otherwise He cannot permit the evil. Geivett summarizes Aquinas's position by a "single proposition: God, being all good, must have a morally sufficient reason for permitting the existence of evil in this world."[41] Therefore, all evil leads to some good in the end because God has so ordained it. As with Augustine, Aquinas argues deductively, beginning with his theology proper. The good God brings out of evil is good in the general sense. Geisler suggests that Aquinas teaches that "not every specific event in the world has a good purpose; only the general purpose is good."[42] In the end, God's power prevails and good overcomes evil. That is, the good is restored.

### Evil as Privation

Evil itself, according to Aquinas, is a privation of the good. Every being "that is not God is God's creature. Now every creature of God is good (I Timothy 4:4): and God is the greatest good. Therefore every being is good."[43] Evil therefore is not a substance in itself, but a lack and in this, Aquinas echoes the Augustinian position of this point. As Hick says,

> But he [Aquinas] renders the traditional definition more precise by giving priority, among the several terms used by Augustine, to 'deprivation' and 'defect'. Evil, is the 'absence' of the good which is natural and due to a thing—as, for example, blindness is the deprivation of a good that is proper to a man but not proper to a stone."[44]

Aquinas summarizes his position by saying, "In fact, evil is simply a privation of something which a subject is entitled by its origin to possess and which it ought to have, as we have said. Such is the meaning of the word 'evil' among all men. Now, privation is not an essence; it is, rather, a negation in a substance. Therefore, evil is not an essence in things."[45] As Brian Davies says, "Aquinas puts it, badness is nothing positive. It is a 'privation of form'."[46] By affirming that evil is a lack of something in the good, it is possible for both Augustine and Aquinas to have a position on evil that avoids making God culpable for its existence. What God creates is good, that is, He does not create any evil. This means that evil is not a created entity with an essence of its own, but rather is something that happens to the good through the free choice of Adam. The understanding that evil is a privation answers the objection that God is creatively responsible for the existence of evil in this world.

### The Cause of Evil

If, however, every being is good, then where does evil come from? Whereas God (the all-good One) cannot create evil substantively (essentially), how is evil related to God? Aquinas maintains that "evil has no formal cause, rather it is a privation of form; likewise, neither has it a final cause, but rather it is a privation of order to the proper end; since not only the end has the nature of good, but also the useful, which is ordered to the end. Evil, however, has a cause by way of an agent, not directly, but accidentally."[47] As Hick observes, for Aquinas, "Paradoxically, then, the cause of evil can only be something good, since evil as such cannot act as a cause. Good is accordingly the cause of evil— but only accidentally and in virtue of some defective power in the agent."[48] It is important, as Geivett notes, to understand that Aquinas's use of the term 'accidently' is designed to teach that "evil arises as the byproduct of some good desired. Evil is produced as an accidental effect of some good that is sought."[49] Aquinas uses the term accidently in an Aristotelian sense.

It is by relating evil to the notion of the accidental that Aquinas was able to avoid having God (the Good) responsible for evil. Aquinas writes, "And thus God, by causing in things the good of the order of the universe, consequently and as it were by accident, causes the corruptions of things according to I Kings 2:6."[50] Gilson explains the thought of Aquinas on this point:

> Now the principle from which God clearly intends in created things is the good of universal order. But the order of the universe demands, as we already know, that certain things be deficient. God, therefore, is the cause of corruptions and defects in all things, only because He wills to cause the good of the universal order, and, as it were, *per accidens*. In sum, the effect of the deficient secondary cause can be attributed to the first cause, free of all defect in what concerns evil and defectiveness.[51]

Aquinas makes it clear that God did not create evil. The cause of evil is "in the action otherwise than in the effect."[52] That is, man is not substantively evil (he is a creation of God). As Brian Davies writes, for Aquinas to say that "something is bad (or evil) is to say, not that it *has* something, but that it *lacks* something. This means that evil could not have been a part of God's initial creation as creation flowed from the mind of God and God's mind lacks nothing.

## Evil and Human Freedom

Both Augustine and Aquinas understand that free will itself did not necessitate evil, but only made evil possible. Aquinas points out that, "Nevertheless the movement itself of an evil will is caused by the rational creature, which is good; and thus good is the cause of evil."[53]

The evil results, as Aquinas adds: "But in voluntary things the defect is not actually subject itself to its proper rule. This defect, however, is not a fault, but fault follows upon it from the fact that the will acts with this defect."[54] Aquinas makes it clear that his suggestion that good is the cause of evil, should not be construed as his saying that God is the cause of evil. He writes, "As appears from what was said [A(1)], the evil which consists in the defect of the action is always caused by the defect of the agent. But in God there is no defect, but the highest perfection, as was shown about [Q(4), A(1)]. Hence, the evil which consists in the defect of action, or which is caused by defect of the agent, is not reduced to God as its cause."[55] As Hick points out, Augustine held that "good is accordingly the cause of evil—but only accidentally and in virtue of some defective power of the agent."[56] Aquinas, as Augustine, argues that evil results from some free negative act (the turning from the unchangeable good to the changeable good) of human will. Thus, God was not the direct, efficient or formal cause of evil. For as Davies argues, Aquinas holds that "God does not creatively will evil. All he wills is good. And he can only be said to will evil in the sense of permitting it, not in the sense of causing it directly."[57]

God has created a world with order and keeps such by His providence, yet as Martin D'arcy notes, Aquinas was not afraid of

> admitting evil within this order. Evil is not created by God; it finds its way in owing to the imperfection of certain types of being. The good which animals pursue cannot be gained without accompanying pain; man cannot, in his present life, be virtuous without effort and painful endurance. Accordingly, this world is not the best conceivable; God could have created more perfect beings, but their ideal would not be our Utopia; it would be completely different. This universe of ours, then, if not the best conceivable, is relatively best, relative to us and to the end and perfection which God had in view.[58]

Here, Aquinas suggests that the good that comes from evil so some kind of soul-making good.

Man's power to choose is the means whereby he can achieve happiness, but as Frederick Copleston observes in his discussion of Aquinas's moral theory, "Perfect happiness, the ultimate end, is not to be found in any created thing, but only in God, who is himself the supreme and infinite Good."[59] In Alexander Broadie's words, Aquinas thinks that man has happiness as his aim, "(w)hich we cannot reject, though through ignorance or incompetence we may in fact act in such a way as to put obstacles in our achieving it. However, the fundamental practical principle 'Eschew evil and do good' is built into all of us in such a way that no person can be ignorant of it."[60] According to

Swinburne, Aquinas's notion that "human blessedness (*beatiudo,* often misleadingly translated 'happiness') ultimately consists in the Vision of God."[61] It is, according to Aquinas, the defect within man that finds him at odds with his own purposes in finding this blessedness.

## Why Men Suffer Now

Men may suffer now, even virtuous men. But as Eleonore Stump points out in her discussion of Aquinas' commentary on Job, "Because Aquinas has always in mind the thought that the days of our lives here are short while the afterlife is eternal, he naturally values anything having to do with the afterlife more than the things having to do with this life."[62] The fact that the righteous suffer does not concern Aquinas. According to Stump, he thinks that "it is precisely those closer and more pleasing to God who are likely to be afflicted the most. Because God can trust them to handle their suffering without despair or other spiritual collapse, he can give them the sort of suffering that will not only assure their final salvation but will also contribute to their additional and ending glory in heaven."[63] In fact, Stump makes the point that according to Aquinas there is some soul-making in Aquinas's view:

> From Aquinas's point of view, the problem that keeps providence from permitting life on earth to be idyllic is the sinful nature of human beings, who are prone to sin even in their thoughts. But it is not possible for people whose thoughts and acts are evil to live happily with God in the afterlife. And so God, who loves his creatures in spite of their evil, applies suffering medicinally . . . . Nonetheless, on Aquinas's account, even a perfectly virtuous person is afflicted with a proneness to evil, for which the medicine of suffering is still necessary and important.[64]

According to Stump, evil for Aquinas is a necessary part of God's dealings with mankind to remind man that, regardless of how virtuous he may be, he still has a propensity to evil.

## Summary

In order to appreciate Aquinas's theodicy, one must remember that he begins with the proofs for God's existence and looks to the future end of man. As Geivett urges, "Aquinas' theodicy cannot be fully appreciated, or even properly understood, apart from grasping his conviction that one could first positively establish that God exists."[65] With God firmly fixed as a metaphysical reality of a particular ontological constitution (at least all-powerful and all-good), evil must be explained in light of that truth. Therefore, Aquinas is certain that, because of God's goodness and providence, all evil that exists (and only that evil exists) from this God will bring good and, therefore, there is no gratuitous evil. Davies concludes, "But God, for him [Aquinas], is wholly good as the source and pattern of all creaturely goodness, from which it follows that there are no standards over and against him in the light of which he must conduct himself."[66] Hick writes that for Aquinas, "'God allows evils to happen in order to bring a greater good therefrom'."[67] Good always obtains from evil. Stump asserts that Aquinas supposes that "*we* can know, at least in general, the good that justifies God's allowing evil. And he [Aquinas] accepts basically the same constraints as those same [sic] contemporary philosophers insist on: if a good God allows evil, it can only be because the evil in question produces a benefit for the sufferer and on that God could not provide without the suffering."[68] This, in fact, makes evil a necessary part of God's work among mankind, for without the evil certain and needed goods would not obtain.

In the end, there is no actual gratuitous evil in Aquinas's theodicy. In fact, all evil that God allows accomplishes something in the sufferer which could not have been achieved otherwise, if not in time, surely in eternity. This conclusion not only raises questions about gratuitous evil but about the greater-good notion in general. As Middleton points out, "Whereas the motivation of the greater good defense is admirable in that it attempts to retain an orthodox doctrine of God as both good and providentially sovereign in the face of evident evil, it is the strategy that is problematic."[69] It is built on an assumption of inference, namely, that an omnipotent and all-good God can not allow anything in His creation that does not serve a good purpose. This is seen in Augustine and now in Aquinas. It is, however, this very assumption that seems to open the greater-good approach to challenge even from a classical theistic position.

## GOTTFRIED VON LEIBNIZ

Gottfried Wilhelm Von Leibniz (1646–1716) in his treatise entitled *Theodicee (1710)* forwards the notion that this is the best of all possible worlds. Leibniz reasons that, (e)ven though one should fill all times and all places, it still remains true that one might have filled them in innumerable ways, and that there is an infinitude of possible worlds among which God must needs have chosen the best, since he does nothing without acting in accordance with supreme reason."[70] Augustine, Aquinas, and Leibniz all believe that God is all-powerful and all-good, and can only create good. Only Leibniz, however, takes it to its logical conclusion and argues deductively. To him, this necessarily means that what God has created is not only good ontologically, it was the best of all the possible worlds. Whereas all three argue deductively in some way beginning with God, Leibniz starts with God's character and what that means for creation.

## The Best of All Possible Worlds

Leibniz maintains that the world God chose out of all the possible worlds was the same world in actuality as it was in potentiality. This was true for every aspect of the world actualized including man's free will, even though man exercised the ability within the decrees of God. Leibniz states:

> Since, moreover, God's decrees consist solely in the resolution he forms, after having compared all possible worlds, to choose that one which is the best, and brought it into existence together with all that this world contains, by means of the all-powerful word *Fait*, it is plain to see that this decree changes nothing in the constitution of things: God leaves them just as they were in the state of mere possibility, that is, changing nothing either in their essence or nature, or even in their accidents, which are represented perfectly already in the idea of this possible world. Thus that which is contingent and free remains no less so under the decrees of God than under his prevision.[71]

Leibniz argues that God in His omniscience (middle knowledge) saw all the possible worlds and actualized the best of those worlds. When He did this, He changed nothing in the actualizing of the world that was known in its state of possibility or potentiality. Of all the possible worlds God could have actualized, this is the world that God chose and it is the best of possible worlds. Hick explains this for Leibniz:

> His [God's] choice was made from an infinity of different universes which were present in idea to the divine mind. Each constituted a complete history from creation onwards, and each formed a systematic whole such that to alter the least feature of it would be to change it into a different universe. It was these comprehensive possibilities that God surveyed, and from among which He summoned one into existence by His creative power.[72]

God, as the all-perfect and all-knowing being, could only do His best, which in this case was to bring into being (actualized existence) the best (not perfect in the same sense God is perfect) of the possible worlds. In the words of Plantinga,

Leibniz, as you recall, insisted that *this* world, the actual world, must be the best of all possible worlds. His reasoning is as follows. Before God created anything at all, he was confronted with an enormous range of choices; he could have created or actualize any of the myriads of different possible worlds. Being perfectly good, he must have chosen to create the best world he could; being omnipotent, he was able to create just any possible world he pleased. He must, therefore, have chosen the best of all possible worlds; and hence *this* world, the one he did create, must be (despite appearances) the best possible.[73]

In fact, H. J. McCloskey says that for Leibniz it was either God would create the best world or no world at all. He points out:

The argument then runs: God exists, Being all-perfect, he must create the best possible world, for there would be an imperfection in God if he chose to create a less good world when a better is possible, for otherwise it would always be possible for God to have created a better world *ad infinitum*, in which case he would not have created any world at all.[74]

Such a world, as Hick points out, cannot be changed in the slightest or it would not be this world. This includes either more or less evil. So this world, according to Leibniz, is not perfect, just the best of all the choices God had and the goods of this world commended themselves to God.

Leibniz is careful not to make the idea of a best world a necessity as this would then open his position to the claim that God is not free, that is, God Himself is determined. He writes:

There is always a prevailing reason which prompts the will to its choice, and for the maintenance of freedom for the will it suffices that this reason should incline without necessitating. That is also the opinion of all the ancients, of Plato, of Aristotle, of St. Augustine. The will is never prompted to action save by the representation of the good, which prevails over the opposite representations. This is admitted even in relation to God, the good angels, and souls in bliss: and it is acknowledged that they are none the less free in consequence of that. God fails not to choose the best, but he is not constrained to do so: nay, more, there is no necessity in the object of God's choice, for another sequence of things is equally possible. For that very reason the choice is free and independent of necessity, because it is made between several possibilities, and the will is determined only by the preponderating goodness of the object.[75]

God considered all the possibilities and chose the best, and this choice was really free for God. Copleston points out that for Leibniz "absolutely speaking, God could have created a different world, but, morally speaking, He could create only the best of possible worlds."[76] God is totally free to create or not create. Once He chooses to create, it is morally impossible for God to create anything but the best of all possible worlds. This is not to be understood as a logical necessity, but rather the good of the object or a moral necessity.

## The Meaning of World

When Leibniz affirms that this is the best of all possible worlds, he is using the word *world* to identify all of created order from start to finish. He explains, "I call 'World' the whole succession and the whole agglomeration of all existent things, lest it be said that several worlds could have existed in different times and different places. For they must needs be reckoned all together as one world, or if you will, as one Universe."[77] That is, "It is a continued creation."[78] This flows from his idea that there were many possible worlds, but out of all the possible worlds, God chose the best and this world as a whole formed one book of that world. If there were to be a better world in the future, then God had not selected the best in His initial creation. As Peterson observes, for Leibniz, the best possible world "is a total possible state of affairs, a complete universe with past, present, and future."[79]

For Leibniz, this means that there is continuity to created order substantively. Although certain accidental changes may occur throughout the entire course of its history, it still must be considered as this world not in a temporal/segmented sense but in an ontological, wholistic sense. Everything that makes up this world is involved to the extent that, "(i)f the smallest evil that comes to pass in the world were missing in it, it would no longer be this world; which, with nothing omitted and all allowance made, was found the best by the Creator who chose it."[80] This must necessarily be true if this is the best of all possible worlds as a result of the argument that the all-perfect God chooses only the best. Therefore, there is only one world actualized, as there can only be one best and this includes the past, present and future.

As Leibniz makes clear, "Now this supreme wisdom, united to a goodness that is no less infinite, cannot but have chosen the best. For as a lesser evil is a kind of good, even so a lesser good is a kind of evil if it stands in the way of a greater good; and there would be something to correct in the actions of God if it were possible to do better."[81] There is nothing to correct. Nicholas Rescher explains that by best Leibniz means that this world "is the 'best possible world' in this somewhat rarefied metaphysical sense of *greatest variety of phenomena consonant with greatest simplicity of laws*. Its being 'the best' has (at any rate, in the first instance) little if anything to do with how men—or men and animals—fare in it."[82]

## The Source of Evil

Like Augustine and Aquinas before him, Leibniz understands the central issue in the problem of evil to be the matter of man's free will. The will has its own power as one does not will to will (no infinite regress of the willing). Reason inclines it, but does not determine it. Leibniz writes, "As for *volition* itself, to say that it is an object of free will is incorrect. We will to act, strictly speaking, and we do not will to will; else we could still say that we will to have the will to will, and that would go on to infinity."[83] This will, however, is not always guided by good judgment. Leibniz continues:

> Besides, we do not always follow the latest judgement of practical understanding when we resolve to will; but we always follow, in our willing, the result of all the inclinations that come from the direction both of reasons and passions, and this often happens without an express judgement of the understanding.[84]

Because the will depends on reason, it should follow that if man always judges rightly, he will act rightly. Bertrand Russell summarizes Leibniz's position: "For if we always judged rightly, we should always act rightly; but our misjudgment comes from confused perception, or *materia prima*, or limitation. And pain accompanies passage to a lower perfection, which results from action. Thus physical and moral evil both depend upon metaphysical evil, *i.e.* upon imperfection or limitation."[85]

Leibniz acknowledges that if one claims that free will has led to suffering, one must explain why the will turned in that direction. It could not be in the will, Leibniz reasons, because God made the will and all that God does is good. Therefore, he concludes that the answer must be found in that which is independent of man's will. This leads him to argue that the weakness is in the ideal nature of man. He writes, "We must consider that there is an *original imperfection in the creature* before sin, because the creature is limited in his essence; whence ensues that it cannot know all, and that it can deceive itself and commit other errors."[86] The nature of man, although it is good, is limited by the fact it was created (finite), which means man is finite in every respect, including knowledge. Therefore, it is impossible for man, as a creature, to know everything. The limitedness (man as a finite creature) of man's ideal nature (his nature was good because it came from God) proved to be the cause of evil. Geivett says, "Evil, in Leibniz's view, is a privative reality. It is an imperfection that comes from limitation."[87] It is not a moral defect or deficiency, but rather an ontological limitedness necessary to man's finiteness that was entailed in the fact he was a created being.

Leibniz continues his explanation, employing an analogy from the field of physics:

> . . . (l)et us compare, I say, the inertia of matter with the natural imperfection of creatures, and the slowness of the laden boat with the defects to be found in the inequalities and the action of the creature; and we shall find that there is nothing so just as this comparison. The current is the cause of the boat's movement, but not of its retardation; God is the cause of perfection in the nature and the actions of the creature, but the limitation of the receptivity of the creature is the cause of the defects there are in his action. Thus the Platonists, St. Augustine and the Schoolmen were right to say that God is the cause of the material element of evil which lies in the positive, and not of the formal element, which lies in privation. Even so one may say that the current is the cause of the material element of retardation, but not of the formal: That is, it is the cause of the boat's speed without being the cause of the limits to this speed. And God is no more the cause of sin than the river's current is the cause of retardation of the boat.[88]

God is not responsible for the limitation, for all created beings, of necessity, have this limitation, as anything created cannot be limitless in all or any respects, for such an attribute belongs only to God who is uncreated. As Ed Miller points out, Leibniz teaches: "(i)t would in fact be *logically impossible* to have a world without evil: Anything created by God would have to be *less* than God just by virtue of being *dependent* on him, and this means immediately that it must be less than perfect, and *this* means immediately the presence of various sorts of imperfections. How could God create something that was perfect, and therefore independent, and therefore uncreated? *It is logically impossible.*"[89] This limitation is not a moral imperfection, but moral imperfection came from this limitedness. As Geivett explains Leibniz, evil "is an imperfection that comes from limitation."[90] This limitation is not evil. As a created entity it could not be perfect in the sense that God (a necessary being) is perfect.

## Free Will

Free will entailing judgment places man above the rest of creation. Choices alone do not make for true freedom of choice. Rather, the ability to make a judgment (moral) about the choices must be added to choices. For Leibniz, free will also meant that the will has its own power. There is not a will that causes the will. As Russell observes,

> He rejected entirely the liberty of indifference—the doctrine that the will may be uncaused—and even held this to be self-contradictory. For it is necessary that every event should have a cause, though it is contingent that the cause should produce its affect . . . . But it is in the goodness or badness of the reason that moral good and evil consist.[91]

Leibniz maintains that the will is free. Man's will, in order to be truly free, must be totally free:

> I am of the opinion that our will is exempt not only from constraint but also from necessity. Aristotle has already observed that there are two things in freedom, to wit, spontaneity and choice, and therein lies our mastery over our actions . . . . There is *contingency* in a thousand actions of Nature; but where there is no judgement in him who acts there is no *freedom*.[92]

The will is free to will as that is the purpose of the will, and the predetermination of God's decrees do not confound (though it may limit) this freedom. For Leibniz, God does decree, but there is no insult to the freedom He has chosen to give man, since free will is part of the best possible world. In fact the notions of best and possible worlds are connected by the idea of free will. Since the best was a world where man had free will, that limited the possibilities of how that world would look, hence the best *possible* world.

So, if God were, in some fashion, to abrogate (or modify) the free will, then the best world would no longer be the world where that happened. In fact, to change anything in the world would be impossible for God. Leibniz asks:

> But could God himself (it will be said) then change nothing in the world? Assuredly he could not change it, without derogation to his wisdom, since he has foreseen the existence of this world and of what it contains, and since, likewise, he has formed this resolution to bring it into existence: for he cannot be mistaken nor repent, and it did not behove him to form an imperfect resolution applying to one part and not the whole.[93]

Once the world has been actualized, it cannot be changed. Elaborating on Leibniz's view of God's foreknowing this world and man's freedom, Millard Erickson points out, "God renders *certain*, but not *necessary*, the free decisions and actions of the individual."[94] Meaning what is is not of necessity. It could have been a different way before this world was chosen by God, but once it was the chosen world, it was certain that things would happen as God knew it to be in its potential state.

## All is Included in This World

On the face of it, this position would seem to eliminate any spontaneous acts of God, such as miracles. Whereas Leibniz believes that miracles did in fact take place within God's created order, he responds to this seeming limitation:

> But one must bear in mind that the miracles which happen in the world were also enfolded and represented as possible in this same world considered in the state of mere possibility; God, who has since performed them, when he chose this world had even then decreed to perform them. Again the objection will be made that vows and prayers, merits and demerits, good and bad actions avail nothing, since nothing can be changed. This objection causes most perplexity to people in general, and yet it is purely a sophism. These prayers, these vows, these good or bad actions that occur to-day were already before God when he formed the resolution to order things. Those things which happen in this existing world were represented, with their effects and their consequences, in the idea of this same world, while it was still possible only; they were represented therein, attracting God's grace whether natural or supernatural, requiring punishment or rewards, just as it has happened actually in this world since God chose it. The prayer of the good action were even then an *ideal cause* or *condition*, that is, an inclining reason able to contribute to the grace of God, or to the reward, as it now does in reality. Since, moreover, all is wisely connected together in the world, it is clear that God, foreseeing that which would happen freely, ordered all other things on that basis beforehand, or (what is the same) he chose that possible world in which everything was ordered in this fashion.[95]

For Leibniz, all agents, actions, and reactions including miracles, prayers and answers to prayers were part of what God saw in the category of possible worlds. His actualizing such a world did not determine how it would be, only that it would be. God saw all the possible worlds which would contain good and bad acts, prayers, vows, needs, answers to prayers and then chose the best world possible out of all the possible combinations. This does not mean that God determined the world in potentiality, but that He saw all the worlds as they played out under the rules of created order and then selected the best to be the world He actualized. John Feinberg observes:

> A second and somewhat related objection relates to God's knowledge of the future. Does God foreknow the future because He foresees what must happen (in Leibniz's case, God foresees what might hap-

pen, for there are limitless options) and then puts His stamp of approval on it, or does God foreknow it because He chooses what will happen and then knows what will happen? In other words, are the possibilities present before God, and then He, without being able to change any of the possibilities, just puts His stamp of approval on one set of possibilities? Or, does God personally create the possibilities, choose the ones He wants as He wants them, and then foresee the future because He has decreed it? Apparently, Leibniz would hold the first of these options.[96]

Feinberg, it seems, is right in his interpretation of Leibniz's understanding of the relationship between God's knowledge and the future. Leibniz sees himself as both a predeterminator (God's foreordination and decrees established the order in which the actual world would function and determined which world would become the actual world)[97] and as a Molinist[98] (God's foreknowledge does not determine man's choices).

## Evil in the Best of All Possible Worlds

Leibniz recognizes that to claim that this is the best of all possible worlds seems somewhat naive in light of the existing evil. Leibniz argues, however, that some would suggest that the best world would be one where no evil or sin exists. He simply replies, "But I deny that then it would have been *better*."[99] His reasoning is that the world is a whole; to change one piece would be to change the whole.

> For this must be known that all things are *connected* in each one of the possible worlds: the universe, whatever it may be, is all one piece, like an ocean: the least movement extends its effect there to any distance whatsoever, even though this effect becomes less perceptible in proportion to the distance. Therein God has ordered all things beforehand once and for all, having foreseen prayers, good and bad actions, and all the rest; and each thing *as an idea* has contributed, before its existence, to the resolution that has been made upon the existence of all things; so that nothing can be changed in the universe (any more than in a number) save its essence or, if you will, save its *numerical individuality.* Thus if the smallest evil that comes to pass in the world were missing in it, it would no longer be this world; which, with nothing omitted and all allowance made, was found the best by the Creator who chose it.[100]

It appears that Leibniz has made an important point concerning the connectiveness within this world and that it is correct to assert that changing the world in one place will have implications for the whole.

He further points out that the case for the presence of evil in this world can be made from an evidential perspective as well. It is "a little evil that renders the good more discernable, that is to say, greater."[101] Having said this Leibniz realized that there was more than a little evil in the world. Hereby, he responds to the one who argues that there is no reason evil should outnumber good by so much. He postulates a greater good in that "if we were unusually sick and seldom in good health, we should be wonderfully sensible of that great good and we should be less sensible of our evils."[102]

As Leroy Loemker says, "Evil *is* because of the good and is impossible except as it is ordered to the good. So there can be no evil which is not known and invited by the highest Good."[103] This line of reasoning, Leibniz suggests, is sensible because we have knowledge of the life to come and the assurance that God always acts in a way that is dutiful, and therefore whatever happens, even the evil, does not destroy the idea of greater good. God does not require the evil and, regardless of how one might make a case, even much evil does not destroy the position that good obtains. The fact is, says Leibniz, that "although it happens very often that it [evil] may serve as a means of obtaining good or of preventing another evil, it is not this that renders it a sufficient object of the divine will or a legitimate object of a created will."[104] What makes it permissible is if evil is "considered to be a certain consequence of an indispensable duty."[105]

> Nothing is open to question, nothing can be opposed to *the rule of the best*, which suffers neither exception nor dispensation. It is in this sense that God permits sin: for he would fail in what he owes himself, in what he owes to his wisdom, his goodness, his perfection, if he followed not the grand result of all his tendencies to do good, and if he chose not that which is absolutely the best, notwithstanding the evil of guilt, which is involved therein by the supreme necessity of the eternal verities.[106]

In the end, God, by duty to Himself, must always antecedently will what is good, for He is good and wills consequently the best from all acts, including evil. Evil only exists because God was being true to Himself by doing His best when creating this world. The best of all possible worlds is not necessarily one without evil but the amount of evil is commensurate with this being, on the whole, the best world. In fact, Leibniz does not argue that this is a perfect world, only the best world.

## The Greater Good

Leibniz holds to the position that although God is not properly responsible for evil, He does in fact permit it and brings a greater good from it. Nicholas Rescher writes:

> Leibniz distinguishes three modes of evil: *physical* evil, which consists of suffering, *moral* evil, sin and *metaphysical* evil, the imperfection of creatures. The first two reduce to the third, for if God admits evil into creation, to create it as such would contravene God's own perfection. Evil of any sort cannot properly be said to be *created* by God; rather it is *admitted into existence* by him as an unavoidable concomitant of the perfections he seeks to realize in his creation.[107]

As for physical evil, Augustine maintains and Leibniz affirms that God wills it "often as a penalty owing to guilt, and often also as a means to an end, that is, to prevent greater evils or to obtain greater good."[108] Leibniz agrees with both Augustine and Aquinas that God uses evil to bring about a greater good, and there can be no other evil (the doctrine of meticulous providence). Further, in all cases, God is not responsible for moral evil (moral evil is never an instrument of God's justice). M. B. Ahern writes, "Leibniz, for example, seems to be correct in laying it down that all actual evil can be justified only as it is a necessary means to a greater good."[109]

## Summary

Leibniz follows the Augustinian tradition by affirming that free choice is the cause of evil in the world. Although God created the will that was good, it was of necessity not perfect because it was created. It is this metaphysical, not moral imperfection, which is responsible for evil in the world. Because God is all-good and all-powerful, He brings good out of evil. While there are differences between Leibniz, Augustine, and Aquinas, Leibniz continues the tradition of the free-will defense and greater-good as God's moral justification for permitting evil in this world. Because this is the best of all possible worlds, one can be sure that the amount of evil in the world is at a bare minimum.

## CONCLUSION

Augustine, Aquinas, and Leibniz agree that evil has resulted through the reality of man's free will. The will is not sinful itself, but it exercises itself in such a way as to choose against, instead of for God. All three, while differing in some of the details, agree that God is able to bring good out of evil. In fact, God uses evil to obtain a greater good.

All three argued (not necessarily on the same grounds) that gratuitous evil does not exist. Unique to Leibniz, however, is his idea that this is the best of all possible worlds.

Although this position has not gained much support over the years, it has theological support and is most promising in advancing a consistent theodicy. The key is understanding Leibniz's view of 'world' by including everything from creation to after life (the state of affairs to come). In fact, Geivett suggests (after quoting Martin Gardner to this effect) that:

> . . . if this assessment is correct, and it does seem that Leibniz can be interpreted in this way, then here again Leibniz stands firmly within the tradition of Augustine and Aquinas by incorporating this eschatological assumption into his solution to the problem of evil. It may well be that Leibniz intended his best-world hypothesis to include the entire space-time universe, past, present, and future, including an eternity following this life where rewards and punishments will be meted out to morally deserving individuals with free wills.[110]

Even though Leibniz's theodicy at its core stands in the "tradition established by his precursors Augustine and Aquinas,"[111] he departs from them in claiming that this is the best of all possible worlds.

Leibniz's point that this is the best of all possible worlds flows naturally from his emphasis on the fact that God is all-perfect. Though God was all-perfect, the world that exists by creation cannot be God, and therefore the world cannot be perfect as God is. Therefore, if there *were* to be a world, certain necessary conditions dictate what would make that world possible. Since Augustine and Aquinas (and others) agrees that a world with creatures with free will in it is better than one without such, Leibniz is within the Augustinian tradition in arguing that best would at least have to entail man having free will. Given that, if it is really to be free will (understood as libertarian freedom), Leibniz argues, there would be a number of directions in which things could go (i.e. there were many possible worlds). God, seeing all the possibilities (due to His omniscience) chose this world (demonstrating His omnipotence), which under the order of free will (which is a necessary part of being a good world), would be the best (God being all-perfect). In this world, man would act freely, but it was this exact world that God determined with all the choices (good and bad), prayers, and other realities. That is, there were other possible choices, but they were not a part of this world; therefore, man did not get the opportunity to make those choices. By God's choosing out of all the possible worlds, God determined which world mankind would live in.

Furthermore, as David Griffin points out, Leibniz believes that, "(b)ecause of the features of possibilities, every possible world includes some evil."[112] Speaking of Leibniz's position, Griffin says, "Hence even the best possible world includes evil. Accordingly, even though there is much sin and suffering in our world, there is less than there would be in any of the other possible worlds."[113] This is part of what Leibniz means when he claims that this is the best possible world, namely that the amount of sin is at a minimum.

When Leibniz is compared with both Augustine and Aquinas in the matter of gratuitous evil, all three claim that gratuitous evil does not exist. Leibniz, however, arrives at his position differently. Leibniz argues that this is the best of all possible worlds based on the fact that God is the all-perfect one. Therefore, He chooses the world where the evil brings about some good. So, Leibniz's position flows from the fact that God is all-perfect. Augustine and Aquinas argue for no gratuitous evil based on the fact of God's omnipotence and goodness. They (and many others who have followed) assume that if God is all-powerful and all-good, then He cannot permit gratuitous evil in His created order. The question is whether this position can be the correct position given the apparent existence of gratuitous evil, i.e., evil that seemingly does not result in a greater good or even any good at all.

## NOTES

1. R. Douglas Geivett, *Evil and The Evidence for God* (Philadelphia: Temple University Press, 1993), 27.

2. Ibid., 28.

3. St. Augustine, *The Problem of Free Choice.* trans. Dom Mark Pontifix in *Ancient Christian Writers*, ed. Johannes Quasten & Joseph Plumpe (Westminster, Maryland: The Newman Press, 1955), 1.1.1. All quotes are cited from this source.

4. Augustine, *The Problem of Free Choice*, 1.2.5.

5. Geivett, *Evil and the Evidence for God*, 14.

6. Jaroslav Pelikan, *The Christian Tradition*, vol. 1, *The Emergence of the Catholic Tradition (100–600)* (Chicago: University of Chicago Press, 1975), 298.

7. Pelikan, *The Christian Tradition*, 299

8. Vernon J. Bourke, *Augustine's Love of Wisdom* (West Lafayette, IN: Purdue University Press, 1992), 33.

9. Augustine, *The Problem of Free Choice,* 2.1.3.

10. Geivett, *Evil and the Evidence for God,* 15.

11. Louis Berkhof, *The History of Christian Doctrines* (Grand Rapids: Baker Book House, 1975), 134.

12. Augustine, *The Problem of Free Choice,* 2.19.53.

13. Ibid., 2.19.50.

14. Robert J. O'Connell, S.J., *Images of Conversion in St. Augustine's Confessions* (New York: Fordham University Press, 1996), 181.

15. Augustine, *The Problem of Free Choice,* 2.19.53.

16. Etienne Gilson, *The Christian Philosophy of Saint Augustine,* trans. L. E. M. Lynch (New York: Vintage Books, 1967), 147.

17. Augustine, *The Problem of Free Choice,* 2.1.1.

18. Ibid., 3.1.2.

19. Ibid., 3.17.48.

20. Gilson, *The Christian Philosophy of Saint Augustine,* 147.

21. Augustine, *The Problem of Free Choice,* 2.1.3.

22. Ibid., 2.18.47.

23. Ibid., 3.4.15.

24. Ibid., 3.4.10.

25. Ibid., 3.3.8.

26. Robert F. Brown, "Divine Omniscience, Immutability, Aseity and Human Free Will," *Religious Studies* 27 (1991): 286.

27. Augustine, *The Problem of Free Choice,* 3.23.66.

28. John Hick, *Evil and the God of Love,* rev. ed. (San Francisco: Harper & Row, 1978), 89.

29. Augustine, *The Problem of Free Choice,* 3.23.68.

30. Richard J. Middleton, "Why the 'Greater Good' Isn't a Defense," 9 *Koinonia* (1997), 83–4.

31. Geivett, *Evil and the Evidence for God,* 17.

32. Norman Geisler and Winfied Corduan. *Philosophy of Religion,* 2nd ed. (Grand Rapids: Baker Book House, 1988), 325.

33. Augustine, *The Problem of Free Choice,* 3.23.69.

34. Ibid., 1.1.1.

35. Berkhof, *The History of Christian Doctrines,* 134.

36. Middleton, "Why the "Greater Good" Isn't a Defense," 82.

37. Thomas Aquinas *Summa Theologiae* 1.2.2. All quotes are cited from Volume One, Part One of the English Dominican Translation of Aquinas (1911) unless otherwise indicated [CD-ROM] (Albany, OR: Ages Software, 1998).

38. Ibid., 1.2.3.

39. Geivett, *Evil and the Evidence for God,* 18.

40. Aquinas, *Summa Theologiae,* 1.2.3.1.

41. Geivett, *Evil and the Evidence for God,* 18.

42. Norman Geisler, *Thomas Aquinas: An Evangelical Appraisal* (Grand Rapids: Baker Book House, 1991), 159.

43. Aquinas, *Summa Theologiae*, 1.5.3.

44. Hick, *Evil and the God of Love*, 94.

45. Thomas Aquinas, *Summa Contra Gentiles* 3.1, trans. Vernon J. Bourke (Notre Dame: Notre Dame Press, 1975), 48.

46. Brian Davies, *The Thought of Thomas Aquinas* (Oxford: Clarendon Press, 1992), 90.

47. Aquinas, *Summa Theologiae*, 1.49.1.

48. Hick, *Evil and the God of Love*, 94.

49. Geivett, *Evil and the Evidence for God*, 20.

50. Aquinas, *Summa Theologiae*, 1.49.2.

51. Etienne Gilson, *The Christian Philosophy of St. Thomas Aquinas*, trans. L. K. Shook (New York: Random House, 1956), 158.

52. Aquinas, *Summa Theologiae*, 1.49.1.

53. Ibid., 1.49.1.1.

54. Ibid., 1.49.1.3.

55. Ibid., 1.49.2.

56. Hick, *Evil and the God of Love*, 94.

57. Davies, *The Thought of Thomas Aquinas*, 96–7.

58. Martin C. D'arcy, S.J., *St. Thomas Aquinas* (Westminster: The Newman Press, 1955), 138.

59. Frederick Copleston, S.J., *A History of Philosophy*, vol. 2, *Mediaeval Philosophy: Augustine to Scotus* (Westminster: The Newman Press, 1962), 399.

60. Alexander Broadie, "Aquinas, St. Thomas," in *The Oxford Companion to Philosophy*, 1995.

61. Richard Swinburne, *Providence and the Problem of Evil* (Oxford: Clarendon Press, 1998), 80.

62. Eleonore Stump, "Biblical Commentary and Philosophy," in *The Cambridge Companion to Aquinas*, eds. Norman Kretzmann and Eleonore Stump (Cambridge: Cambridge University Press, 1993), 263.

63. Ibid., 263–64.

64. Ibid., 263.

65. Geivett, *Evil and the Evidence for God*, 21.

66. Davies, *The Thought of Thomas Aquinas*, 97.

67. Hick, *Evil and the God of Love*, 97.

68. Eleonore Stump, "Aquinas on the Suffering of Job," in *The Evidential Argument from Evil*, ed. Daniel Howard-Snyder (Bloomington: Indiana University Press, 1996), 51.

69. Middleton, "Why the 'Greater-Good' Isn't a Defense," 90.

70. G. W. Leibniz, *Theodicy*, ed. by Austin Farrer and trans. by E. M. Huggard (LaSalle, IL: Open Court, 1951), 128. This edition will be the text cited below.

71. Leibniz, *Theodicy*, 151.

72. Hick, *Evil and the God of Love*, 155.

73. Alvin Plantinga, "God, Evil, and the Metaphysics of Freedom," in *The Problem of Evil*, eds. Marilyn McCord Adams and Robert Merrihew Adams (Oxford: Oxford University Press, 1996), 86–7.

74. H. J. McCloskey, *God and Evil* (The Hague: Netherlands: Martinus Nijhoff, 1974), 79.

75. Leibniz, *Theodicy*, 148.

76. Frederick Copleston, *History of Philosophy*, vol. 4, *Descartes to Leibniz* (Westminster: The Newman Press, 1974; Image Book, 1985), 326.

77. Leibniz, *Theodicy*, 128.

78. Ibid., 139.

79. Peterson, *God and Evil*, 92.

80. Leibniz, *Theodicy*, 128.

81. Ibid.

82. Nicholas Rescher, "Logical Difficulties in Leibniz's Metaphysics," in *The Philosophy of Leibniz and the Modern World*, ed. Ivor Leclerc (Nashville: Vanderbuilt University Press, 1973), 185.

83. Leibniz, *Theodicy*, 151.

84. Ibid.

85. Bertrand Russell, *A Critical Exposition of the Philosophy of Leibniz* (London: George Allen & Unwin, 1967), 198.

86. Leibniz, *Theodicy*, 135.

87. Geivett, *Evil and the Evidence for God*, 26.

88. Leibniz, *Theodicy*, 141.

89. Ed L. Miller, *Questions that Matter*, 3rd ed. (New York: McGraw-Hill, 1992), 356.

90. Geivett, *Evil and the Evidence for God*, 26.

91. Russell, *A Critical Exposition of the Philosophy of Leibniz*, 193.

92. Leibniz, *Theodicy*, 143.

93. Ibid., 151–52

94. Millard Erickson, *Christian Theology*, vol. 1 (Grand Rapids: Baker Book House, 1983), 358.

95. Leibniz, *Theodicy*, 152–53.

96. John Feinberg, *The Many Faces of Evil*, 2nd ed. (Grand Rapids: Zondervan Publishing House, 1994), 50.

97. Leibniz, *Theodicy*, 146–47.

98. Molinists follow the Spanish Jesuit theologian Luis de Molina (1535–1600) in holding that God has what has been called middle knowledge. God not only knows all facts of actuality, but He also knows all possibilities in all that has potential. This means that free choices can be made and God knows them because He knows all possible free choices His moral creatures will make, yet He determines none of them. God's knowledge is thus complete yet non-coercive. It this way, man's free choice is preserved as well as God's omniscience.

99. Leibniz, *Theodicy*, 128.

100. Ibid., 128–29.

101. Ibid., 130.

102. Ibid.

103. Leroy E. Loemker, "Leibniz and the Encyclopedists," in *The Philosophy of Leibniz and the Modern World*, ed. Ivor Leclerc (Nashville: Vanderbilt University Press, 1973), 294.

104. Leibniz, *Theodicy*, 137.

105. Ibid.

106. Ibid., 138.

107. Nicholas Rescher, *The Philosophy of Leibniz* (Englewood Cliffs: Prentice-Hall, 1967), 153.

108. Leibniz, *Theodicy*, 137.

109. M. B. Ahern, *The Problem of Evil* (New York: Schocken Books, 1971), 73.

110. Geivett, *Evil and the Evidence for God*, 27.

111. Feinberg, *The Many Faces of Evil*, 27.

112. David Ray Griffin, *God, Power, and Evil: A Process Theodicy* (Philadelphia: Westminster Press, 1976), 132.

113. Ibid.

# Chapter 3

# Review of Contemporary Greater-Good Theodicies

The G-G theodicies of John Hick, Richard Swinburne and Michael Peterson have been selected for review because of their recognized work in theodicy. Each one has contributed much to the ongoing work of theodicy, particularly in answering the atheist evidential argument from evil. In spite of all the work that has been done, however, it still appears that the work of theodicy has not reached its completion. The following reviews are intended to illustrate how G-G theodicies explain certain important issues relative to a theodicy. Each review contains a brief critique on certain points. Several issues in particular will receive particular attention: gratuitous evil, free will (power of moral choice), God's omniscience, the state of man in the afterlife, and whether or not this is the best of all possible worlds. Other G-G theodicies might well have been included, however, these three seem to be a good representation of G-G theodicies in general.

## JOHN HICK

Hick begins his theodicy by affirming the traditional view of God as the all-good and all-powerful God insisting that in the Irenaean view "man, the finite personal creature capable of personal relationship with his Maker, is as yet only potentially the perfected being whom God is seeking to produce."[1] He believes this is the most promising starting point for theodicy. Hick urges, "Let us now try to formulate a contemporary version of the Irenaean type of theodicy, based on this suggestion of the initial creation of mankind, not as a finitely perfect, but as an immature creature beginning the long process of further growth and development."[2] Consequently, for Hick soul-making is both primary in God's intention for man and an explanation of why suffering must be allowed in this life. Through suffering the soul is perfected, and the perfected soul is the greater good that comes from human suffering.

**The Fall**

Whereas man was not created in a 'ready made' spiritually mature state, Hick argues that man must grow into the perfected state. Therefore, Hick, in the tradition of Irenaeus, suggests that man's spiritual maturing involves a two-stage process. At least in principle[3], he follows Irenaeus' notion that there is a difference between "the image of God" and the "likeness of God", which gestures to Hick's two-stage maturing process. He explains it as the process where individual persons are led from "human *Bios*, or the biological life of man, to the quality of *Zoe*, or the personal life of eternal worth which we see in Christ . . . ."[4] Through the struggle within a hostile environment over the last four thousand years or so, "[U]ncounted millions of souls have been through the experience of earthly life, and God's purpose has gradually moved towards its fulfillment within each one of them, . . . ."[5] According to Hick, man is made by divine power in the "image of God", but only through the struggle encountered in the hostile environment in which man lives is it possible to achieve the second intention of God, namely man developing into the "likeness of God."

The first stage, which came about by divine power, includes "the development of man as a rational and responsible person capable of personal relationship with the personal Infinite who created him."[6] This stage is what Hick identifies by the phrase "image of God." Of Hick's position, Geivett says "It would be impossible, even for divine omnipotence, to create individuals in an already perfected state."[7] Whereas for Hick the "personal life is essentially free and self-directing,"[8] it is not possible that it should be subjected to the controlling or determining power of God.

The second stage is signaled by the term "likeness", which points to "the certain valuable quality of life which reflects finitely the divine life"[9] and cannot be accomplished by God's omnipotence. This second stage is what Hick refers to as the soul-making stage. The value of life in this world is not determined primarily by either the pain or pleasure it brings but "by its fitness for its primary purpose, the purpose of soul-making."[10] For the soul-making process to move forward, man must be placed in an environment where temptation and struggle exist as a means to the soul-making end. As Hick writes, "The value-judgement that is implicitly being invoked here is that one who has attained to goodness by meeting and eventually mastering temptations, and thus by rightly making responsible choices in concrete situations, is a good in a richer and more valuable sense than would be one created *ab initio* in a state either of innocence or virtue."[11] As Marilyn M. Adams points out, Hick sees God's soul-making project culminating "in a process of spiritual development in which autonomous created persons, with their own free participation, are perfected, fashioned into God's likeness, formed towards the pattern of Christ."[12]

M. B. Ahern raises an objection to this. He points out, "The theory requires that every evil should be logically related to this perfection and, indeed, logically necessary for this perfection. It is hard to see how this can be."[13] If the maturing process is what this vale of tears is all about, then why is there so little of the maturing process manifested? With all the suffering in this world, the developing of the good character and authentic love for God should be more evident. In fact, it seems just the opposite—men are moving away from God. As Frederick Sontag observes, "Our world has the pain and stress needed for spiritual growth, but enough is enough, and it would appear God turned the pressure up so as to destroy some while educating only a few."[14] Sontag's point is well taken as few are actually improved spiritually in their love and understanding of God because of the difficulties they face. It would seem, if Hick is right on this, the number who are formed into the image of Christ would be much higher than appearances indicate. If stress and trouble are in fact designed by God to mature the soul, it would seem that the perfecting process would be more effective than what evidence suggests.

## The Importance of Man's Freedom to Love

Hick argues that the perfecting process becomes a reality by the exercise of man's free choice in learning what is the good as he faces temptation, struggles and risks. It is not that it is his free choice to be matured, but only that through his free choice the second phase of God's creative purposes are actualized through individual man's struggle in a fallen world. In the words of Stephen Davis. Hick argues that "what God wants is for us humans *freely* to love and obey God. Furthermore, the best virtues are those that are earned and learned rather than simply given."[15] Hick insightfully notes that God's purpose for men "is not only that they shall freely act rightly towards one another but that they shall also freely enter into a filial personal relationship with God Himself."[16] If God pre-selected only those choices men would make to do right—this would include loving God—then man's love for God would not be free. In fact, it would not be love. Hick points out that "He [God] would have pre-selected our responses to our environment, to one another, and to Himself in such a way that although these responses would from our point of view be free and spontaneous, they would from God's point of view be unfree."[17] It would be logically impossible, Hick concludes, for God to manipulate nature and environment so that man would choose to love Him, although it might be logically possible for God to make free man always to do right. If God made man so that man would love Him, then man's actions would not be free in his relationship to God, thereby seriously eroding the idea of both free will and love. Furthermore, Hick argues, if God manipulates man so that man can only love Him, there would be something "inauthentic about the resulting trust, love, or service."[18]

While logically God could have created a world where man would not sin, it would be logically impossible to create man so that he *would* love God. Love must be a totally free act or it is not love. Hick argues that it is of profound importance to be free to choose the good in order freely to develop morally. Authentic love and worship require the freedom to choose that path.

Hick's point is that coerced love and worship form an oxymoron. As Davis comments, according to Hick, "[W]hat God wants is for us humans *freely* to love and obey God."[19] Man must really be free to love and worship God if it is to be authentic. It is precisely this filial personal relationship that defines what is meant by the "likeness of God." This explains why free will is so central to Hick's theodicy.

### Necessity of Epistemic Distance

If man is really free to love God, Hick claims that there must be an actual distance between the infinite and the finite so that man will sense no pressure to love God. He writes, "In creating finite persons to love and be loved by Him God must endow them with a certain relative autonomy over against Himself. But how can a finite creature, dependent upon the infinite Creator for its very existence and for every power and quality of its being, possess any significant autonomy in relation to that Creator?"[20] In other words, there must be some "epistemic distance"[21] between the Infinite One and the finite ones if there is to be any true sense of freedom on the part of the created ones.

According to Hick, epistemic distance means that "the reality and presence of God must not be borne in upon men in the coercive way in which their natural environment forces itself upon their attention."[22] Epistemic distance is God setting man at an epistemological distance from himself so that man's freedom to choose to love God would be totally free—no subtle influence from God. This distance is not total distance, however, as it has been constructed in such a way that man can have some knowledge of God, but "only in a mode of knowledge that involves a free personal response on man's part, this response consisting in an uncompelled interpretative activity whereby we experience the world as mediating the divine presence."[23] This, he suggests, means that in a sense the world must not have some overpowering influence upon men whereby they would have no option but to acknowledge and love God. This is not to say that one cannot see God in the universe, but only that the acknowledgment must be of such a nature that it permits a true freedom of choice, where man is free either to be aware or not be aware of God. Whatever is visible of God in the universe, it must in no way bear unnecessarily influential upon man. Only then would man be truly free in his experience to choose to love God. Only under this state of affairs can man be said to be a free moral being who can enter into an authentic filial relationship with God. In the words of G. Stanley Kane, "According to Hick, if men were to live in the direct and immediate presence of God, they would not be cognitively free with respect to belief in God."[24] As Kane notes, in the end epistemic distance is "simply another term for lack of knowledge, or more bluntly, ignorance."[25]

According to Kenneth Surin, Hick's, epistemic distance only grants man the "cognitive freedom"[26] to acknowledge God or not acknowledge God with not the slightest pressure from God. Unfortunately, Hick does not explain how this would be accomplished or what it would look like in the real world, nor how it fits with certain declarations found in the Bible.[27] It is difficult to know with confidence whether Hick's "general opposition to natural theology"[28] gives rise to epistemic distance or if epistemic distance requires his view on natural theology. Either way the notion of epistemic distance lacks agreement with much of western Christian theological tradition.[29]

Another concern associated with Hick's notion of epistemic distance is the implication it has for the will. It assumes that the virtue of the will choosing right or good is predicated upon the kind of knowledge with which it has to work, not so much the act of the will itself. That is, the act of the will in man choosing to love God can only be authentic if the knowledge on which the will acts has a cognitively neutral relationship to the subject. This position maintains that if God had made himself known in some manifest way, then that love would not be authentic. Carried to its logical conclusion, this means that a child who loves his parents because they have provided for, cared for, and re-enforced their love for him could not be authentic love, because his love would not be truly free. The fact is, Hick constructs his idea of epistemic distance without logical parameters and, therefore, with an infinite range turning on ambiguity.

## The Greater Good Obtains

Hick maintains that in the end the good obtains however, when questioned regarding horrific evils he equivocates. For example, Nazi atrocities often come to mind. As James Wetzel points out, theodicists like Hick "want to say about the status of evils that they are supposedly outweighed by a greater good." He goes on to say that "Hick vehemently denies that his appeal to divine design should be taken to diminish or deny the gravity of evil."[30] In one place Hick argues that when bad things happen man may simply miss the good that comes from it. Hick says, "It is true that sometimes—no one can know how often or how seldom—there are sown or there come to flower even in the direst calamity graces of character that seem to make even the calamity itself worthwhile."[31] But then he confesses that the contrary could be true:

> It may also fail to happen, and instead of gain there may be sheer loss. Instead of ennobling, affliction may crush the character and wrest from it whatever virtues it possessed. Can anything be said, from the point of view of Christian theodicy, in the face of this cosmic handling of man, which seems at best to be utterly indifferent and at worst implacably malevolent towards him?[32]

When addressing the question of the Nazi program of the extermination of the Jews, Hick maintains, "It would have been better—much much better—if they had never happened. Most certainly God did not want those who committed these fearful crimes against humanity to act as they did. His purpose for the world was retarded by them and the power of evil within it increased."[33] Here, it appears that Hick is willing to admit that evil sometimes works counter purpose to the plan of God, in which case the principle of meticulous providence does not always hold. In this case, gratuitous evil would be a reality.

So which is it—gratuitous evil or no gratuitous evil? Hans Schwarz charges that Hick can give "no answer as to the why of the Nazi crimes,"[34] which indicates Hick's theodicy stumbles at a most important point—gratuitous evil. When pressed into consistency with a theodicy dening gratuitous evil, Hick refuses to give in and simply confesses that his only response is a "frank appeal to the positive value of mystery."[35] Hick is sure that the greater good is obtained as a God of love would permit no other. He argues, "It would be an intolerable thought that God had permitted the fearful evil of sin without having already intended to bring out of it an even greater good than would have been possible if evil had never existed."[36] By this Hick affirms that evil is necessary to the plan of God as it enables God to do something He could not have otherwise done. Yet, Hick also protests that he is not claiming that "each evil which occurs is specifically necessary to the attainment of the eventual end-state of perfected humanity in the divine Kingdom."[37] If this is so, does this mean that some evil does not accomplish its purpose, that is to say, it is pointless?

In the end, Hick admits that while concrete answers may be difficult, nonetheless, gratuitous evil does not exist. He writes, "Moreover, I do not now have an alternative theory to offer that would explain in any rational way or ethical way why men suffer as they do. The only appeal left is to mystery."[38] He argues that "there could not be a person-making world devoid of what we call evil; and evils are never tolerable—except for the sake of greater goods which may come out of them."[39] Hick is bothered neither by the circuity of his argument nor by the contradiction of his position.

## Universalism

Hick admits that suffering does not always complete its task in this life. His conclusion is:

> This world, with all its unjust and apparently wasted suffering, may nevertheless be what the Irenaean strand of Christian thought affirms that it is, namely a divinely created sphere of soul-making. But if this is so, yet further difficult questions now arise. A vale of soul-making that successfully makes persons of the desired quality may perhaps be justified by this result. But if the soul-making purpose fails, there can surely be no justification for 'the heavy and the weary weight of all this unintelligible world'. And yet, so far as we can see, the soul-making process does in fact fail in our own world at least as often as it succeeds.[40]

If soul-making is not accomplished in this life, then at some point after death a suffering will accomplish the perfection of the soul. As Hick suggests, this causes us to rethink the doctrine of hell. He concludes that the "needs of Christian theodicy compel us to repudiate the idea of eternal punishment."[41] For Hick, the only way the good purposes of a loving God can be met in suffering is if all men are saved (made perfect). He concludes that God must accomplish the soul's perfection after the death. Souls not won to God in time through suffering will be brought to God after death through suffering "within some further environment in which God places us."[42] Hick admits that this is an idea not "far from the traditional Roman Catholic notion of purgatorial experiences"[43] by which the soul ultimately reaches moral perfection. This, however, is not exactly what Hick has in mind. He does acknowledge that if the suffering in time fails to accomplish the soul-making process, then it can only be that the soul will be perfected after death, for if one soul fails then the God of love has failed. According to Hick, this may happen in what he calls "a series of lives, each bounded by something analogous to birth and death, lived in other worlds in spaces other than that in which we now are."[44] Hick explains his view of man reaching his spiritual perfection in the afterlife by positing a middle ground between purgatory and reincarnation. S. Davis asserts that Hick's posture with universal salvation, argues that "in the afterlife God will continue to respect our freedom; no one will be forced into the Kingdom, so to speak. But God has an infinite amount of time to work with and an infinite number of arguments to use."[45]

Other questions remain for Hick's theodicy. If soul-making is by free choice within the time-space context, then it would also have to be by free choice in the future (some kind of an environment after death that has suffering attached to it or even some form of reincarnation). If it is by free choice, how can one be sure that the "soul-making" will be accomplished after death? What is it about the suffering after death that accomplishes something, which could not be accomplished in time? Soul-making cannot be in any way that God forces it to happen, because that would be contrary to the central plank of Hick's theodicy—free will. Furthermore, it cannot be that somehow God is more evident to man after death, because that would be contrary to the notion of epistemic distance which, according to Hick, is essential to authentic love and worship. If God in some way influences this maturing of the soul, then the resulting love and worship would be of less quality than those matured under epistemic distance. If God bears Himself upon man after death, and man acknowledges God as a result of God overpowering man with His presence, then man's love would not be authentic because it would not be truly free will. Furthermore, as M. and R. Adams point out, "If souls make better progress in alternative post-mortem environments, however, we may ask why God did not place us in such settings from the beginning."[46]

In addition, Hick's soul-making theodicy appears weightless in the issue of natural evils. As Barry Whitney writes, "The problem of explaining why God allows physical evil is, perhaps, an even more difficult question than the problem of moral evil." Whitney also mentions that "a number of serious critical questions have been levied against Hick's theodicy at this point."[47] He admits that Hick attempts to answer these questions in his second edition of *Evil and the God of Love*, but having examined this edition, one is still hard pressed to find consistent answers to these questions. It is hard to see how some natural evils contribute to the soul-making notion in Hick's theodicy.

## The Suffering of Innocents and Soul-Making

As Geivett notes, for Hick "natural evil is regarded as a means of providing those environmental conditions that would be most instrumental to God's purpose of soul-making."[48] This might make sense, if natural evil were only thought of in impersonal terms. However, when the faces of human beings are placed on natural evil, this argument is difficult to understand. For example, the matter of children suffering from starvation because of a famine resulting from a drought seems to have no individual good to the starving children. Remaining questions fall along the lines of those natural evils that seem to play no part in soul-making, such as the thousands who starve to death because of a famine in Africa. There is no way that a three-year-old can benefit from the suffering, but it is the three-year-old who experiences the stomach pains. How are we to understand (even in the broadest sense) that such suffering provides an environment leading to some soul-making advantage, even for those who survive the famine? How could this be explained in eschatological terms of the greater good? Whereas soul-making is essential for the Kingdom, would this not mean that the three-year-old would need to enter the purgatorial state in order for his soul to be perfected, if suffering is the only way this can become a reality? Surely he is not perfected at this age by his own agonizing death. Something seems out of joint at this point, especially when Hick emphasizes—as he does—the God of love. Why would God not give everybody an equal opportunity in time to accomplish the stage-two maturing process? This would seem the least that a God of love would do.

## Summary

In the end, Hick's theodicy not only has theological differences that weaken its appeal to the classical theist, it also appears to have several inconsistencies as a system. Moreover, his universalism does not rescue his theodicy from its soul-making weaknesses. Aside from the theological issues, his failure to explain what appears to be gratuitous evil forges an untenable theodicy as it fails either to justify the ways of God or to give substantial understanding to the ways of God relating to evil. This has led Kane to conclude that Hick's theodicy is "either self-defeating or is merely a speculative conceptual scheme having no demonstrated capacity to explain the evils that actually exist in our world."[49] In the words of Schwarz, "Hick is unable to offer a plausible theodicy."[50] Geivett expresses his theological concerns over Hick's theodicy because Hick is "so willing to give up universally acknowledged conditions of orthodoxy within the Christian tradition."[51]

On whatever points one may find agreement with Hick, his theodicy as a whole fails as a satisfactory theodicy. It suffers from internal contradiction and requires a commitment to certain theological concepts which fall outside the pale of what is generally accepted within orthodox theology (such as universal salvation of mankind). Furthermore, Hick's theodicy fails to provide an adequate explanation for natural evils and those evils involving the innocent or disadvantaged. Moreover, at one point he seems to make provision for gratuitous evil and at another point he denies its existence. For all his assurances to the contrary, Hick's theodicy, Irenaean or not, is still a G-G theodicy.

As Middleton notes, although Hick "claims to propose a theodicy that follows not Augustine, but Ireneaus and provides an alternative to Augustinian theodicy, his resolution of the problem of evil constitutes another version of the greater good defense."[52] It is Madden and Hare who succinctly summarize the failure of Hick's Irenaean theodicy:

> (i) This solution is simply inapplicable to some physical evils, insanity being perhaps the best example. (ii) At best it can only account for a small amount of evil and cannot account at all for the maiming of character which too much evil often produces. . . . (iii) The price that is paid for spiritual growth even when it does occur is often too high to be justly exacted. (iv) Moreover, it is not clear why God, if he is all-powerful, could not have created spiritually significant people in the first place. . . . (v) If courage, endurance, charity, sympathy, and the like are so spiritually significant, then the evil conditions which foster them should not be mitigated.[53]

## RICHARD SWINBURNE

Richard Swinburne weighs in on the theodicy quest because, in his estimation, "[w]ithout a theodicy, evil counts against the existence of God."[54] He thinks the "Christian doctrine of Providence is itself a central Christian doctrine," which can be defended against objections "when given its specifically Christian form."[55] Furthermore, Swinburne's understanding of the traditional task of theodicy[56] is not necessarily to give "an account of God's actual reasons for allowing a bad state to occur, but an account of his possible reasons (i.e., reasons which God has for allowing the bad state to occur, whether or not those are the ones which motivate him)."[57] He believes that God's good purposes are or "will be realized in the world"[58] and that the "good states which (according to Christian doctrine) God seeks are so good that they outweigh the accompanying evil."[59] Furthermore, Swinburne believes that suffering is a means to develop one's character. He writes, "It is good, as we have noted earlier that we should have the opportunity over time freely to form our characters, to determine the kind of people we are to be."

## Libertarian Freedom

At the center of Swinburne's theodicy is the theological concept of free will, which for him is the libertarian understanding of freedom.[60] Swinburne acknowledges that the Free Will Defense "forms a central plank of [his] own theodicy"[61] as understood within the libertarian tradition. Concerning libertarian freedom, Swinburne points out that "the Christian theological tradition is that all Christian theologians of the first four centuries believed in human free will in the libertarian sense, as did all subsequent Eastern Orthodox theologians, and most Western Catholic theologians from Duns Scotus (in the fourteenth century) onwards."[62] By libertarian freedom, Swinburne means that the agent's intentional action is not fully caused by either some process of natural causation (i.e., in virtue of laws of nature) or in some other way (e.g., by an agent such as God acting from outside the natural order).[63] He is convinced that the free will defense "becomes more plausible only if 'free will' means libertarian free will."[64]

According to Swinburne, if the only view of free will is that of the compatibilist, then God is ultimately the cause of evil unless "it can be shown that any actual bad choice is a necessary condition of some good state of affairs . . . ."[65] He suggests the compatibilist position makes the task of defense very difficult because it requires showing that "allowing the bad to occur is *logically* necessary for the attainment of good."[66] Swinburne reasons that demonstrating evidentially such a state of affairs promises to be a most difficult and unnecessary task for the theist (which is precisely the premise of this present work).

For Swinburne, the greater good lies in the free will of man even though man may choose wrong. If evil results from man's free will (and it has), evil in God's universe is morally justified on the grounds that the greater good is man having free will. Swinburne maintains that it is, in fact, this libertarian freedom that stands at the center of understanding evil, both in terms of Adam's sin and all who follow. He qualifies this by pointing out "that there must be a lot of other good served by our suffering than the good of Adam's responsibility for future generations."[67] Swinburne accepts the fall as "a historical Fall," but does not give it the "prominence that Augustine gave to it."[68]

In fact, his sympathies lie closer to the Irenaean tradition than the Augustinian. As Bruce Russell comments, "There are many similarities between Swinburne's theodicy and that of John Hick. (Hick himself sees Swinburne's theodicy as being of the same Irenaean type as his)."[69] Swinburne writes, "[A]nd plausibly enough—at any rate given the view of Adam as a weak character which Irenaeus and other early theologians advocated and which is far more plausible given our knowledge of evolutionary history than the rival view—the first human yielded at some time to his bad desires and so was also the first sinner."[70] With this view, Swinburne appears to deny any sympathy with the Calvinistic doctrine of total depravity and the fact men are all born sinners. He rejects this notion on "moral grounds" when he says, "I cannot be guilty in respect of the sins of another."[71] He does, however, see a relationship between Adam and those who came after. By "inheriting, genetically his desires and his free will; and by inheriting, no doubt in part culturally, his moral awareness, we later humans inherited that sinfulness" Swinburne notes.[72] Nonetheless, according to him, each person will be judged as a sinner solely on the basis of his own choices, but each person does not start out as a morally depraved being—a posture that places Swinburne out of step with many within the western theological tradition.

### God's Ability to Know

Swinburne argues that "[O]n the assumption that God's knowledge of the future is limited by the libertarian free will which he [God] gives to humans, even God cannot know in advance for certain the actual amount of harm one individual will suffer at the hands of another in a given situation."[73] Swinburne believes that God is omniscient with qualification: "An omniscient being is one who knows everything logically possible for him to know, anything the description of his knowing which does not involve a contradiction."[74] However, "He will not necessarily know everything that will happen unless it is already predetermined that it will happen."[75] What God can know (at least) is all past and present events as well as all future events He has determined. What He cannot know is the future choices of His moral agents. As Jerry Walls observes, "According to Swinburne, God knows everything that is possible to know, but the future actions of free persons are not knowable in principle. So not even God can know with certainty what actions free persons will perform."[76] Swinburne thinks that God can "predict human behavior correctly most of the time, but always with the possibility that men may falsify those predictions."[77] Swinburne argues that suggesting God foreknows all the possible worlds he can create, all the free beings, and under what circumstances each would choose to do good or bad unnecessarily complicates and frustrates the theist's work of theodicy.

Concerning middle knowledge, Swinburne finds problems. His controversy with middle knowledge arises over the question of whether or not there is any truth-value to counterfactuals of freedom.[78] Swinburne contends there are no counterfactuals of freedom with truth-value and, therefore, not even "an omniscient being could know which counterfactuals of freedom were true or false and thus act to put creatures only in those circumstances in which they will freely choose rightly."[79] Therefore, God cannot know any counterfactuals of creaturely freedom, which means that all God knows with respect to the choices of contingent beings is that they will choose. He cannot know what they will choose, however; He may have a high rate of success predicting what they might choose. Furthermore, if there is an infinite number of beings and circumstances from which to create this world, Swinburne asks, why did not God choose only those beings and those circumstances in which they freely choose to do good?[80] This, however, would be a cut and paste world which would not be a real world..

If, as Swinburne maintains, God does not know the future choices of His moral creatures, then how would God know if their particular choices would bring good or evil? Since Swinburne argues for the greater-good justification of evil and denies gratuitous evil, it arguably appears that if God does not know the future choices of his moral beings, it would be impossible for Him to prevent any evil that will not serve some good. In order for God to prevent gratuitous evil, He would have to know what the choice is ahead of time in order to prevent any evil that will not serve His good purposes. It appears necessary that God know the future choices of His moral agents. The only way around this rationale would be if God could change the past. That is, after He finds out about the choice, He can go back and change what has happened—a position that seems most difficult to defend both philosophically and theologically.

## Greater Good Will Obtain

Not only is the general greater good found in the reality of man's free will as the general order of things, but also, for Swinburne that a good obtains from different kinds of evil. He believes it is possible to demonstrate that the good obtains, arguing that evidence points to the fact that the good obtains and is observable to man. For Swinburne, Stephen Wykstra's Condition of Reasonable Epistemic Access (CORNEA) position is "too bold a claim."[81] According to Wykstra, one may not always see the good obtained, but this should not concern the theist, as God's ways are much deeper than man's ways. Swinburne correctly states Wykstra's position saying that "we have reason to suppose that if there is a God, His understanding of moral goodness will be so much deeper than ours that it is to be expected that we should think that there are bad states which serve no greater good, when in fact they do serve the greater good."[82] Swinburne counters with this pointing:

> The trouble with this version of the argument is that while our moral beliefs (and factual beliefs, we must add) may indeed be in error in relevant respects, we need some further argument to show that they are more likely to be biased in the direction of failing to understand that some apparent bad states really serve greater goods, rather than in the direction of failing to understand that some apparent good states really serve greater bad states.[83]

The conclusion for Swinburne is that if Wykstra's position is to hold, it must be demonstrated that the human mind is more apt to view things incorrectly than correctly, where "correctly" means the way God sees.

Swinburne postulates that one must look at the larger picture, whether the net gain in human history favors the bad or the good. This is not to say that each evil is not necessary, but that any particular evil may not be sufficient in and of itself to bring about the greater good. Nonetheless, without the particular evil, the outweighing good could not obtain. His argument is that the good outweighs the bad, even if only by a little bit. All evil, on the balance of things, is outweighed by the good. God is fair in allowing the evil because He the Creator God. Swinburne qualifies this by stating that "God has a right to do something if and only if he does no wrong to anyone else by doing it."[84] Furthermore, no one can claim that God is unfair unless "the bad states were too bad or not ultimately compensated."[85] However, Swinburne adds, "The crucial point is that God must not over time take back as much as he has given. He must remain on balance a benefactor."[86] Swinburne is confident that when put in these terms, the argument demonstrates that the greater good obtains.

If one accepts Swinburne's theodic framework, a question still remains: If God does not know the future choices of his moral agents, how is it that one can be assured that the *greater* good always obtains? If God does not know the evil that men will choose, neither will He know the good they will choose and how that good might offset some evil. Consider this scenario: $A$ commits a good act ($G$) at $t_1$ so that at $t_1$

God knows about *G* and does what he can do within the consistency of Himself and the world He created to promote the good that *A* chooses. At $t_2$, however, *A* chooses to use *G* as an opportunity to choose to do an evil act (*E*). The question is, if God has only limited knowledge of future choices of his moral creatures, will not God inadvertently promote *G* not knowing that *G* is going to be used to accomplish *E*? This appears problematic. God, according to Swinburne, is always acting to promote the good or to bring about a greater good out of evil, but He is forced to do so without the benefit of the knowledge of future choices of others that will impact the situation.

Suppose Bill gives Susan, who is in a desperate financial situation, $100 (G). Susan agrees to pay it back in three weeks. However, she chooses to spend her money elsewhere. At the end of three weeks Susan is unable to pay Bill (E). At this point, Bill chooses to forgive the debt (G), but he then chooses to use the forgiveness to coerce Susan to provide him with a sexual favor. Susan senses no way out, so she gives Bill what he wants and loses her virtue (E). Instead of Susan's character being built up (the initial help with the $100), her virtue is destroyed, which can hardly be considered a greater good. According to the limited knowledge scheme, God would have promoted the first good, which in the end was used for evil. This is a reverse of what is often used as an example, but it works both ways. This seems to be a problem for the greater-good justificatory scheme.

## Natural Evil Is Not Gratuitous

Concerning natural evil, Swinburne considers it necessary in order for man to know how to do evil or good to his fellows. "For example, Swinburne writes, "I believe that the occurrence of natural evils (i.e., evils such as disease and accidents unpredictable by humans) is required for humans to have the power to choose between doing significant good or evil to their fellows, for the reason that the observation of the process which produces natural evil is required to do significant evil to their fellows. Without that knowledge the choice between good and evil will not be available."[87] Stump, who has serious reservations about Swinburne's view, points out that Swinburne's major premise rests on the assumption that "men can have knowledge of the consequences of their actions only by induction on the basis of past experience."[88] Past evils are important for man to understand what constitutes suffering so he can avoid or cause the same. This position, however, does not seem to hold. After man learns from the natural evil that the natural evil will no longer be necessary, since man will have learned the bad consequences. Yet much of the same natural evil continues. Swinburne argues continued observation of the evils in nature is necessary. This is part of the greater good because such knowledge is "a further good beyond the mere possession of knowledge."[89] It is not clear at this point if Swinburne is only arguing for the superiority of such knowledge or for the necessity of experience as the sole source of such knowledge. Moreover, what begins as natural evil, once man has gained the practical knowledge from that evil—if he continues in that evil—becomes a moral evil not a natural evil. This is to ask how can a second person's act of murder be justified, as it is not natural evil but rather moral evil?

Swinburne thinks that some of the most difficult evil happenings can be explained by what he calls the good-of-being-of-use approach. At times, someone's suffering is the means by which others are spared the same suffering. "Consider someone hurt or killed in an accident," Swinburne writes, "Where the accident leads to some reform which prevents the occurrence of similar accidents in future (e.g., someone killed in a rail crash which leads to the installation of a new system of railway signaling which prevents similar accidents in future)."[90] This does not give the invitation to someone to do evil so good may come of it, he argues. He appears to qualify his position when he adds, "Nor am I yet passing any judgement about whether the good is as great a good as the bad is bad. Nevertheless, I am claiming, the supreme good of being of use is worth paying the price."[91]

Further, Swinburne urges that this notion of the good-of-being-of-use applies even to corporate evils, such as the slave trade.

> (God's)allowing this to occur made possible innumerable opportunities for very large numbers of peoples to contribute or not to contribute to the development of this culture; for slavers to choose to enslave or not; . . . . There is also the great good for those who themselves suffered as slaves that their lives were not useless, their vulnerability to suffering made possible many free choices, and thereby so many steps towards the formation of good or bad character. And for the victims there remain the possibilities of compensation and reward after death.[92]

This gives men an opportunity to struggle for justice in light of such moral injustices, which means that the slave trade provided an opportunity for others to act justly in opposing such an evil. However, this does not justify their wickedness on the grounds that it gives others opportunity for good. Swinburne adds, "Yet again before anyone misunderstands—only God our creator has the right to allow bad people to promote the slave-trade. Humans had the duty to fight very hard against it; and a good God would very much want them to do that."[93] In this case, suffering that comes to large numbers of people through a social injustice would give others an opportunity to develop virtuous qualities by combating such injustice. Furthermore, those who suffer under such conditions will be compensated in the future, according to Swinburne. He sees even large scale evil, such as slavery, as a means for God to bring about the greater good. Still, it is unclear how such intense evils can be judged as justified because of their "bringing about the good which they make possible."[94]

Even with much suffering, Swinburne continues, the fact remains that men still choose to live rather than die, which means that suffering is seldom counted as being so bad one wants to die. What this indicates, Swinburne suggests, is that "even if they think that at present the bad outweighs the good, they live in hope of better times. Thereby they express their belief that a life of good as a whole and over time would be worth having even if its present state is on the balance bad."[95] In the end, he affirms that "God will only cause harm for the sake of good . . . ."[96] This, Swinburne suggests is evident in the way man looks at life; that is, he believes that in tomorrow lies the hope the good will prevail because this is the way life has proven to be.

Swinburne also appeals to this view as at least one explanation for the suffering of animals. He suggests that "all the ways in which the suffering of *A* is beneficial for *B* are also beneficial for *A*—because *A* is privileged to be of use. The fawn caught in the burning thicket is privileged to be of use to other deer; . . . he has enabled others to save themselves."[97]

Admittedly, Swinburne's efforts to demonstrate inductively from the evidence that gratuitous evil does not exist and the greater good prevails does have merit in some cases. The weakness, however, is revealed once again in that it seems impossible for the theist to demonstrate that the greater good *always* prevails, thus raising a question of legitimacy for the greater-good justificatory framework. Unless it *always* prevails, then the possibility of gratuitous evil exists.

### The Good Comes Either in This Life Or the Life to Come

If life really gets bad (as it appears in some cases), God has the option of bringing death and compensating the individual in the afterlife. Swinburne notes, "If the bad, in particular the suffering, endured by any individual during that period outweighs the good, God does have the power to compensate that individual in an afterlife."[98] This of course would only be an argument if one of the following conditions is met: all men are ultimately saved, or all men enjoy some good albeit at different levels in the life to come. Swinburne hints at the latter when he suggests that "God, being good, would not punish a sinner with a punishment beyond that he deserved; and I suggest that, despite majority Christian tradition, literally everlasting pain would be a punishment beyond the deserts of any human who has sinned for a finite time on Earth."[99] For the incorrigibly wicked soul, Swinburne denies everlasting sensory punishment, rather concluding that "annihilation, the scrap heap, seems an obvious final fate for the corrupt soul."[100] If the wicked are annihilated, it appears the good does not obtain as Swinburne argues earlier. Since it is better to live than not to live. All the suffering in the lives of the wicked fails to achieve its purpose time, and God could not even compensate in the afterlife. In the end, it seems that some suffering, contrary to Swinburne's objections, is gratuitous.

Swinburne confesses that he is guided by two principles in determining his understanding of the future state of man. "The first is that the fate of man for eternity can, and often does depend on his own choices in this life. The second is that no man in the end is ever deprived of that fate (among those fates on offer) which he really seeks."[101] While Swinburne continues to affirm that it is choices in time that determine one's fate after death, he leaves the door open for those of the "right will" to be given more time (after death). He concludes that God gives us a "limited period of earthly life in which by our actions we can choose our character; he will leave us free to choose, and he will give each with his resulting character the kind of life appropriate to such a character. What more could we want?"[102]

While Swinburne considers what he calls the good pagan, he withdraws from any notion that anyone would fail the beatific vision of God except the completely corrupt soul, however that comes to be. The good pagan's destiny is determined by the "good will" factor. Pointing to those who die without the Christian message, he writes:

> Nevertheless, the man of good will has his heart in the right place. Despite his lack of good desires and important true beliefs, he deserves reward for the firmness of his good will. And the most appropriate and best reward would be to allow him to acquire the true moral beliefs and right unfrustrated desires which will give full blessedness . . . . And anyway, such a will is so precious a thing that a God who seeks man's eternal well-being would naturally allow it to be perfected, since that is the agent's basic choice, and allow him after this life through change of belief and desire to plead the atoning sacrifice of Christ and thereby join the Church and enjoy the bliss of Heaven.[103]

This is not to be confused with purgatory, which teaches that those in that state will be perfected. Swinburne is arguing for the possibility that God will give the good pagan proper information which they had not received in life. Suffering in this life brings about the right form of the soul. Yet, in the case of the good pagan it is simply more knowledge in the afterlife. A question remains. If knowledge is sufficient in the afterlife, why not in this life? In other words, why not this kind of knowledge in this life, which would mean no need for suffering at all?

Swinburne wants this stage of the afterlife to be a time when the individual receives the right information, while the individual is still required to make a choice to move forward to Heaven by the work of Christ. It is not, however, necessarily the case that each individual will. Although Swinburne does not admit or deny it, this state of the afterlife would require some form of suffering—in order for Swinburne to be consistent—since preparation for Heaven (the beatific vision of God) cannot take place apart from suffering.

Furthermore, Swinburne's idea of being compensated in death seems to work only if: (1) the individual who dies has the right character through personal choices in time; (2) there is opportunity to develop right character after death. The first choice excludes (at least) infants and the mentally retarded. With the second, the theodicy requires (by Swinburne's own admission) a doctrine of afterlife outside the mainstream of orthodoxy. Furthermore, if the one perpetrating the evil is a corrupt soul, what punishment will he face for his wickedness in time? Hardly will a corrupt soul be compensated if he is annihilated. Even Swinburne thinks that life is better than death, but this is not death or life, this is annihilation. Annihilation hardly seems like a just recompense for causing a lifetime of suffering, such as shooting someone in the spine and the consequent quadriplegic state of another while the one who caused the suffering is never brought to justice. When pressed hard, Swinburne's attempt to demonstrate that evil always brings about a greater good, even in large amounts at particular times, travels far beyond either the evidence or imagination.

## Summary

Swinburne has worked to develop a theodicy constructed on the foundation of man's libertarian free will. God will respect the true human freedom where choices really make a different. To do otherwise would mean God fails His obligations to His creation. In defense of his theodicy, Swinburne addresses different kinds of evil in order to demonstrate evidentially that there are reasons to believe that good always obtains, concluding that gratuitous evil does not exist. God's knowledge is limited when it comes to the future choices of his moral creatures, and God cannot know counterfactuals of freedom. Swinburne's theodicy unfolds within the context of a world (not necessarily the best world) which has been voluntarily ordered by God. Furthermore, as most G-G theodicies do, Swinburne's theodicy, taken as a whole, appears to suffer from a lack of coherence.

## MICHAEL PETERSON

A theodicy may include (and most of the time does include) making a case for the Christian worldview, not just the one theological claim that God exists. As Peterson says, it is rather "asserting a whole set of logically interrelated claims regarding the divine nature and purposes. He (the theist) might even understand the single claim 'God exists' to be invested with this larger interpretive scheme and therefore entailing all sorts of other claims about God's ways with the world."[104]

For Peterson, developing a coherent whole is as necessary as answering the primary question of evil. The merits of the claim that God exists need to be judged on "how well the overall theistic position fares in comparison to other worldviews, both religious and secular."[105] Consequently, he attempts to address the problem of evil from a broad worldview perspective. Peterson thinks the task of the theist is not a matter of simply proposing *"merely possible* reasons God might have for permitting evil, a theodicy seeks to articulate *plausible* or *credible explanations* that rest on theistic truths and insights."[106] Therefore, Peterson wisely encourages the theist to be conscious of his worldview when doing the work of theodicy.

### The Evidential Version of the Problem of Evil

According to Peterson, many still believe "that evil provides a basis for some kind of nondeductive argument or broadly inductive argument against theism. The trick is to arrive at a formulation of an evidential argument from evil that significantly advances the discussion."[107] He admits that this is a more difficult but not impossible task as it "asks the theist to make sense of evil in light of his belief in God. In this case, the theist must answer the critic's charge that cites some alleged fact about evil as the *evidence* that supports the conclusion that it is more probable, given the evidence, to believe that God does not exist."[108]

In order to approach this task in a way that increases the possibility of its success, Peterson identifies three different forms of the evidential

argument from evil. He points out three objections the atheologian
might present as evidence against God's existence:

(E₁) Evil exists;

(E₂) Large amounts, extreme kinds and perplexing distributions of
evil exists;

(E₃) Gratuitous or pointless evil exits.[109]

Different atheologians have thought that all three arguments argue successfully against God. When any one is conjoined with "God exists,"
the probability of the claim "God exists" is questioned.

Peterson thinks that if (E₁) is what the theist must answer, he postulates that the theist could have relative success as "theists typically
agree that even quite considerable evil can be allowed by a morally
perfect deity as long as it is necessary to either bringing about a greater
good or preventing a greater evil."[110] He admits that it is a "dubious
assumption that God would not allow the existence of any evil whatso-
ever."[111] Therefore, Peterson suggests that the broad objection to God's
existence, based on the fact that some evil exists, can be rather handily
and successfully countered by the theist.

Responding to (E₂), however, presents the theist with a more difficult but not impossible challenge, says Peterson. The substance of the
objection in (E₂) is that "it is not the sheer existence of evil per se that
counts against the existence of God but the fact that there are so many
evils that are very severe and present in patterns defying comprehension."[112] As Peterson mentions, "Some theists have pointed out that this
argument rests on the assumption that the theistic deity would allow
only certain amounts, kinds, and distributions of evil. Yet it is hard to
know how to establish how much evil is *too much* for God to allow."[113]
True as this may be, Peterson holds that this still leaves the theist with
the Herculean task of demonstrating that every kind of evil as well as
the seemingly disproportionate distribution of evil serve some greater
good. The assumption is that if the all-good and all-powerful God allows evil, then it must only serve some greater purpose no matter how
great the evil.

If, however, it cannot be demonstrated that a greater purpose is
served, then the evil would be pointless (gratuitous evil), and God
would appear powerless in the face of this evil. This would count
against a G-G theodicy. Peterson concludes that the inescapable force
of (E₂) is such that "the burden falls upon the shoulders of thinking
Christian theists to articulate a concept of God which is more sophisti-

cated and profound than popular theism envisions."[114] In other words, Peterson concludes that it is important to establish a more precise view of God if one is to respond satisfactorily to the atheistic objection related to ($E_2$).

Although the evidential argument entailed in ($E_2$) is forceful, Peterson thinks that the issue of gratuitous evil ($E_3$) is undoubtedly the most crucial to the theist. He writes, "So, it is gratuitous or pointless evil, if it exists, that provides crucial evidence against the existence of a supremely powerful, wise, and good God."[115] If the gratuitous evil objection is answered, this would contribute to a satisfactory solution to ($E_2$). In order to answer the objection of ($E_3$), one needs either to demonstrate evidentially that all evil obtains the good (and thus defeat the claim that some evil is gratuitous) or develop a theistic worldview in which gratuitous evil does not count against God.

When answering the atheistic objection from gratuitous evil, Peterson maintains that William Rowe[116] presents the most formidable formulation of this version of the problem. He notes, "Rowe's argument has virtually been the paradigm for the evidential argument from evil since the late 1970s."[117] Peterson notes that Rowe's argument begins with the assumption that gratuitous evil exists, which is based upon *prima facie* evidence from the world and concludes that God does not exist. According to Peterson, Rowe's view of gratuitous evil is an evil

> that an omnipotent, omniscient being could have prevented without thereby losing some greater good or permitting some evil equally bad or worse. A gratuitous evil, in this sense, is a state of affairs that is not necessary (either logically or causally) to the attainment of a greater good or to the prevention of an evil equally bad or worse. According to this line of thinking, the only *morally sufficient reason* God can have for permitting any evil is that it must be necessary either to the attainment of a greater good or to the prevention of an evil equally bad or worse.[118]

Here Peterson points to the inherent difficulty of the G-G approach. If God allows only that evil by which the good is ultimately obtained, then it is incumbent upon the theist to demonstrate evidentially that this is so. In light of the fact there appears to be much evil that shows no sign of obtaining the good, then the greater-good approach has answered the more general problem—evil exists ($E_1$), but it has exacerbated the problem created by denying gratuitous evil ($E_3$).

Peterson acknowledges that most theists have approached the problem by trying to "rebut or mitigate the force of Rowe's first premise and thus stop the argument from working."[119] In spite of their efforts, the "evidential argument from gratuitous evil is now widely considered the most formidable objection to theistic belief."[120] In fact, Peterson claims that "the most potent atheistic rebuttals to theistic specifications of greater goods revolve around the claim that at least some evils or some kinds of evils do not seem necessary to any greater good."[121] Whereas "theists have typically taken a *greater-good approach* as integral to their search for a morally sufficient reason for why God allows evil,"[122] the theist must either demonstrate evidentially that gratuitous evil does not exist or rethink the *greater-good approach.* According to Feinberg, Peterson thinks "the better approach to solving this problem is not to deny the factual premise, but to admit its truth and to reject the theological premise."[123] The factual premise is that gratuitous evil exists and the theological premise is that God could not (or would not) allow gratuitous evil to exist (meticulous providence).[124]

As Peterson notes, the theist has generally attempted to prove the former. This has been done, however, by philosophical sleight of hand (circular reasoning) as the theist employs a deductive (*a posteriori*) approach to an evidential argument. For Peterson, "One flaw in many theodicies is that they tacitly assume that God exists and then argue against gratuitous evil with this confidence smuggled in. But within the framework of the problem of evil, this is an illicit assumption, since God's existence is the very thing in question."[125] In an attempt to avoid circular reasoning, Peterson addresses the problem of evil by developing a theodicy that acknowledges the existence of gratuitous evil while demonstrating that gratuitous evil does not count against God. He thereby challenges the idea that God would permit evil in His creation only if He would bring some greater good from the evil. Peterson questions this theological notion as unjustified within classical theism.

## Libertarian Freedom

Peterson argues that libertarian freedom makes gratuitous evil a real possibility and then shows how gratuitous evil is a reasonable (not logically necessary) correlative to libertarian freedom. He writes:

> [When we] consider that God chose to create free rational and moral agents who would exist in an independent, stable order—even though this creation entails the possibility of gratuitous evil—we see a God who does not hesitate to permit conditions (e.g., a natural order within which free creatures can significantly operate) under which such goods can be achieved, even though these same conditions may give some men grounds for atheism.[126]

Natural law provides the structure within which man's freedom operates and thereby keeps matters from becoming unmanageable and unstable. The unfortunate downside of all of this freedom is some horrendous evils experienced by mankind. However, through this natural order God is also able to achieve some good from evil.

Peterson's point is that, "God cannot eliminate the frightening possibility of gratuitous natural evil as long as he chooses to sustain natural order which, in turn, sustains a great many natural and moral goods."[127] That is, for Peterson the evil comes with the good, and to tamper with the natural law and moral order would seriously compromise man's free will and, for Peterson, "Free will is most significant—and fitting for the special sort of creature man is—if it includes the potential for utterly damnable choices and actions. This is part of the inherent risk in God's program for man."[128]

Still, Peterson adheres to the idea that God uses at least some evil accomplish His soul-making or character-building purposes. Therefore, some evil is justified. But there can only be true soul-making potential from evil if man lives in an environment where he is really free to choose between the good and the evil. This makes this world the only *kind* of a world (not necessarily the best of its kind) that God could create, according to Peterson. Precisely because this kind of world provides the opportunity for man to develop his moral character, on the balance of things this world (even with its gratuitous evil) is arguably a world that is worth being in existence. The net gain of the greater good makes this creation valuable.

Although Peterson sees this as a world in which God accomplishes much good, He does not believe that this is the best of all possible worlds or that this is the only world God could have created. It is not that this world must have evil in it; given the facts of creation order, it is understandable why there is evil. Peterson rejects the idea of meticulous providence, arguing that "it cannot be demonstrated that God is obliged to eliminate the gratuitous evils which man has an awesome power to create."[129] In fact he asserts that "a theistic case against gratuitous evil casts grave doubt on the reliability of human experience and on the moral and rational categories which condition it, and thus runs the risk of being self-defeating."[130] A world where man has real freedom is a better world than one in which he does not have true freedom. This means, however, that this makes gratuitous evil possible.

### God's Omniscience

Peterson points out that "one interesting benefit of this conception of gratuitous evil as a possibility which is *logically* linked to free will is that it does not necessitate limitation of any of the divine attributes, not even omnipotence."[131] Among the divine attributes Peterson names as important are perfect goodness, omnipotence and omniscience. He defines omniscience as *"at any time, God knows all propositions that are true at that time and are such that God's knowing them at that time is logically possible, and God never believes anything that is false."*[132] The critical point in his definition is "logically possible." According to Peterson (and Swinburne) some things are logically impossible for God to know, such as future choices of his free moral creatures. Since such knowledge is logically impossible for God to know, it cannot count against His omniscience. God cannot know the logically impossible any more than He can do the logically impossible. In this way, Peterson affirms that God is omniscient, yet does so in a way that is more consistent with those who hold to the openness of God view rather than the view of classical theism.

Peterson argues that his understanding of omniscience is a necessary corollary to his understanding of free choice:

> If we find the conclusion unacceptable (that is, if we believe that human beings do possess libertarian free will), then a reasonable response would be to adopt a definition of omniscience that includes the requirement of logical possibility . . . . The conclusion will be, then, either that no created beings ever make any free choices at all or that God is unable—*logically* unable—to know these decisions with certainty before they are made.[133]

Since God cannot know anything false, all things that God knows are true. Whatever God knows must happen, or else God would hold a non-truth or misbelief.

Peterson's logic is that if omniscience means that God knows all things, then whatever God knows *must* come to pass. Since future choices of His moral creatures are future, if God knows them prior to the choice being made, then, since they must come to pass, man does not have true freedom of choice. If God has always known that this author would be typing on his computer on a warm summer day in Maine and God only knows true propositions, then this author has no choice but to be typing on his computer on this day. If he were not, then God would have had false knowledge (at least in respect to this author's typing at this time), which means God would not be omniscient. The theist cannot have it both ways. He must choose between God knowing all things and man with no freedom of choice or God being logically constrained in His future knowledge (about future events related to human choices) and man having freedom of choice. Peterson admits that the idea of logical constraints on God's knowledge regarding contingents still needs more investigation and discussion to see if "it constitutes a serious problem for theistic philosophy and theology."[134] But, if Peterson is right, he has defended his understanding of theism against the charge from gratuitous evil. The central issue at this point, however, is whether one will accept the notion of libertarian freedom and its impact on Peterson's understanding of God's omniscience.

### Dealing With the Issue of Gratuitous Evil

According to Peterson, the theist has two options regarding the matter of gratuitous evil. One is to deny the existence of gratuitous evil and argue that it is only *prima facie* gratuitous evil. The second is to affirm the actual existence of evil (as opposed to only the appearance) and to try to demonstrate that gratuitous evil does not count against a morally perfect Being. On the one hand, if the theist elects for the first option (which most G-G theodicists do), then he will need to give some evidential justification about why it is possible to conclude that God accomplishes a greater good from all evil. If, on the other hand, the theist claims that gratuitous evil does exist, as Peterson suggests, then the theodicist's task is to present a case about why it is philosophically and theologically possible for gratuitous evil not to count against the character of God.

Peterson uses Rowe's argument from gratuitous evil to demonstrate the importance of the theist dealing with the issue of gratuitous evil. Peterson believes Rowe has presented the theist with the most formidable argument from gratuitous evil. Rowe states that there is no good that we know of that "justifies an omnipotent, omniscient, perfectly good being in permitting" unjustified evil, and in fact, "no good at all justifies an omnipotent, omniscient, perfectly good being" permitting unjustified evil. Therefore, "there is no omnipotent, omniscient, perfectly good being."[135] Rowe's examples concerning Bambi and Sue serve to illustrate what he calls gratuitous or unjustified evil. If gratuitous evil exists, then according to the G-G theodic claims, God does not exist. However, the G-G theodicy is constructed on the assumption that gratuitous evil does not exist.

Arguably, this very assumption of G-G theodicies weakens its overall power to convince the atheists that their argument from evil is flawed. If the theist assumes that God *cannot* allow gratuitous evil, then the burden of proof is on him to show that God *does not* allow unjustified evil. Furthermore, that task cannot be accomplished by simply appealing to God's character as proof in the evidential argument, unless the evidence for God's character is on the same order as the evidence for evil. Peterson thinks that the best approach is not to deny gratuitous evil, but rather to acknowledge its existence and then show that it does not count against the moral perfection or the omnipotence of God. Peterson does not claim that all evil is gratuitous; in fact, he thinks that one can understand God using evil to build moral character in voluntarily-responding humans. God does not cause the evil, but by His permitting it, He uses some of it for good. This good, on the balance of things, is valuable enough to make this world a worthwhile creation. On this point, it seems Peterson has argued correctly.

## The Doctrine of Hell

Peterson thinks affirming the reality of gratuitous evil is necessary for understanding the doctrine of hell in a classical theistic context and for having it form a consistent part of the larger Christian worldview. He writes:

> Furthermore, it is reasonable to believe that the terrifying human potential for evil includes the possibility of some person's willing and loving evil to the extent that hell becomes the emergent, dominant choice of his whole life. Hell is simply the natural culmination of the things which he has voluntarily set in motion. Just as God cannot override a person's every evil choice, He cannot contravene the larger, cumulative evil orientation of one's life.[136]

He believes that "hell is the logical extension of the idea that man has the radical power to create gratuitous evil."[137] Peterson argues that if "God is going to allow us to exist as significant free beings, capable of the highest achievements, then He must allow us also the most depraved and senseless errors—even if they lead to hell."[138] This appears to resonate with C. S. Lewis who wrote, "I willingly believe that the damned are, in one sense, successful, rebels to the end; that the doors of hell are locked on the *inside*."[139]

God does not change the flow of bad events/acts, because to do so would deny His creative choice to give man free will and place man in an environment with natural order. This means that there are real and sometimes negatives consequences to those choices. To abstain from changing the way things are is not a charge against God's omnipotence, but a testimony to His faithfulness to His creation. As Peterson sees it, this is not a charge against God's omnipotence or goodness but rather it is a testimony to God's faithfulness to His creation because He has given free will and it really matters, which is to say, God respects it.

## A Challenge to the 'Greater-Good' Theodicy

Peterson's position challenges the traditional G-G theodicy approach by identifying what he believes to be the fundamental weakness, namely the basic premise on which it is constructed. His theodicy seeks to avoid that premise, that the all-good, all-powerful, all-knowing God in His providence would prevent any and all evil that could be prevented without causing a greater evil or preventing a good that outweighs the evil. This premise, Peterson argues, forces the theist to deny the existence of gratuitous evil. Peterson sees this as "self-defeating."[140]

Others are inclined to view Peterson's theodicy with guarded approval. Ronald Nash suggests that if Peterson's arguments are sound, gratuitous evil does not "tip the scales of probability in favor of the atheologian."[141] In fact, Nash thinks there would seem to be "good reasons to conclude that the stalemate is over and that the probabilities favor theism."[142] After examining Peterson's position, Feinberg says, "Moreover, his [Peterson's] handling of gratuitous evil contains interesting subtleties and is most stimulating intellectually. All of this is praiseworthy, and I believe his appeal to the free will defense does justify the existence of much gratuitous evil for one committed to a free will theology like Arminianism."[143] What needs to be shown, if Peterson's overall theodicy is to gain acceptance in broader theological groups, is that his theodicy is not exclusively dependent on Arminian theology.

## Summary

Peterson builds a theodicy on the notion of the libertarian freedom of man. Man is really free to disobey and even choose hell. God's natural law and moral order establish the context within which God works among men. As a rule, He does not interfere with the choices of men for this would go contrary to the order He has established. Therefore gratuitous evil exists, but it does not count against God, for to intervene and bring about a good would be going against the way God created the world to be. However, not all evil is gratuitous as God does often bring good out of evil. Whereas God is faithful to His creation, He will not violate the order of free will. Unfortunately, Peterson moves close to the openness of God view as part of his libertarian view of man's freedom but stops just short of endorsing it. It appears, however, that one need not accept Peterson's view of God's omniscience in order to accept he position on gratuitous evil. Gratefully, what Peterson has put forward does make a significant contribution to the work of theodicy. Its most promising contribution is that it offers an alternative to accepting the basic self-defeating premise of G-G theodicies and acknowledges that gratuitous evil exists without counting against either the goodness or power of God.

## CONCLUSION

After considering the three G-G theodicies, it is apparent that the agreement does not go much beyond the denial that this is the best of all possible worlds. Hick differs theologically in his consideration of the fall. Holding to what he calls his Irenaean perspective, he argues that man was not created mature and the fall resulted. God uses evil to accomplish the task of soul-making. Whereas God does nothing without purpose, including allowing all kinds of evil, ultimately all souls will be perfected. If perfection is completed in this life, it will be completed in the life to come. This leads to a view that even Hick admits sounds very much like the idea of purgatory, although he does not call it that. All souls will eventually be perfected, either by the suffering in this life or in the life to come, but in either case it will be efficacious because ultimately all will be perfected. For Hick the love of God guarantees the end.

Swinburne builds a G-G theodicy that develops around the libertarian free will of man and the openness of God. He rejects Plantinga's free-will position because it requires middle knowledge. Swinburne believes it is logically impossible for God to know what the future decisions of his moral beings will be. For Swinburne, gratuitous evil does not exist. He seems unclear about the notion of eternal damnation and gestures to a moderating position but does not specifically state what that is. He gives examples of where good obtains from evil but fails to argue conclusively that such is true in all cases of evil. For Swinburne these examples only show how God possibly might use evil.

Peterson, while arguing for a modified soul-making theodicy, holds to an Augustinian view of the fall and hell, while at the same time affirming a libertarian view of human freedom. This places him very close to the openness view of God's omniscience, which at this point has failed to demonstrate its agreeableness with classical theism. Peterson also affirms that gratuitous evil exists and denies meticulous providence but offers an explanation why the existence of gratuitous evil does not count against God's moral perfection. It is because God is faithful to His creation and His creation order. God will not interfere with the order He has established, even though some of His moral beings turn against Him. Although God did not design man to choose evil, whereas man did choose evil, God allows man the freedom of choice and in love provides a way of redemption for those who choose to have their relationship restored to God. However, those who choose hell will get it.

These three main theodicies charted below (see fig. 1) summarize the position of each with respect to the key issues that shape one's theodicy and to help compare the different philosophical and theological components of the respective theodicies. The purpose is to give an overview of the philosophical and theological positions held by the three different theodicists for general understanding only. There is no attempt to suggest that the various theological or philosophical positions are necessary to the respective theodicy.

Notice that the two committed to the premise that gratuitous evil does not exist also have rather contrived views of the afterlife as well as some differences on either the view of the fall or the importance of the fall. Apart from the weaknesses and strengths pointed out in the above sections, there seem to be some theological questions with Hick and Swinburne. Peterson affirms the reality of hell and eternal punishment of the wicked. While Hick's discussion is not clear God's omniscience, Swinburne opts for the openness of God view of omniscience and Peterson is very close to this view. However, Peterson admits that this position needs more attention before accepting it totally. Although weaknesses may be thought to exist in each of the above theodicies, each has made a major contribution to the ongoing discussion and formation of theodicy. Interestingly, what seems to be increasingly clear is that the greater-good justificatory framework is perhaps the greatest liability to the work of theodicy.

**Fig. 1. Three 'Greater-Good' Theodicies Compared**

| | John Hick | Richard Swinburne | Michael Peterson |
|---|---|---|---|
| **Fall** | Myth | Historic, but not central | Historic |
| **L F** | Yes | Yes | Yes |
| **G O** | Unclear | Openness | Uncommitted openness |
| **G E** | No | No | Yes |
| **BPW** | No | No | No |
| **G-G** | Yes | Yes | Modified |
| **S-M** | Yes | Yes | Yes |
| **Afterlife** | Universalism | Annihilation of the wicked | Heaven & Hell |

Key:
**Fall**: As a historic event where men fell from a pristine state, to an sinful state
**L F**: Libertarian Freedom
**G O**: God's Omniscience
**G E**: Gratuitous Evil
**BPW**: The Best of all Possible Worlds
**G-G**: Some form of greater-good as part of the theodicy
**S-M**: Some element of soul-making as part of the theodicy
**Afterlife**: What happens to the perfected soul and the corrupt soul at death

## NOTES

1. John Hick, *Evil and the God of Love*, rev. ed. (San Francisco: Harper & Row, 1978), 211–2.

2. John Hick, "An Irenaean Theodicy," in Encountering Evil, ed. Stephen T. Davis (Atlanta: John Knox Press, 1981), 42.

3. In fairness to Hick, the most we can say is that he agrees in principle with Irenaeus, because Hick admits that the distinction between 'image' and 'likeness' is "exegetically dubious." Hick, *Evil and the God of Love*, 254.

4. Ibid., 257.

5. Ibid., 256.

6. Ibid., 255.

7. R. Douglas Geivett, *Evil and The Evidence for God* (Philadelphia: Temple University Press, 1993), 34.

8. Hick, *Evil and the God of Love*, 255.

9. Ibid., 254.

10. Ibid., 259.

11. Ibid., 255.

12. Marilyn McCord Adams and Robert Merrihew Adams, "Introduction," eds. *The Problem of Evil* (Oxford: Oxford University Press, 1990), 18.

13. M. B. Ahern, *The Problem of Evil* (New York: Schocken Books, 1971), 65.

14. Frederick Sontag, "Critique," in *Encountering Evil*, ed. Stephen T. Davis (Atlanta: John Knox Press, 1981), 56–7.

15. Stephen T. Davis, "The Problem of Evil in Recent Philosophy," *Review and Expositor* 82 (Fall 1985), 541–42.

16. Hick, *Evil and the God of Love*, 272.

17. Ibid., 274.

18. Ibid., 273.

19. Davis, "The Problem of Evil in Recent Philosophy," 541–42.

20. Hick, *Evil and the God of Love*, 281.

21. Ibid.

22. Ibid.

23. Ibid.

24. G. Stanley Kane, "The Failure of Soul-Making Theodicy," *International Journal for Philosophy of Religion* 6 (Spring 1975): 5.

25. Ibid.," 7–8.

26. Kenneth Surin, *Theology and the Problem of Evil* (Oxford: Basil Blackwell, 1986), 93.

27. Psalm 19: 1–2 which states that the "Heavens declare the glory of God: and the firmament shows His handiwork. Day unto day utters speech and night unto night reveals knowledge." This is the very text that Paul quotes demonstrating that all have heard the good news that God is (Romans 10:13–17). Romans 1: 19–20 assures "because what may be known of God is manifest in them; for God has shown it to them. For since the creation of the world His invisible attributes are clearly seen, being understood by the things that are made, even his eternal power and Godhead; so that they are without excuse." Ecclesiastes 3:11 indicates that God has put eternity in their hearts. Lastly (not comprehensively) one should consider Genesis 3:8 which indicates that the Lord communicated directly with Adam and Eve in the Garden. All of these

texts make it extremely difficult to find any theological sense in Hick's notion of epistemic distance.

28. Geivett, *Evil and the Evidence for God,* 33.

29. It is true that there are many in the western tradition who disallow natural theology, but it is usually on the grounds that because of the fall, man is cognitively at a disadvantage in knowing God from creation. However, this is much different than suggesting that God created man at an epistemic distance from the beginning as a necessary condition for man's love for God to be free and therefore authentic.

30. James Wetzel, "Can Theodicy Be Avoided?" *Religious Studies* 25 (1989): 8.

31. Hick, *Evil and the God of Love,* 330.

32. Ibid., 331.

33. Ibid., 361.

34. Hans Schwarz, *Evil: A Historical and Theological Perspective,* trans. Mark W. Worthing (Minneapolis: Fortress Press, 1995), 203.

35. Hick, *Evil and the God of Love,* 335.

36. Ibid., 176.

37. Ibid., 375.

38. Ibid., 333–4.

39. John Hick, "An Irenaean Theodicy," In *Encountering Evil,* ed. Stephen T. Davis (Atlanta: John Knox Press, 1981), 50.

40. Hick, *Evil and the God of Love,* 336.

41. Ibid., 342.

42. Ibid., 347.

43. Ibid.

44. John Hick, *Death and Eternal Life* (New York: Harper & Row Publishers, 1976), 456.

45. S. Davis, "The Problem of Evil in Recent Philosophy," 542.

46. M. and R. Adams, "Introduction," in *The Problem of Evil,* 20.

47. Barry Whitney,. *What Are They Saying About God and Evil?* (New York: Paulist Press, 1989), 43.

48. Geivett, *Evil and Evidence for God,* 35.

49. Kane, "The Failure of Soul-Making Theodicy," 2.

50. Schwarz, *Evil,* 203.

51. Geivett, *Evil and the Evidence for God,* 226.

52. Middleton, "Why the 'Greater Good' Isn't a Defense?" 85.

53. Edward Madden and Peter Hare, *Evil and the Concept of God* (Springfield, IL: Charles C. Thomas Publisher, 1968), 70.

54. Richard Swinburne, *Providence and the Problem of Evil* (Oxford: Clarendon Press, 1998), x.

55. Ibid., xii.

56. On this point, he thinks that Plantinga misses the traditional use of 'theodicy' and makes an unwarranted distinction between 'theodicy' and 'defense'.

57. Swinburne, *Providence and the Problem of Evil*, 35.

58. Ibid.

59. Ibid.

60. Philip L. Quinn, "Philosophy of Religion," in *The Cambridge Dictionary of Philosophy*, 1995, notes that in the Free Will Defense (which he claims is the position of both Swinburne and Plantinga), that "its key idea is that moral good cannot exist apart from libertarian free actions that are not causally determined."

61. Swinburne, *Providence and the Problem of Evil*, 15.

62. Ibid., 35.

63. Ibid., 33–34.

64. Ibid., 34.

65. Ibid., 34.

66. Ibid., 32.

67. Ibid., 110.

68. Ibid., 41.

69. Bruce Russell, "The Persistent Problem of Evil," *Faith and Philosophy* 6 (April 1998): 126.

70. Swinburne, *Providence and the Problem of Evil*, 109.

71. Ibid.

72. Ibid., 109.

73. Ibid., 232–3.

74. Ibid., 3.

75. Ibid., 3.

76. Jerry Walls, "Will God Change His Mind? Eternal Hell and the Ninevites," in *Through No Fault of Their Own?* eds. William V. Crockett and James C. Sigountos (Grand Rapids: Baker Book House Company, 1991), 66.

77. Richard Swinburne, *The Coherence of Theism* (Oxford: Clarendon Press, 1977), 176.

78. Wayne A. Davis, "Counterfactuals," in *The Cambridge Dictionary of Philosophy*, 1995, explains, "Counterfactuals, also called contrary-to-the-fact conditionals, subjunctive conditionals that presuppose the falsity of their antecedents, such as 'If Hitler had invaded England, Germany would have won' and 'If I were you, I'd run.'"

79. Swinburne, *Providence and the Problem of Evil*, 130.

80. Swinburne, *Providence and the Problem of Evil*, 129.

81. Ibid., 26.

82. Ibid., 27.

83. Ibid.

84. Ibid., 223.

85. Ibid., 236.

86. Ibid., 230–31.

87. Richard Swinburne, "Some Major Strands of Theodicy," in *The Evidential Argument From Evil*. Daniel Howard-Snyder, ed. (Bloomington: Indiana University Press, 1996), 31–2.

88. Eleonore Stump, "Knowledge, Freedom, and the Problem of Evil," in *The Problem of Evil*, ed. Michael L. Peterson (Notre Dame: University of Notre Dame Press, 1992), 321.

89. Swinburne, *Providence and the Problem of Evil*, 66.

90. Ibid., 103.

91. Ibid.

92. Ibid., 245.

93. Ibid., 245–6.

94. Ibid., 239.

95. Ibid., 241.

96. Ibid., 231.

97. Ibid., 240.

98. Ibid., 233.

99. Richard Swinburne, *Responsibility and Atonement* (Oxford: Clarendon Press, 1989), 181.

100. Ibid.

101. Ibid., 199.

102. Ibid., 200.

103. Ibid., 191.

104. Peterson, *God and Evil*, 87.

105. Ibid., 105.

106. Ibid., 85.

107. Ibid., 67.

108. Ibid., 69.

109. Ibid., 24.

110. Peterson, *God and Evil*, 72.

111. Michael Peterson, *Evil and the Christian God* (Grand Rapids: Baker Book House, 1982), 69.

112. Peterson, *God and Evil,* 71.

113. Ibid.

114. Peterson, *Evil and the Christian God*, 72.

115. Peterson, *God and Evil*, 72.

116. William Rowe, "The Evidential Argument from Evil: A Second Look" in *The Evidential Argument from Evil*, Daniel Howard-Snyder, ed. (Bloomington: Indiana University Press, 1996), 262, notes: "My purpose here is to look again at an evidential argument from evil that I first presented in 1979. Since that time I have made several changes in that argument in an effort to make it clearer and to patch up weakness in earlier statements of it." The formulation of this argument appeared first as "The Problem of Evil and Some Varieties of Atheism," *American Philosophical Quarterly*, 16 (1979), 335–41. In this article he uses as his example for pointless suffering the case where a fawn (Bambi) is trapped in a forest fire and dies an awful, lingering death. Later, he revisits this subject, and it is in this article that he uses as his example of pointless suffering, a five-year old girl (Sue) who is raped, beaten and killed by strangulation.

117. Peterson, *God and Evil*, 74.

118. Ibid., 72.

119. Ibid., 74.

120. Ibid., 85.

121. Ibid., 104.

122. Ibid., 103.

123. Feinberg, *Many Faces of Evil*, 264.

124. The principle of meticulous providence means that God does not allow gratuitous evil. According to Peterson, this principle in the end forces the theist to claim that there is no gratuitous evil which contradicts the evidence from experience.

125. Peterson, *Evil and the Christian God*, 86.

126. Ibid., 122.

127. Ibid., 116.

128. Ibid., 104.

129. Peterson, *Evil and the Christian God*, 124.

130. Ibid., 92.

131. Ibid., 105.

132. Michael Peterson and others, eds. *Reason and Religious Belief.* 2nd ed. (New York: Oxford Press, 1998), 73.

133. Ibid., 77.

134. Ibid., 78

135. Rowe, "The Evidential Argument from Evil: A Second Look," 263.

136. Peterson, *Evil and the Christian God*, 124–5.

137. Ibid., 125.

138. Ibid.

139. C. S Lewis, *The Problem of Pain* (New York: Macmillan, 1962; reprint, New York: Simon & Schuster, 1996), 114.

140. Peterson, *Evil and the Christian God*, 92.

141. Ronald Nash, *Faith and Reason* (Grand Rapids: Zondervan Publishing House, 1988), 221.

142. Ibid.

143. Feinberg, *The Many Faces of Evil*, 269.

# Chapter 4

# Why Greater-Good Theodicies Fail

The previous chapter reviewed three contemporary G-G theodicies leaving none of them without some criticism (some more serious than others). In general, each of the three revealed some commitment to a greater-good justificatory framework and affirmed soul-making (to varying degrees) as an important part of the good. Furthermore, free will of the libertarian tradition formed an important component in all three theodicies. Only Swinburne and Peterson explicitly expressed some commitment to the openness of God. Regarding the future state of man, Hick admitted that his soul-making theodicy logically required him to affirm universalism with some purgatorial-like element. Swinburne, on the other hand denied any eternal sensory punishment for the wicked, arguing that it would be unfair because the punishment would not fit the crime. It would not be becoming to a good God to respond to temporal badness with eternal punishment. Nonetheless, because choices in time really do have implications for eternity, Swinburne suggested that a more fitting punishment (at least in his mind) would include the annihilation of the wicked (the really wicked—the corrupt soul), and some type of second chance, especially for the uninformed but right-hearted pagan. On this point, Swinburne is not really clear; in fact, he is conspicuously ambiguous about what the future state of nonbelievers would look like, stating only that it would not be any form of enduring sensory punishment. In this triad of theodicies, only Peterson maintained a more traditional view of hell. Regarding the nature of this world, all three maintained that this is not the best of all possible worlds, or at least there is no way to know whether or not it is the best of all possible worlds. The most instructive difference, however, appeared in the critical area of gratuitous evil. Hick and Swinburne stayed along the traditional lines, adhering to the idea that gratuitous evil does not exist. Only Peterson developed his modified G-G theodicy by maintaining the actual possibility of gratuitous evil.

There is a growing consensus among evangelicals that the subject of gratuitous evil presents itself as a tenacious problem within the evidential version of the problem of evil. As David O'Conner points out, "There is a great deal of evil in the world, much of it seemingly pointless. Intuitively, then, there seems to be a discordance between certain facts of inscrutable evil and the theistic conception of the world as God-made."[1] It is just this inscrutable evil that seems so resistant to philosophical taming within the context of the evidential version of the problem of evil. Horrific evil is precisely the greatest challenge to G-G theodicies, since it requires the theist to demonstrate empirically that the good obtains from such terrible evils in order to maintain the belief that gratuitous evil does not exist. The difficulty of this task is reflected in the many varied attempts at proving the good obtains from all evil, including the horrific evils. The idea that the only evil allowed by God is that evil from which He can bring about a greater good or prevent a greater evil necessarily requires the rejection of the notion that some evil is gratuitous. It will be argued that it is this very premise that is the seed of destruction internal to G-G theodicies. A more fruitful approach appears to be what Petersons suggests, namely a theodicy that does not depend on the greater-good assumption. Before offering such a theodic proposal, this chapter will parse the greater-good assumption itself and suggest a list of weaknesses inherent in the concept.

## THE WORK OF THEODICY

It appears that the theist has two options regarding the evidential version of the problem of evil. First, the theist can deny the reality of gratuitous evil, thereby preserving God's moral goodness and power by emphasizing His unmitigated sovereignty. While this option sounds good at first, further examination reveals that such an argument is not based on the evidence but rather upon the initial premise of the theist. In this case, the counter evidence (evidence that seems to deny the possibility of the claim that God exists) is taken by the theist and explained in a way that makes it consistent with (supports) his initial premise. This premise is that the all-good, all-powerful God does not allow any evil for which He does not bring some greater good or prevent some greater evil. Support for this position, however, does not come from the evidence in man's experience, and it is questionable whether such a position can be supported from the Bible.

Since the non-existence of gratuitous evil is precisely the point to be proven, to assume the conclusion in the premise involves circular reasoning. From a logical point of view, this weakens the force of the argument and existentially causes it to run contrary to the experience of man (at least in appearance). After all, this is the question. It is not so much that God does not exist as that He cannot be God as traditionally defined and still exist? Arguing that evil does not count against God because God cannot permit gratuitous evil is circuitous.

The atheist begins with the traditional understanding of God, looks at evil and claims that evil is inconsistent with the existence of an all-good, all-powerful God. The theist looks at evil and believes that it does not matter what you see, that it cannot count against God precisely because He is the all-good, all-powerful God. Furthermore, God brings some greater good from the evil He allows, thus justifying Him morally for allowing the evil. The explanation of the theist suggests to the atheist that, if this is the case, then the theist should be able to establish his position from the evidence. Unfortunately, those theists who have attempted such an evidentiary enterprise have not been very successful.[2] Whereas the theist claims there is no gratuitous evil, he must be able to demonstrate in all cases (even, or especially, in the case of horrific evil) that God has brought or will bring some good from the evil that justifies His power and goodness to permit that evil. This is an empirically impossible task. Such an attempt, at best, only shows how God *might* use some evil, but it fails to demonstrate that all evil can be explained in these terms.

As Peterson points out, the serious challenge from the atheist is not that there is some evil in the world, but that there is so much evil and some of it is so terrible. It seems that the Free-Will argument seems satisfactory to explain why there is evil in God's creation in the first place, namely, that evil is the consequent (not necessary consequent) of God giving man the power of moral choice. The more pressing problem, however, is why evil seems so pervasive and destructive to humanity if a loving and omnipotent God is in control? The suggestion that God only allows the evil from which He can bring about a greater good or prevent a greater evil may answer the question, but in doing so, places a tremendous (and I would say unnecessary) evidentiary burden on the theist. Now the burden of proof lies on the theist since he who makes the claim has the burden to prove the claim.

If God uses all evil for good, then the theist must answer whether or not the evil is only *incidental* to the good or *necessary* for the good. If *incidental* to the good, then the theist must show that God is justified in permitting something so painful if it is only *incidental* to the good. If, on the other hand, evil is *necessary* to the good, then the theist has a whole new set of problems—to demonstrate that the good could not have come about without the existence of evil in this world. If there is a necessary good that can only obtain through God using evil, then it appears there is something omnipotence cannot do, namely, bring about a necessary good without evil. Denial of this conclusion seems difficult to support.

Even if the necessary evil is the result of man's power of moral choice, then man of necessity had to sin or else the necessary good would not have obtained. Moreover, if the good is the character building or some other category of good, without evil that good would not have been present in God's world, making the goodness in this world at least in part dependent on evil. It seems reasonable to argue that a world with more goods is better than a world without those goods. Furthermore, since this is the way it turned out (and the argument is that God's goodness and power have seen to it that it worked out this way), then a world without evil would have been a world less than what God's goodness and power could have brought to pass on their own. This seems like a difficult position to maintain as it seriously erodes the very point assumed that God is all-power and all-good.

The second option, which is the one similar to that taken by Peterson (and some other theists), posits that gratuitous evil is actual, but it also maintains it does not count against God as the all-good, all-powerful Being. This approach maintains that God uses some evil for the soul-making (character-building) of His moral creatures but claims that not *all* the evil contributes to the process of soul-making (or some other moral good). In this case, not all evil leads to some good. The argument here is not that God works all evil out for good, thus justifying the evil, but rather that God has made the world to work in a certain way (natural law and moral structure) to which He is morally obligated. Moreover, God's moral justification for permitting evil rests in His faithfulness as Creator instead of His omnipotence. Evil has come about by man misusing his freedom. Therefore, it is God's moral obligation to Himself and His world that exempts Him from moral culpability for evil in general and gratuitous evil in particular. God is not morally responsible for the bad choices nor is He responsible for man's good choices. He is morally obligated to honor the freedom He has given man that makes both kinds of choices possible.

Gregory Boyd has crafted a theodicy called "A Trinitarian Warfare Theodicy" that affirms the reality of gratuitous evil. He rejects the idea that evil is "allowed for a specific greater good."[3] He notes that the idea that God can "bring more good out of their evil than he could without" is "traditional, but problematic."[4] Although Boyd's theodicy tries to correct the error of the greater-good assumption (which I applaud), he does so at a theological cost which a considerable number in evangelical Christianity are unwilling to pay. Most problematic is that he supports an openness view of God's omnipotence. He does so by attaching his view to what he calls "neo-Molinism", a view which seems somewhat opaque and unnecessary. He denies that this is the best of all possible worlds and does so on the grounds that "it seems implausible that this actual world constitutes the one possible world in which free agents choose the least amount of evil."[5] As argued in other places in this book, in spite of the fact that many good theologians reject the idea of the best of all possible worlds, it still appears that to do so creates unnecessary theological tension at best and conflict at worse when developing a consistent theodicy.

## To Override or Undercut

Broadly speaking, the theist has two approaches for responding to the evidential argument from evil. One is to develop an argument he believes will soundly *undercut* (defeat) the atheistic argument. The other option is to form independent arguments for God's existence that would offer sufficient reasons for *overriding* the argument from evil. The former, if possible, would be the more effective of the two.

Bruce Russell asserts that "recent attempts at *undercutting* these arguments [from the atheist] will fail, though attempts at *overriding* them may succeed."[6] In order to appreciate the distinction he has made one does not need to agree with Russell's conclusion, namely that "because the hypotheses which are offered to save theism are unlikely on what we know, theism is defenseless against the evidential arguments from evil."[7] While Russell thinks it is possible for the theist to find arguments that override the arguments from evil, he is not convinced it will happen. Nonetheless, an approach that overrides the atheist's argument is on a different order from a strategy to undercut his argument. It seems however, that a theodicy must give primary attention to the task of undercutting.

The two different approaches arguably address two separate issues. The strategy of undercutting aims at confronting the argument side of the debate. This side deals with demonstrating to the atheist that evil is not a fatal defeater to the claim that God exists. In other words, it undercuts the atheist's argument. Overriding the argument from evil considers the *faith* side of the debate. Many theists are vexed with questioning thoughts in the face of horrible evils, especially when challenged by others who note that such seems to count against God's existence. The overriding arguments may convince the theists that he has other sufficient reasons to override the evidence from evil. By this, he is able to quiet those momentary haunting doubts. The latter only assures the theist (and the atheist if he is listening) that the theist is not irrational in his affirmation that God exists. It is not irrational to believe in God's existence even though it has little apologetic value. The undercutting approach is designed to demonstrate not just the rationality of the claim that God exists, but its truthfulness. Apologetic in nature, the undercutting focuses on arguments for why evil does not count against God. This strategy focuses on arguments for God's existence (and other evidence) that muffle arguments against His existence. The theist affirms he has good and sufficient reasons to believe that God exists while demonstrating the argument from evil fails to make its case against God.

The difference between these two issues is similar to what Barry Whitney calls the "faith solution" and the "rational solution." "The faith solution appeals to faith as the ultimate (and the only legitimate) solution to the theodicy issue: God has given or permits the evil and suffering we must endure for good reasons, it is held, reasons that are beyond complete human comprehension."[8] What Whitney calls the 'faith solution' really only answers the personal faith side of the debate, which may have value for the theist, but again it says little to the atheist. The theist maintains that the presence of evil in God's world does not create a problem for him; therefore, he will go on believing regardless of the evidence. There is no suggestion here that such a position is without merit for the individual theist; however, it has little convincing apologetic power on the argument side of the debate. Furthermore, one must calculate the cost when appealing only to the faith solution. If the theist can maintain his position without answering the evidence that seems to count against his position, then he has no objection when the atheist does the same thing.

The apologetic aspect is built on what Whitney calls the "rational solution." Whitney, maintains that the "rational solution" achieves more than simply answering the atheist's argument; it offers a foundation for the "faith solution" of those who believe. He notes, "I suggest that without some rational underpinning, some viable theodicy, coping can be seriously hindered by poor or non-existent explanations for the suffering with which we seek to cope. I contend that we can cope better if we have some understanding of the reasons for the evil and suffering which affects us."[9] The two approaches are not mutually exclusive. The faith solution, apart from some rational solution, tends to appear fideistic to the atheist.

The faith solution has merit, but only as an answer for the theist. As Nelson Pike points out,

> A theologian who accepts the existence of God (either as an item of faith or on the basis of an *a priori* argument) must conclude either

that there is some morally sufficient reason for God's allowing suffering in the world, or that there are no instances of suffering in the world. He will, of course, choose the first alternative. Thus, in a theology of the sort now under consideration, the theologian begins by affirming the existence of God and by acknowledging the occurrence of suffering. It follows *logically* that God has some morally sufficient reason for allowing instances of suffering. The conclusion is not, as Philo suggests, that there *might* be a morally sufficient reason for evil. The conclusion is, rather, that there *must* be such a reason. It could not be otherwise.[10]

No one denies the faith solution has value for the theist, but few would agree that it has much influence as an apologetic in the evidential argument from evil. It is this which has drawn the theist into the discussion it the first place. It appears that the major task for the theist is to develop a theodicy that aims at undercutting the argument from evil, for everything hinges on that—both the faith solution and the apologetic response. Furthermore, unless there is some apologetic response to the evidential argument, the theist will only solve the problem (a faith solution based upon a prior theological commitment) for himself (who obviously looks at the world differently than the atheist) without a real impact on the atheist. Pike's point that the theist is required to show a morally sufficient reason for evil seems inescapable. Unfortunately, the most common theistic approach to this end has been the greater-good justificatory premise that arguably commits the theist to more than can be reasonably accomplished. In fact, the implications and logical conclusions of the greater-good premise seem to indicate that it is not the most advantageous theodic route for the theist.

## G-G THEODICY EXPLANATIONS

The difficulty of demonstrating evidentially the actuality of the greater-good premise has not been lost on some theists. Some maintain the position based upon the fact of God's sovereignty. God is sovereign in such a way that all individual choices of men are only those which God directly permits. His plan is such that it includes the evil and this is all that is needed in terms of a theodicy. In fact, for such theists, a theodicy is only mere speculation without benefit because it is impossible for man to understand the ways of God. It is enough to know that He is sovereign. Others have opted to try to save the greater-good premise by developing theological responses. One common response holds that the good obtains in all cases, but often man simply does not see it because it is beyond his ken. Another approach, based on Romans

8:28, is when the theist maintains he has warrant for believing the good obtains and looks no further for justification. All of these responses are attempts at avoiding the evidence from human experience, and they involve either questionable exegesis or application of biblical truth.

### God is Sovereign

The appeal to God's sovereignty as the basis for the G-G theodicy is an inferential argument. There is nothing wrong with inferential arguments as long as there is sufficient warrant to support the claim drawn from the evidence. In this case, the claim is that there is no gratuitous evil in this world. The evidence is the numerous Scriptures that speak of God as the Sovereign One. There is no objection to the claim that God is sovereign, as the Bible is clear on this matter. The question is whether or not the application of sovereignty in the G-G theodicies is actually warranted.

First, some confusion exists among Christians as how sovereignty should be defined. As Peterson observed, Christians must work for more precise definitions when speaking of God. Sovereignty is often used interchangeably with providence and omnipotence. Clearly, the three terms do not speak of the same attribute or property of God. In fact, providence does not appear to be an attribute of God, but rather the way in which God acts because He is God. God's providence has to do with His daily governance over His creation. Sovereignty can best be defined as divine autonomy. Because God is sovereign, He is the supreme ruler since all His pre-creation and creation choices were not influenced by anyone or anything outside Himself. God's choice to create and to create the way He did, as well as His counsels concerning creation, are solely His choices. What His sovereignty chooses, His omnipotence perfects. Omnipotence relates to the extent and kind of God's power. There is no person or thing that has more power than God. He is all-powerful not because He can do anything (such as the logically impossible), but because His power is circumscribed by none. While these three terms are connected, they are not interchangeable.

Second, how should sovereignty be applied in the case of gratuitous evil? Does it necessarily mean that if something happens on this earth without a divine purpose, this somehow strikes at the truth of God's sovereignty? It seems to me that the answer is no. To maintain otherwise leads to questionable ends. If a person commits adultery, is it gratuitous evil or is it an evil that God in His sovereignty planned? The plan would have had to be from before creation or at the moment of creation. The end is that God planned for a person to commit adultery, the very thing that God says is sin. God becomes the author of sin.

Furthermore, the adultery was planned to bring about a good (under the G-G theodicy), so now sin brings about good, so more sin would bring about more good. Since the sin actually happened, it was the will of God. So now God wills the very thing He condemns. It appears that there is no way out of this conclusion if one follows the logic of applying God's sovereignty in this way. In the end, God is responsible for the existence of the very thing He condemns. In the end, if this is how sovereignty is defined and applied, it collides with other non-negotiable doctrines of Christianity (such as God is not the author of sin since this would make it a created thing, something with its own essence).

### The Good is Beyond Our Ken

Stephen Wykstra argues that in all cases the good obtains from evil, but in some cases, the good is beyond man's ken (that is, beyond man's range of vision). He defends this position in his response to the challenge of Rowe. His objection to Rowe's argument turns on Rowe's appeal to the fact that one often does not see all evil resulting in some greater good. Wykstra, however, argues that Rowe makes an epistemic error because he errs in his assumption concerning the principle of the Condition of Reasonable Epistemic Access (CORNEA). According to Wykstra,

> CORNEA says that we can argue from 'we see no X' to 'there is no 'X' only when X has 'reasonable seeability'—that is, is the sort of thing which, if it exists we *can reasonably expect* to see it in the situation. Looking around in my garage and seeing no dog entitles me to conclude that none is present, but seeing no flea does not; and this is because fleas, unlike dogs, have low seeability; even if they were present, we cannot reasonably expect to see them in this way. But should we expect God-purposed goods to have the needed seeability? Arguing from the disparity between a creator's vision and ours, I urged not: Rowe's case thus fails CORNEA's seeability requirement.[11]

Wykstra's argument is rather simple. God sees things differently than man sees them, and this is what one would expect given that God is infinite and man is finite. Therefore, the "seeability" of the good from some evil is that one would not expect man to see it even if it were present. God brings the good from the evil. Whereas God's ways are not man's ways, it is reasonable that the good would be beyond man's ken. Therefore, Wykstra argues, the good is present, but under the circumstances one should not expect to see it. Consequently, not seeing the good does not mean it is not present; therefore, there is no justification for denying its reality.

In order to judge the acceptability of Wykstra's argument, we must determine in what way appearance is different for God than it is for man. First, there is no argument that God sees matters more comprehensively than man because He knows all things. What must be demonstrated is that God sees things differently than man, and that this fact applies the case of evil where the good obtains. Is it simply an epistemic issue or is something else involved? There are three possible ways to understand Wykstra's idea. One, God sees the good while man does not see it because the good obtains by God's intervention and only God knows how He will intervene in order to bring about the good. This refers to how the good obtains. Two, God sees the good and man does not, because God knows that the good will obtain. He sees farther into the future and thereby sees what man does not see in the flow of natural order. God is in eternity and man is in time. Three, God sees good differently than man sees good. This is an issue of definition. If it is (1), the problem of man's seeing is still not solved for if it is just a matter of means, eventually the good would still become evident and man would see it. If it is (2), and the good is far down the road (why man cannot see it), then when the good does obtain, some man would see it. If it is so far down the road that the person who suffered is not the one rewarded, then this would seem to be an abrogation of the scriptural principle of reward and recompense. The one who suffers should also be the one who sees the good. Furthermore, if it is so far removed from the suffering, how can one be sure that the good comes from the evil? If (3), then God sees good differently than man, which raises the question of how man knows when he has done good as God sees it. Whereas God is the One man is to please, not understanding good as God does would leave man always wondering if he had done good. Furthermore, if man and God understand good differently then religious language is equivocal, throwing all communication between man and God into confusion.

Two other observations seem to call Wykstra's rebuttal into question. The first is his example of seeabilty under the principle of CORNEA. In his example, not seeing the flea is not an epistemological problem but an ontological one—the size of the flea against that of the dog. Fleas do have seeability, but Wykstra's is actually trying to defend no seeability. It appears that he has engaged in the fallacy of false analogy. This is not to say that an example cannot be given, but the one he gives seems to miss the mark. The reason man does not see the good coming from evil is his limited cognitive abilities against God's, not the amount of the good itself. The reason Wykstra does not see the flea in the garage is because of the size of the flea, not his cognitive powers. If he looked real hard, it would be possible to see the flea even in a garage, because it *does* have seeability, albeit rather low. Following Wykstra's analogy the good obtained from evil could be seen; it would simply mean that one would have to look harder to see it. Even if one grants Wykstra his point that God sees things differently than man, what follows is a concern about other areas of life. Do theists also suggest that God sees justice or morality differently than man? This may not be a strong concern, but it needs to be addressed. Why should suffering be the only aspect of life that falls into this category?

The second observation is Wykstra's complaint that Rowe's examples are prejudiced in Rowe's favor (his examples are too difficult). One could not deny this, but it would only be a legitimate objection if, in fact, Rowe uses an example bearing no consistency with reality. The fact is, if the example is within the range of human experience, Rowe has every right to introduce it. In fact, there are many cases in everyday life that similar to Rowe's example of the young girl being horribly abused. It is just these kinds of evil that raise the question from the atheist—where is the good? Therefore, Wkystra's argument seems to fail on several counts and, consequently, is little help to those who wish to hold on to a greater-good justificatory framework in response to the argument from evil.

### All Things Together For Good

The case for G-G theodicies would be helped immeasurably if one had a propositional statement in the Bible affirming its premise. According to some theists such a verse is Romans 8:28. This verse affirms that "all things work together for good to those who love God and are called according to His purpose." Does this verse teach that God brings good out of all evil? No. Several exegetical matters are crucial to understanding the force of this text and what it has to say regarding evil in this world.

First, the context limits the benefits of the statement to believers only and specifically limits the good to those who love God. If it were true that, in the general flow of things, all suffering turned out for one's good, then why tell the Christian it is true only for those who love God? The fact that believers are singled out indicates that the principle is particular to them and no one else. No matter how or when one understands the good obtaining—this life or in the life to come—this verse does not teach the meticulous providence and should not be quoted as support for the G-G theodicy.

The context of Romans 8 arguably speaks to suffering that comes to the Christian as result of his righteous living. Paul points to this fact in verse 36 when he says "For Your (God's) sake we are killed all the day long; we are counted as sheep for the slaughter." In fact, the Bible offers two broad categories of suffering as experienced by the Christian. The first is suffering for righteousness sake while the second is suffering because of the fallenness of this world. Romans 8 only points to suffering for righteousness sake, not for any kind of suffering. Furthermore, it is silent on causal issues with regard to suffering. It simply declares that when Christians suffer for righteousness sake, they can be assured that God in His providence will bring some good from it.

This is consistent with other texts in the Bible teaching the same truth. For example: Matthew 5:11 ("for My sake"); II Timothy 3:12 ("desire to live godly"); James 1:3 ("the testing of your faith"); and I Peter 1:7 ("genuineness of your faith"). Furthermore, consider the following examples: Job suffered because of his righteousness (Job 1:10); Joseph because of his faithful proclamation of God's dreams to him (Gen. 37:19—"Look, this dreamer is coming"); Shadrach, Meshach, and Abed-Nego for not worshiping the gold image (Dan. 3:8–25); and Daniel for praying to God (Dan. 6:10–23). When Christians suffer for righteousness sake, God is at work to work things together for their ultimate good, but it is in spite of the evil not because of the evil. And, it is only under such conditions that one should look to Romans 8:28 for comfort. According to II Corinthians 1:3–7 Christians can be assured that the Father of mercies and God of all comfort is present to encourage and comfort them in their time of suffering. The force of the Romans 8 text is that we should live boldly for God, knowing no resulting form of suffering can separate us from the love of God that is in Christ Jesus our Lord (Rom. 8:37–39).

Another verse often introduced into the discussion is Genesis 50:20, which records Joseph's response to his brothers' fear of him. In reply, Joseph comforts them and assures them that he has no intention of avenging their dastardly deed of selling him into slavery many years before. He says, "But as for you, you meant evil against me; but God meant it for good" (Gen. 50:20). This text only tells what happened in this particular circumstance, and it is unwise to build a doctrine on a strictly narrative text. This is Joseph's testimony after the fact about how God reversed the evil intent of his brothers. It does not say that God purposed this to happen in order to bring about the good, only that He did bring about the good. One would need strong warrant to move from the evidence of Genesis 50 to the claim made by the G-G theodicies. It seems that Joseph's evil treatment from his brothers resulted from his righteousness—they called him the dreamer. Also, Joseph makes no mention of the other suffering he encountered while in Egypt. If these conclusions are right, there is no propositional statement affirming the greater-good assumption. There may be other approaches to defend the G-G theodicy, however, it seems that any new defense will prove equally as impotent in shoring up the greater-good premise. It also seems safe to say at this point that an appeal to Romans 8:28 as deductive grounds on which to support G-G theodicies is unwarranted.

## WEAKNESSES IN THE G-G THEODICY

While the theist maintains that the greater good always obtains, the atheist responds by noting instances of suffering that God could have prevented without eliminating some greater good or allowing some evil equally bad or worse (or so it seems). At this point the task of the theist boasting of the greater good is much greater than before, as he must show that the good did obtain and that is an evidential task. However the theist responds, he must address two issues that he did not need to address before. (1) He must demonstrate by some means that, in fact, God does in *all* cases of evil bring about a greater good. That is, *all* evil permitted (whatever evil is observed in this world, in whatever proportions, in whatever degree and to whomever it comes) results in some good that could not have been obtained without the evil, and, therefore, no evil is pointless. (2) The theist must demonstrate that God could not have prevented *any* evil that is, because if He did, some good would not have obtained or an equal or worse evil would have taken place. This seems almost an impossible evidentiary task. It requires that one present sufficient evidence, the preponderance of which would make the case convincing. Moreover, it will not do simply to offer possible ways in which the good might obtain in some cases, as the nature of the theist's claim is that *all* evil that is, is permitted by God for the purpose of bringing about a greater good or disallowing a greater evil. All the atheist has to do is to find cases (and there are many) where it is reasonable to conclude that the good did not obtain in order to raise serious doubts about the theist's claim. As if this task were not enough to subvert the credibility of the G-G theodicy, there are other attending difficulties.

## It Suggests That Evil is Necessary to Good

The greater-good justificatory framework as a response to the evidential argument from evil appears to have a number of attending problems. The affirmation is that God only permits that evil into this world from which He can bring about a greater good or prevent a worse evil. What assumptions must be true in order to accept this affirmation and what are the logical conclusions if they are true? Peterson argued that any solution to the problem of evil should not be done in theological isolation. The theist must make sure that whatever answer he gives is consistent with a complete Christian worldview. What is said about God in relation to evil will have implications for most other major doctrines of classical theism.

First, it is posited that God allows all evil that comes into the world because from it He will bring about some greater good. The question is whether the good that God brings from the evil is a necessary good. Is this good essential to God's plan for humanity or is it just a good that happens because the evil is allowed? The logical answer is that it is essential to the plan of God. If not, why allow all the suffering if the plan of God would be just as complete without the resulting good? So, what are the implications of this for the theist? He has now made the evil necessary, for the good could not obtain without the evil and the good must obtain because it is necessary. If the good is necessary, and it is dependent on the evil, then the evil is also necessary. If the evil is necessary, then God must determine the evil in order to assure it will come to pass so that the good can obtain. This makes God directly responsible for the evil, not in a contingent way, but in a necessary way.

This implies that God cannot bring about certain goods without particular evils, for if any evil will do, God should pick the least of the sufferings. Also, if God can bring about the good without the evil, then he should for if He can and He does not, then He is not the good God being defended. One could argue that if God needs particular evils to bring about certain goods, then God is not omnipotent. In this case, the all-good, all-powerful God is unable to bring a good without the help of evil. Immediately one can see how theologically convoluted this becomes. It diminishes God and makes evil a necessary part of His plan, thus destroying the Free Will Defense used ever since Augustine. This means man did not rebel freely in the Garden. He was determined to do it because God needed the evil to bring about some good for this world. Furthermore, this reasoning undermines the truth about the God it seeks to defend—His omnipotence. If the theist responds that the evil is not necessary to the good obtained and the good is not necessary to the plan of God, then the evil is gratuitous. God could have produced the good without the suffering, but in that He allows the suffering His goodness is now in question. If the good is necessarily dependent on the evil and the good is necessary, then His omnipotence remains in question. Either way serious theological questions follow.

There is no evidential proof that certain evil is *necessary* to a corollary good, or that *all* evil always obtains a greater good. To claim such is the case seems far beyond the preponderance of the evidence.[12] In fact, it is impossible to prove that the evil is necessary to the good just because good comes from the evil any more than it is possible to make the case that the particular good is necessary. This mistake in logic assumes that just because B follows A there is necessarily some causal relationship between A and B. Further, it openly confesses that what *is* constitutes what *ought* to have been or even *must* be.

It is obvious that there is a large difference between claiming that good comes from evil and arguing that the evil is *necessary* to the good. It may be possible, at least in some cases, to demonstrate that good comes from evil. However, it is a very different task to argue that evil is necessary to the good. If one argues that the good is not necessary, then the G-G theodicy must respond to why God allows such suffering for something that is not necessary. The greater-good approach may be able to offer some evidence for good from evil, but it seems it is unable to demonstrate that it is necessary to evil, true in all cases of evil, or explain why there is so much evil in the world. What happens in the end is that the appeal to God's sovereignty and power as the grounds for supporting the greater good assumption actually undermines those very attributes the G-G theodicy seeks to protect.

### The End-Justifies-The-Means

The logical conclusion of the greater-good premise is that it promotes a type of argument that turns on the end-justifies-the-means philosophy. As R. Z. Friedman says, "The end, in other words, justifies the means. Yet this is the complete antithesis of the moral task which religion gives to God."[13] Norman Geisler counters this argument[14] when he writes that the "theist does not say that a good end justifies God's *performing* evil acts, but it only justifies God's *permitting* such acts."[15] He goes on to say that "God is interested in bringing the greatest good for the greatest number, but not at the expense of performing or promoting any evil."[16] The argument, however, is not that God *performs* evil, only that He allows it. If God allows evil to bring about a greater good, then the end is the good and the means is the evil. No one is accusing God of performing the evil. This argument maintains that the good comes from this or that evil, and that the good would not exist apart from this or that evil. If God is omnipotent and omnibenevolent, then what He permits must be the best because He can prevent what is not best. In such a case, evil becomes the path to good, so it would seem the best action would be to let evil runs its course, for in the end it will be good.

In this vein, Friedman's observations seem proper, "As an individual in possession of the knowledge of good and evil I ought to act to alleviate the suffering of the innocent, but as a theodicist perhaps I ought to accept the power of evil to produce good and allow the process to run its course without my 'interference'."[17] He goes on to say, "The theodicist's claim that evil produces good and is therefore not really a challenge to the existence of and goodness of God may undermine the claim, central to that tradition which gives rise to this defense of God, that man knows the difference between good and evil."[18] His point is that, in the end, there is no difference between good and evil because out of evil comes good. Richard Middleton agrees. He notes, "If the greater good defense is true, although we might feel sorrow over these events [Bosnia, Rawanda, Auschwitz and Dachau] when viewed in isolation, nevertheless we ought ultimately to praise God for them, since seen in their proper perspective they are necessary to some greater good which could not be accomplished without them."[19] If Middleton's observations are correct, this creates no small amount of theological tension, as it logically leads to the position that evil must be left unrestrained if the good is to obtain. Again, Middleton raises the point, "If the greater good defense were truly believed, it would undercut motivation for both petitionary prayer and redemptive opposition to evil by generating a self-deceptive apathy instead of a biblically inflamed passion for justice and shalom."[20] Moreover, Friedman thinks that since "the logic of theodicy may force us there, we find ourselves in direct conflict with the view of moral agency contained in the Fall, that man having eaten of the forbidden tree is in possession of the knowledge of good and evil."[21]

Those who hold to a greater-good premise can protest strenuously against this conclusion. Yet, it seems this is very much a case of the end justifying the means. In the end, the G-G theodicy seems to look very similar to some forms of social Darwinianism, (although that is clearly not the intent of those putting forward the G-G theodicy). Simply putting God in charge of the whole thing does not change the morality of it all, only the mechanism by which it is realized. If the argument is that God allows the evil because from it He brings about a greater good, then it is difficult to escape the charge of consequential-ism.

## G-G Theodicy Undercuts Social Justice

If good comes from evil (the end justifies the means) and the good is necessary, then why stop the evil? In fact, to stop the evil would be to prevent the good, which logically means that God would need to find another place to allow the evil where there will be no interference. Further, if all evil leads to some good not obtainable without the evil, then at what point should God's people obey God's command to stand against evil? As Middleton urges, "Believing the greater good defense would result in nothing less than ethical paralysis."[22] In fact, this might lead to a position suggested by Freidman:

> To be consistent, perhaps the next time we are asked to support fam-ine relief for African children we should simply decline and respond that because the birth rate in the world of nature has already insured the survival of the human species and does not really need these children for its purposes. A morally indifferent universe does not know of moral distinctions, judgements, and designations. There is neither innocence nor evil in such a universe, only events.[23]

Scripture, however, is replete with commands for God's people not do evil and to prevent it wherever it is found. The weak, the orphan, the widow, the fatherless are not to be taken advantage of (Deut. 27:19). In instances where it does happen, God's people are to do everything in their power to stop the evil. In fact, the book of Amos primarily centers around the failure of Samaria to uphold social justice and God holding them accountable as He holds all accountable for such moral passivity.

Some may argue, however, that God in His wisdom and knowl-edge uses men through social justice to stop evil that is pointless and this is the good. In this case, two problems arise. One is that this would destroy man's choice to do the good, which makes commands to do good meaningless. If the evil has to be stopped because it will not lead to a good, then in order for it to be certainly stopped, it will have to be determined by God. If it is determined by God, then it is not man's choice to obey—only to do what has been programmed, as an actor on the stage recites the words of another. The second problem is that the idea of good would be relativized. Under these conditions, it cannot be the particular evil itself about which God is concerned, only that evil as it relates to *that* person in that circumstance (since all social injustice is not prevented by man). If it is not prevented by any means, it must lead to some greater good. The command in the Bible, however, is that social injustice is to always be prevented; that is, it is a universal command. Where God intervenes through His people (or some other means) to prevent social injustice in one place and not in another place (geographical), one can only conclude (if there is no gratuitous evil) that it is not the evil but the individual circumstances that determine God's intervention (either directly or indirectly) in relation to the necessary good. This would seem to make the Scripture's commands to be actively engaged in social justice a relative and not an absolute command to say nothing of the fact that it would not be a choice to obey since it would be necessary to stop the evil because it would not bring about some good.

In such cases, it might be argued that God allows the evil in some lives and, through the efforts of others, stops the evil where it serves no purpose. This also contradicts the biblical mandate to love our neighbor as ourselves. How can one reconcile the command to stop social injustice because God demands it and then suggest that God allows it because it will lead to a greater good? Arguments of this nature postulate that God allowed slavery for a period of time and when it could not longer serve some good, He raised up men to stop it. This seems blatantly contradictory. It makes no difference in the present argument if God permits or causes the evil; His command is clearly against social injustice.

For those who hold to the openness of God, another difficulty arises. How would God know ahead of time whether the evil would be beneficial since it depends upon the future choices made by man and He cannot know what choices people will make? If God does not know the outcome of the future moral choices of His moral creatures, He cannot possibly know the consequences of those choices, therefore, He will not know which choices to permit and which ones to prevent. In fact, without this knowledge, He might stop a good from coming to pass as well as permit some evil that would not bring about some good.

From man's perspective, one might even argue that promotion of evil could be condoned, a similar idea Paul addresses when he writes, "What shall we say then? Shall we continue in sin that grace may abound? Certainly not!" (Rom. 6:1–2). Should men do evil that good might obtain? The answer would be the same—certainly not! It is clear that when taken to its logical conclusion the greater-good premise destroys the notion of social justice. Although Swinburne argues that those who countenance the greater good position are not suggesting that people do bad things so that good will come of it, he does not address the matter of why anyone should try to stop evil. Yet, if certain goods cannot obtain without certain evils, then would it not be to the disadvantage of someone suffering, if another stopped the evil that was meant for his good? As Arthur Flemming notes,

> All of us morally ought to prevent or minimize evil consequences whenever we can. Benevolence would then apparently require that we reduce the evil that there is in the world as far as possible. Yet if the theistic worldview [greater-good justificatory framework] is correct, the mixture of good and evil in our world is optimal. On that hypothesis, wouldn't one only change things for worse by intervening to remove evil?[24]

If certain evil is necessary to certain goods, how will the theist know which evils to permit and which evils to prevent? Whereas under the greater-good justificatory framework the theist cannot always know when the good is achieved (Wykstra's solution), there would not even be a way by which he could design a paradigm on which evils to permit and which ones to try to prevent. Therefore, one would never know if he were preventing an evil or preventing a good. This would convolute the notion of social justice and confuse the definition of good and evil. In one case, good is stopping the evil while in another case, good is achieved by permitting the evil. Without charging anyone who holds this position of supporting the idea of *karma*, it does appear that this posture brings one dangerously close to this notion.

### G-G Theodicy Raises Questions About Prayer

If, as the G-G theodicy maintains, the only evil permitted by God in this world is that from which He can bring about a greater good or prevent a worse evil, then what about prayer? Suppose a Christian is suffering from cancer. The actuality of cancer, which counts as an evil (physical), means that God has allowed it. However, God only allows the cancer to bring about a greater good or to prevent a worse evil. Nonetheless, someone brings the name of this person before the church and asks for prayer that God might heal the person from cancer. Here a problem arises. Why should the church pray that God will stop an evil that He has allowed. Does this not question God's purposes since is a purposeful (maybe even willed) event? Furthermore, if God answers the prayer of the church, then the initial good He intended never comes and the world is without a necessary good all because the church prayed. The matter becomes even more difficult if the purpose is to prevent a worse evil. If God answers the prayer of the church and the evil is stopped, then all the church has accomplished is bringing a worse evil upon humanity.

Some might try to answer the question by saying that the evil is God's permissible will, while good health is His perfect will. The question that follows is which will is stronger? It would seem that the permissible will is strongest, which means that He perfect will is subservient. The implications for the eschaton are potentially alarming. When the G-G theodicy is seen in light of prayer, it raises some serious questions for those who believe that prayer is more than a Bingo game and a matter of matching the numbers on earth with the numbers in heaven.

**The Concept of Good Is Relativized**

Another problem involves the use of the word good. In G-G theodicies the word *good* is shrouded in ambiguity, made relative to something else and not a straightforward or absolute concept. A straightforward concept is the statement, "Feeding a starving child is *good*." Here, the sense of goodness stands by itself as a moral good in the absolute sense. But, when the good is placed in relationship to another act, it becomes a comparative notion relative to the situation and/or those in the situation. The following statement is a relative notion: "It is good that John got such a good buy on the car." If the man who had to sell the car did so at a loss (making it a good buy for John) because he had to sell the car due to his son's sickness (which had taken all his money so he could not make the car payment), then it was not good in that sense that John got such a great buy on the car. The good was only relative to John's power to purchase, but it entailed a condition not good to the man selling the car.

In this way, good is relativistic. This is the way in which it is used in the G-G theodicies when pointing to some good that obtains. Good is not used in the intrinsic sense but in a relative sense giving rise to ambiguity at best and equivocation at worse. The idea is a consequential good, which involves a relative notion and cannot be judged by itself but only by the consequences. Furthermore, this notion of good leaves open the question about when or how the good obtains and requires an understanding of the larger context in which evil and good take place. For example, what may appear to be good might really be evil, and what is evil could be good when viewed from a different perspective. A father shoving his son across the yard and the son breaking his leg could appear to be evil, but if the father was pushing his son out of the way of a deadly snake, the act is actually good. Used in this way, good depends on what one takes into account when determining how something is viewed in terms of its good and bad value. Some things may appear good and yet they are actually evil in terms of consequences. If one is to condone the evil in light of the consequences (greater-good), then it is fair to say that the theist must be willing to live with the converse.

Given this scheme of things, what appears to be good could, in the flow of things, actually turn out to be evil. At this point, the entire debate is thrown into confusion. An example of the good that obtains evil would be: A gives B an aspirin to relieve a serious pain, the aspirin causes an allergic reaction which constricts the throat and the person becomes oxygen deprived resulting in a Persistent Vegetative State. Or, a medication relieves one problem, but ten years later results in a painful condition for which there is no relief. In these cases, the act is permitted and praised but leads to suffering, which means that good is evil according to the principles of argument in the G-G theodicy. Furthermore, perspective is important when determining the good. For example, Hitler thought that the good of the Arian people being freed from Jewish presence was a greater good than allowing Jews to live.

Some might object to these examples, contending that they do not make the point since in some cases the intent was not evil but good. An objection on the grounds of intent, however, does not hold, as a lot of evil has no evil intent by the one committing the act and yet is still called evil/suffering. For example, a pedestrian may be struck by a car and killed; however, the driver did not intentionally try to kill the pedestrian but the person is nonetheless dead regardless of intent. Intent is not a moral defense in an argument to support the claim that evil or suffering do not result. The only thing that the G-G theodicy claims is that the consequences lead to good; nothing is said about intent. To determine what is good based on intent alone makes moral judgments totally relativistic, leading to situation ethics.

### Who Receives the Good?

If one grants that the good obtains, the next logical question is good for whom? According to the principle of "eye for eye, tooth for tooth" (Ex. 21:24), the one who suffers is the one to whom the good should accrue. As Eleonore Stump notes:

> It seems to me that a perfectly good entity who was also omniscient and omnipotent must govern evil resulting from the misuse of significant freedom in such a way that the sufferings of any particular person are outweighed by the good which the suffering produces *for that person*; otherwise, we might justifiably expect a good God somehow to prevent that *particular suffering*, either by intervening (in one way or another) to protect the victim, while still allowing the

perpetrator his freedom, or by curtailing freedom in some select cases.[25]

Stump's point is well taken (she is not arguing for gratuitous evil, however) since it is reasonable that the one suffering is the one who should receive the benefit. If there is no gratuitous suffering, there ought to be some evidence that the individual sufferer does in fact benefit from the suffering. In light of this, it is not enough to say that some good somewhere at sometime for someone is reasonable justification for God allowing the evil.

One can think of situations in which it is difficult to argue that a particular evil obtains a good for the individual who is suffering. Consider the case of a man working in the woods by himself. His bulldozer overturns on him. No one hears his cry for help. If he does not get help soon, he will bleed to death. In excruciating pain, the man floats in and out of consciousness. After three hours of agony, he dies and because he is not a believer, he goes to eternal punishment. It is impossible to see how the good obtains to this man. It seems insufficient to argue, as Swinburne and others do, that from his suffering others learn not to work in the woods by themselves. Here, the most that can be argued is that the good obtains to another and not the one suffering. And further, what if the man had three small children and a wife, where is the good for them?

There is also the question of horrific and large scale suffering, such as slavery in the United States or the Holocaust. For whom did the good obtain in these cases. If one argues with Wykstra that the good is beyond our ken, more problems develop. Surely, if an evil of this magnitude is permitted because of some greater good, the good would have to be in proportion to the evil. How could anyone miss this good? Furthermore, if suffering is for the purpose of soul-making, it would be necessary for the good to obtain for the one suffering. So, it is logical that the G-G theodicy maintain that the good does obtain to the ones suffering and not for another.

One might argue that the good obtains to the one suffering but at a much later point in the sufferer's life. Let's maybe five or ten years later. This too raises questions. How can one be sure that the good is in fact directly linked to the suffering from five years ago? Surely there could be many other intervening events in the five year period which could also account for the state of affairs five years later. Further, how can one be sure that the particular good in question would not have occurred if the suffering had never taken place? How can one be certain that the good is somehow only possible because of a particular suffering event five years previous? It cannot be demonstrated evidentially.

## Lacks Objective Criteria to Measure Good Against Evil

Another apparent problem for the greater-good premise is the lack of objective criteria for determining when the good outweighs the evil. How is it determined when the good is greater than the evil? How is a value assigned to the act and the consequence even in cases where people think that they can see the greater good? As Russell points out in his critique of Hick and Swinburne, "I cannot agree that it [the greater good] is *so* valuable that it could justify someone in permitting suffering like that endured by the little girl in Flint."[26] How does one calculate how much good is needed to make the evil justified? Or, is it just an arbitrary notion subject to anyone's interpretation? The notion of greater implies either a quantitative or qualitative measure that requires some means of measurement.

When a measurement is affixed to the discussion, one is faced with a less than desirable conclusion. Consider working from some sort of a numerical value system by assigning a numerical value to suffering and the same with a good. Let's assign the value of -4 to being beaten (a negative value because it is evil) and the value of +5 to reflect the consequential greater good (a positive value because it is good) and assume that the greater good is obtained. In this case, the net value gain of +1 indicates that the good obtains, which is the basic premise of the G-G theodicy, namely that a greater good obtains. Consider a second case in addition to being beaten, a person is also raped and then dismembered while alive. This evil, which one can assume is worse because it involves additional suffering, (assuming that the beating was of equal force in each case). For this suffering we will assign the value of -7 because it is a worse evil and it involves more suffering. In order to represent the obtaining of a greater good, the prevailing good will be assigned a value of +8. In both cases, we have assigned proportionate positive value to represent the greater good obtains from each respective evil. Both the -4 and the -7 represent real evil events as the +5 and +8 represent real goods. This means that the good obtained in the first case is not of the same magnitude as the good obtained in the second case, or there is a greater good in the second case than in the first. This means that the good obtaining from being beaten and raped is greater (+8) than only being beaten (+5). Logically, it follows that it is better to be beaten and raped than only beaten since the good is greater (something no one actually believes).

Some may object to this example by pointing out that the net gain is the same. This misses the point. Remember that the numerical value for increased good has to be moved up to save the greater-good approach. Unless this move is totally arbitrary, there must be some justification for increasing the numerical value to +8. The only justification is if the actual good increases. Surely a good of the value +8 is better than +5, which is to say the world is better with +8 goods than with only +5 goods. This illustrates the fact that the concept of good in the greater-good approach is neither objective nor constant and therefore less than meaningful. There is no way to determine what kind of good outranks a particular evil or how much good is needed in order for the greater good to obtain. There is no divine equation to use in order to know what good (or how much good of a particular type) must obtain in order for it to be greater than the corollary evil.

### Fails to Answer Mental Attitude Evil

Arthur Flemming also raises another question, which appears to have some force against the greater-good premise. This one addresses the issue of evil that has no actual or overt consequence. A case in point would be where an evil is only thought and not actually committed. This seems to leave some evil outside the explanation of the greater-good approach. Jesus taught that to lust after a woman was to commit adultery (Matt. 5:28). As Flemming suggests, "Attempted theft or assault or murder is an evil in itself, but each becomes worse if the attempt succeeds."[27] From a theistic perspective, the thought can also be evil even though it does not become as bad as it might have been if acted upon. Consider the evils of hate, envy and the like, which may never manifest themselves in a way that causes suffering. How is it that good ever comes from such mental attitudes?

### It Limits God

The idea that this is not the best of all possible worlds is standard fare in G-G theodicies. After all, if this were the best of all possible worlds, then there would be no room for any greater good to obtain, either in this life or the life to come. Geisler and Corduan develop the idea that this is not the best of all possible worlds but rather the way to the best of all possible worlds. That is, through sin and subsequent redemption, God is able to bring about a better world for humanity—in general terms. While denying that this is the best of all possible worlds, they claim that "this kind of world with free beings who do sin is the best of all possible ways of obtaining the best of all possible worlds, and that no other world or nonworld would have been morally better than this world."[28] The present world is the best it can be under the circumstances, but the circumstances are far from the best. The good achieved by evil is a better state for redeemed mankind.

These two authors concede that this is the best world under the circumstances, which includes the fact that man really has freedom. In fact, they argue that this is the "worst of all possible worlds."[29] Since God allows only that evil that results in the greater good, then for more good there must be a considerable amount of evil. That is, "The actual amount of evil in the world must be the upper limit. If the evil in this world is the necessary condition for bringing about the best of all possible worlds, then we must be experiencing the maximal amount of evil necessary."[30] This sounds a little like the let's sin-more-that-grace-may-abound approach. However, this middle-of-the-road approach comes under the same criticism as other G-G theodicies.

Geisler and Corduan claim that "God must do his best."[31] Stated in a fuller way they say, "God must do his best or else it is evil for him. Hence, if God produced anything less than a world that could be produced by an absolutely perfect Being, then God is not an absolutely perfect Being."[32] Their argument runs like this:

1. God is an absolutely perfect Being.

2. Producing less than the best possible world would be an evil for an absolutely perfect Being.

3. But an absolutely perfect Being cannot produce evil.

4. God produced this world.

5. But this world as is and as has been is not the best possible world.

6. Therefore, there must be a perfect world to come (of which this present world is a necessary prelude to its production).[33]

The *best* for Geisler and Corduan is in the eschatological sense, which requires evil as a means of bringing about the best world in the future.

In the end, they argue, that "it is impossible for God to create directly a world with achieved moral values of the highest nature. He must first allow evil as a precondition of the greatest good. Hence, this world with freedom and evil is the best way to produce the morally best possible world."[34] This sounds similar to Hick's view of a soul-making theodicy. Furthermore, Geisler and Corduan use the word *world* to speak only of this present state of affairs, meaning that there is more than one world in God's plan. This, at least, includes this one and the world to come. Geisler and Corduan, speak of *best* in the sense of an eschatological moral perfection. They argue that this world with sin is necessary to the world to come (the Kingdom seems to be that of which they are speaking). God could not have created the best world without a world with evil in it as a necessary precondition to the best world, one with no evil. In the end, God did His best in initial creation, which was not really the best but the best He could do at the time.

The Geisler-Corduan view also raises the question that if evil leads to good, how could a world where no evil exists be the best—the world to come (in their thinking)? This is like some form of dialectic by which a moral evolutionary process is driven by evil out of which comes good and a better world. As with all evolutionary schemes, it is difficult to know at what point the optimum good has been achieved and the process brought to a conclusion. Whereas the process involves an increase in the number of beings, it seems possible that one more evil could result in another good and a better world. Since the possibilities are infinite, by cutting short the process from evil one also cuts short the possibility of corollary good. In a world where no evil is present, good will be limited (it would remain at its present level—no increase) which means it cannot be the best world. It does not matter how one defines best or good in this present argument. It is enough to know that the greater good comes from evil and there is a world (the one to come) where there is no evil. This seems to hold God hostage to evil in order to have the good God knows is best for man, but God is unable to create it apart from using evil. If this is the case, then God is not omnipotent in His creative powers.

## SUMMARY

If the above analysis is correct, then it appears that all traditional G-G theodicies are in need of recasting. In order for God to have morally justifiable reasons for permitting evil, in all cases the greater good must obtain. If an evil occurs two things must logically follow: (1) The evil must be the will of God or else it will not have happened. In that case, God wills the very things He calls sin. (2) The greater good must obtain. Whereas a world with more good is better than a world with less good, and whereas the good comes from the evil, it is better to have evil than not to have evil. If this is the case, then refraining from evil personally or preventing evil culturally actually robs the world of some good that would have obtained if the evil would have been committed. One might object to this line of argument by pointing out that man has the opportunity to do good by stopping the evil—a greater good. If this is so, then two questions are raised. The one involves the evil that is not stopped, or not stopped until it has persisted for an extended period of time. (One can think of slavery or the extermination of Jews under Hitler as examples. What good was obtained before the good of someone stopping the evil?) Second, how is one to know which evils are permitted for the purpose of man stopping and which ones are permitted from which God Himself will bring about the greater good?

Others might posit that the greater good is the glory of God. If a person or group of persons stop the evil, then God is glorified because His moral will is being done on this earth. How can it be that His moral will is to stop the evil and His sovereign will is for the evil to occur so that the good might obtain? Another possibility is that if the evil is not stopped, man (as a wicked sinner) simply gets what he deserves anyway and this is justice that brings God glory (and this is the greater good). At this point, one could raise some serious theological concerns. First, how would this apply to Christians who suffer in this world? Second, is physical suffering the penalty of sin? Third, it seems to have a hard pass when speaking about the suffering of little children. Furthermore, if the good is the glory of God, then one can bring glory to God by either doing good or evil. The position of G-G theodicies is that God only allows that evil in the world from which He can bring about a greater good or defeat a worse evil. If an evil occurs, it must be allowed by God in order to bring about a necessary good (necessary because if it were incidental, if would have no purpose and, therefore, would be gratuitous—something G-G theodicies deny). Since the good is necessary, the evil is also necessary, and this requires that it be willed by God. When a person commits adultery and destroys a family, this is the will of God to bring glory to Himself. Whether doing good or evil, I can bring glory to God. Whereas bringing glory to God is the greater good, and I want to bring glory to God, I can do it by either doing evil or doing good. Something does not sound right about all of this.

A number of disturbing theological and philosophical concerns surface upon close scrutiny of the G-G theodicy. The position that God permits all evil in this world as necessary to the obtaining of some greater good or to prevent some evil greater contains difficulties at best and inconsistencies at worse, both within itself and within the larger Christian theological context. The greater good premise itself is dubious, and furthermore, requires the denial of gratuitous evil, forcing the theist into the impossible task of demonstrating this from the evidence or from the Bible. This seems to be an unfortunate claim by the theist, as his only means of supporting his claim is to assume his conclusion as the basis for making his argument. It is this claim of the greater good (and the corollary denial of gratuitous evil) that this author believes is the Achilles heel of the G-G theodicy. Therefore, in the next two chapters we will look at a possible alternative theodicy called the "Creation-Order Theodicy."

## NOTES

1. David O'Conner, *God and Inscrutable Evil* (New York: Rowman & Littlefield Publishers, 1998), 1. This book is highly recommended by Daniel Howard-Snyder. In the book, O'Conner interacts with some of the most recent positions on theodicy with a focus on the subject of gratuitous evil. It is a worthwhile book. Even though it may not come down firmly on one side or the other, it does a remarkable job of drawing the lines of distinction within the argument and critiquing several major positions.

2. It will be remembered that Swinburne understood exactly what the theist must do, but his attempt at trying to point out how evil does work for the good fell far short of being convincing. Hick, does not attempt to demonstrate from the evidence that gratuitous evil does not exist.

3. Gregory Boyd, *Satan and the Problem of Evil* (Downers Grove: InterVarsity Press, 2001), 179.

4. Ibid.

5. Ibid., 125.

6. Bruce Russell, "Defenseless" in *The Evidential Argument from Evil,* ed. Daniel Howard-Snyder (Bloomington: Indiana University Press, 1996), 204.

7. Ibid., 204.

8. Barry Whitney, *Theodicy: An Annotated Bibliography on the Problem of Evil-1960–1990* (Bowling Green, OH: Bowling Green State University Philosophy, Documentation Center), 1998, 7.

9. Ibid., 8.

10. Nelson Pike, "Hume On Evil," in *The Problem of Evil*, ed. Marilyn McCord Adams and Robert Merrihew Adams (Oxford: Oxford University Press, 1996), 48–9.

11. Stephen John Wykstra, "Rowe's Noseeum Arguments from Evil" in *The Evidential Argument From Evil,* ed. Daniel Howard-Snyder (Bloomington: Indiana University Press, 1996): 127–8.

12. The argument here is not that the claim cannot be made, only that it cannot be made on the strength of the evidence.

13. R. Z. Friedman, "Evil and Moral Agency," *Philosophy of Religion* 24 (1988): 7.

14. Geisler is actually defending against the objection to his position that this is the best way to the best world, but the argument is the same in either case.

15. Norman Geisler, *Philosophy of Religion* (Grand Rapids: Zondervan Publishing House, 1974), 395.

16. Ibid.

17. Friedman, "Evil and Moral Agency," 9.

18. Ibid.

19. Richard J. Middleton, "Why the 'Greater Good' Isn't a Defense," 9 *Koinonia* (1997): 88.

20. Ibid., 91.

21. Friedman, "Evil and Moral Agency," 9.

22. Middleton, "Why 'Greater Good' Isn't a Defense," 91.

23. Friedman, "Evil and Moral Agency," 13.

24. Arthur Flemming, "Omnibenevolence and Evil," *Ethics* 26 (January 1986): 281.

25. Eleonore Stump, "The Problem of Evil," *Faith and Philosophy* 2 (1985): 411.

26. Bruce Russell, "The Persistent Problem of Evil," *Faith and Philosophy* 6 (April 1989), 26.

27. Arthur Flemming, "Omnibenevolence and Evil," *Ethics* 26 (January 1986): 270.

28. Geisler and Corduan, *Philosophy of Religion*, 371.

29. Ibid., *377*.

30. Ibid., 378.

31. Ibid., 311.

32. Ibid., 312.

33. Ibid., 343.

34. Ibid., 353.

# Chapter 5

# Foundations for a Creation-Order Theodicy

The existence of God is not a question of personal opinion or preference as it deals with a matter of reality. Either God exists or He does not exist, and the affirmation of either constitute a philosophical affirmation rather than a religious affirmation. The statement affirms something about the state of affairs referred to as reality. God cannot be a part of reality and not a part of reality in the same way at the same time. Therefore, depending upon what is, one or the other statement must be false while the other is true. It is the same as an affirmation about the existence of tigers. Either tigers exist or they do not exist. Depending on where you are living, your belief about their existence could make a measurable difference. If they do exist, a statement affirming their existence would be a true statement, whereas denying their existence would be a false statement. So it is with a statement about God's existence—it deals with reality first and religion second.

Furthermore, the existence of God is not a question about personal preference. That is, it is not the same kind of issue as who would like to be president. Simply preferring God to exist has no place in the argument. When considering the question of God's existence, it must be clear that the force of this question deals with the fact of reality and not one's preference regarding His existence. What must not be lost in the discussion is that what is at stake is one's view of reality. Reality is what it is, and either our perception of it is correct or incorrect. Moreover, if God does not exist, then all that has been constructed on the notion that He does exist must be discarded immediately as it would have no value for living in reality. Further, all reasons ever held as good and sufficient to warrant belief in God's existence must be rejected as fool's gold. One the other hand, if God does exist then what one does with the information is extremely important.

## HELPFUL CLARIFICATIONS

Before getting too far into the discussion of theodicy, it will be helpful to revisit the definition issue again. First, most often affirmations about reality enlist the word "believe" so the affirmation is that one believes this or that about reality. Unfortunately, when the word "believe" is conjoined to the word "God", "believe" is christened as a religious word, making the statement a mere religious affirmation. If one says that he believes God exists, it is viewed quite differently from someone saying that he believes tigers exist. The first is seen as only a religious statement while the second is not. Attaching the word God to "believe" automatically prejudices all that follows as nothing more than a religious statement which is ultimately only a statement about one's religious commitments—merely a private judgment. This, in turn, makes any affirmation of belief that God exists a statement of private value, not a statement of fact about reality. Unfortunately, whenever the object of belief is God, a bias exists in hearing what is said. Such a bias is without epistemological justification and, therefore, must be resisted by the theist at all times and in all places.

Moreover, it is important to distinguish between affirming one's belief in the existence of God and one's belief in that God. The assertion that God exists carries with it no explicit religious connotation. A person can affirm belief *that* God exists without confessing any personal commitment to that God. On the other hand if a person confesses that he believes *in* God, then something quite different is being said. The first statement conveys what a person thinks about the nature of reality,[1] while the second reveals some personal commitment to God, which is clearly a religious statement. Of course the second statement would reasonably be made only by one who also affirms the first. It is often the case that the two notions are confused.

It should be pointed out that any affirmation about personal commitments by itself says little or nothing substantively about the existence of God in terms of reality. It is quite possible for God not to exist even though people make some religious commitment to the idea of God. In fact, nothing of epistemological substance is gained for the larger question of God's existence just because someone says he believes in God. Ample examples of notorious religious testimonies affirm notions that are contrary to reality, yet people are very committed to them. Saying that one believes something exists does not say anything substantively about reality. One must examine the reasons why a person believes this or that concerning reality.

Second, the word "God" serves double duty in everyday conversation, at least in the English speaking world. One function for "God" is to speak of the *nature* of a being whose essence is God. When used in this sense, the word God refers to a cluster of essential attributes forming a particular nature. The other use for the word God is to reference a being as *a person* in contradiction to another being. In spite of an overlap, there is clearly a difference, and it is one that must be maintained. To say God sent His Son to be the savior of the world is to use the word "God" to point to a person who acts. On the other hand, when the Bible says that God is just, the emphasis is on the essence of the being. Sometimes the term is used to point to the being; at other times it identifies the nature of the being. It is not that these are unconnected, only that there is a different emphasis.

When a statement is made to the effect that God limits Himself, the question is which of these two usages is in view. It certainly cannot be that God limits God in terms of essence, for God would not be God. Rather, the intent of the statement is that God the person, limits the expression of His essence under certain circumstances. God cannot limit who He is ontologically (a logical impossibility), but He can choose to limit the expression of possibilities as God as seen in the Incarnation. It is logically impossible for God to use His power to cause Himself substantively to be something less than God. Any possible limited expression of God's nature, however, must not be limited in such a way or to such an extent that it would result in the manifestation presenting a distorted view of God or entailing a contradiction of God*ness*.

In the discussion of evil, the first order of business is to determine whether or not there are good and sufficient reasons to justify belief that God exists as a part of reality. Considering what a person might do personally if he believes God exists is another matter altogether.[2] The question associated with the argument from evil is the question dealing with God's existence in an objective sense. In the end, the theist must determine whether or not the presence of horrible evils (the part of reality in which man lives) strong enough to defeat all other evidence for God's existence. Both the positive and negative evidence must be examined to determine if the claim that God exists is irrational and indefensible in light of terrible evils such as the Holocaust. Put another way, is it more likely that God does not exist than that He does exist?[3]

The atheist's project of disproving God's existence, however, does appear to say something about the positive evidence for God's existence. People do not attempt to disprove that which no one believes or only a small number of people believe. However, belief in God's existence enjoys a rather extensive well-documented history in the world, motivating individuals to great feats, compassionate acts as well as providing the subject for many great works of art. While this in and of itself does not prove that God exists, it does encompass a large portion of history which cannot simply be ignored by the atheist. It is true that a person's belief is not necessarily justified by the length of history of those who have believed, but historical continuity of a particular belief among so many people, increases the probability that there is some objective justification for such a belief. To say the least, belief in the existence of God is a very tenacious belief, arguing that there must be some good and sufficient reasons for such a belief. In fact, one might argue that the vigorous attempts to defeat the belief God exists strongly suggests that there are good and sufficient reasons for people to believe *that* God exists. Moreover, if there were not good and sufficient reasons for people to believe in God's existence, surely it would not take much to defeat such a claim. Historically, all attempts to defeat belief in God's existence by attacking the traditional arguments for God's existence have not proven very successful for the atheist. However, the positive evidence for God's existence is not grounds for dismissing the argument from evil.

It appears some strong positive evidence against God is required to defeat the good and sufficient reasons people have for believing God exists. It is true that the appeal to evil/suffering does appear to be a strong argument against God's existence. This is not a new objection, so why has it not convinced people to give up belief in God's existence by now? What remains instructive is the fact that while evil/suffering (some very hideous indeed) have been part of mankind's experience, over the years this has not proven strong enough to overthrow belief in God's existence. Furthermore, as seen in recent history such evil often turns people to call on God. On September 11, 2001, when the Trade Towers were destroyed killing thousands of innocent people, the first thought of the technologically sophisticated America was to ask God for help, not deny His existence. People did not deny God existence. Instead they talked about praying to God. In this case, terrible evil did not prove to people that God did not exist, but rather how much they needed His protection. It should be pointed out that this does not minimize the argument from evil, but rather places it in a proper historical/existential context. In and of itself, this is not a proof for God's existence. It only points out that evil has not convinced large numbers of people to deny the existence of God.

What the atheist needs to defeat reasonable belief in God's existence is some evidence that would count conclusively against God's existence and be a final defeater of all arguments for God's existence. This evidence would need to be of such a caliber and so compelling that it would render belief in God's existence as both irrational and unwarranted. It would be something like the evidence needed by reviewing a tape of the play in order to overturn an official's call on the football field. According to the atheist, the argument from evil does just that, in spite of its poor track record over the centuries. Notwithstanding this fact, the theist must admit that it does appear *prima facie* that the presence of horrible evils argues against the existence of God. Furthermore, the argument from evil is more than atheistic propaganda. Even some within the ranks of theism struggle with reconciling the two realities: evil and God. Whether or not the argument from evil has convinced many, it still presents the theist with a legitimate argument that must be answered. Not only for the atheist but for the Church as well. Theism claims to have the answers to life, and suffering is one of those great questions of life.

Unfortunately, the standard fare G-G theistic response lacks its own success in answering the argument from evil. In fact, we have seen the G-G theodicy, with its numerous theological and philosophical concerns, has actually strengthened the atheist position by committing the theist to deliver an answer that requires empirical evidence, which is most difficult to produce. The theist's task of developing a theodicy that avoids this difficulty while remaining true to a classical theism remains unfinished. The theist must not only demonstrate that human suffering is not conclusive evidence against God's existence, but he must also show how it is consistent with theism.[4] That is, the theist must not look simply to counterbalance the argument from evil but actually undercut the argument.

## BASIC ELEMENTS OF THE CREATION-ORDER THEODICY

Whereas, it is the existence of the God of theism that is attacked, it is only reasonable to defend the God of theism.[5] Further, this understanding of a theistic God comes from the Bible, so it follows that it is also reasonable to take whatever the Bible says about God as true. Therefore, information about God from the Bible may be used by the theist in his response to the argument from evil. One cannot use the Bible to construct the objection and then deny the defense the same right to consult the Bible. If the whole argument against God comes from an understanding of God as presented in the Bible, then to be consistent, one cannot deny the use of the Bible in the defense when it speaks to the matter of God. After all, any answer that comes must come from a theistic world view.

## The Nature of God and Creation

Minimally defined, God is the omnipotent, omniscient, omnibenevolent One. Either this God exists or He does not exist. If He does not exist, then there is no discussion. Why debate that which does not exist? If He exists, then He exists as the God identified (all-powerful, all-knowing, all-good) in the objection. Ideas about the theistic God come from either what is true to reality or what is not true to reality. If they come from what is not true to reality, then there is no reason to have a discussion as it would be meaningless. While this does not answer the argument from evil, it does seem to clarify the real task of theodicy. (It is not to prove God's existence since the argument must assume His existence to have an argument.) The task of the theist is to demonstrate how God can be morally justified in permitting evil in this world. This would undercut the atheist's argument. The responsible theist crafts a theodicy that is philosophically sound, theologically consistent, and existentially satisfying for the sufferer and sufficient to answer the objections from the argument from evil. The problem facing the work of theodicy is the apparent unreconcilable tension that develops precisely because both God and evil are part of reality as known to man. It is true that God belongs to the circle of uncreated reality and evil to the circle of created reality, but these two realities intersect and interact.

Evil exists because God created something good. Evil cannot exist by itself as it has no essence of its own (Augustine). It is a lack in that which is good. In this sense, evil is not a thing, but rather a condition of privation in something that is good.[6] Prior to any act of creation (angels, man, the universe) there was only God. Furthermore, since all that existed eternally is God (who is absolute goodness), whatever He created had only His nature (absolute goodness) to guide the process and His mind to design the product. Consequently, one cannot separate the nature of God from the nature of what was created. This is not to say that the nature of God and creation are identical, only that whatever God created reflects His perfect character for no other pattern existed. This, however, is not to imply that creation was perfect in the same way that God is perfect. That would be impossible as God is uncreated and immaterial, while the world is created and material. By virtue of its created*ness* it cannot be uncreated*ness*.

There is an essential difference between the created and the uncreated substance. Nonetheless, what God created was controlled and informed only by His perfect nature, for there was nothing else after which to pattern it for all there was was God. This means that within the category of created, what God created was perfect to the degree and kind that a created thing can own perfection. It is a logical impossibility for God to create a perfection belonging only to that which is uncreated. Furthermore, had God never created anything, it would be impossible for evil to exist. Whereas God by definition is eternal and complete it is logically impossible for any lack within His nature (this is why Aquinas argued that evil came from good). However, creation did not necessitate evil's existence, it only made it possible. Since evil cannot be understood apart from creation and since creation is perfect (without moral flaw), understanding evil requires both an understanding of God in His creative relationship to creation and of what creation necessarily entailed in order to be a workable and interactive creation.

### God and Man

The story of trinitarian theism begins in Genesis. It is also the proper place to begin the work of theodicy. In the early chapters of Genesis God provides information on the basic *modus vivendi* (a feasible arrangement that circumvents difficulties) to which He voluntarily commits in order to establish a predictable and meaningful relationship with man. Just as it is necessary to understand the rules by which a game is played beforehand, so it is necessary to understand under what terms and conditions God creates making mutual interaction between God and man possible. Such terms and conditions establish how the infinite personal God can meaningfully and predictably interact with finite personal man. God, who is eternal (without a past from which He came, or a future in which He will become), must of necessity be on a different ontological order than man who is a contingent being. God never came into existence and will never go out of existence. Creation had a beginning (although it appears to not have an end), a fact that owes its reality to God. Prior to the existence of matter, the triune God existed in trinity. Within this trinitarian complex the Father, the Son and the Holy Spirit enjoy a perfect relationship with one another. Jesus expressed something of this relationship when He was here on earth. As He prayed to the Father the night of His betrayal, He spoke of the glory which He had with the Father "before the world was" (Jn 17:5). Whatever else glory may include, Jesus is speaking of a social and shared interaction that existed between the persons of the Godhead before the material realm existed. In this way Jesus differentiated between the relationship He had as God only and the relationship He experienced as the God-man.

Clearly, the personal relationship among the persons of the Trinity enjoys a different ontological level than the personal relationship between God and man. When God (the Trinity) acts through and towards those within the Divine community, the essence of God is unrestricted in manifestation. Therefore, one can speak of God acting/interacting without restriction within the Trinity. That to which the Father relates in others is the same—God—and therefore, the fullness of expression is possible within the uncreated circle of reality—the Trinity. The second condition in which the personal God acts/interacts involves that which is outside His essence, namely the circle of created contingent reality— His creation in general and personal man in particular. Man, who is made in the image of God, is not God. While there is compatibility between God and man, they do not share the same ontological order. God, who by sovereign choice created man as a personal moral being, suggests that God intended to interact relationally with man in *similar* fashion to His relation within the Trinity. Whereas God is sovereign, He alone determines the manner by which He interacts in a person-to-person relationship, so that it is meaningful even though His moral agents are space/time contingent creatures. This possibility requires some limitation of the expression of some of God's attributes in this relationship. However, the limitation in no way involves any moral attributes of God or the moral use of any attributes of God.

Such parameters do not limit God the person in who He is essentially. He remains God in all respects, however, with reference to how He works within created order. He limits Himself in the interest of establishing a meaningful person-to-person relationship with man. Furthermore, this relationship, unlike that of the Trinity, takes place within a space/time context. This requires some *modus vivendi*, whereby the eternal God operates relationally within the space/time context with a moral being less than Himself—man. God, who is sovereign, chooses to limit the full expression of some of His attributes for the sake of true communication and community with man. Anything else requires God to be always at such a distance from man that such distance would inhibit a meaningful relationship with man. This is hinted at in Deuteronomy 5:23–27; 18:15–19. This is not limiting any divine attribute. It is rather the limitation of the expression of the attribute in relational interaction with man. For example, it is generally agreed that in the Incarnation, the Son of God limited the full expression of His deity (Phil. 2:6–8; Heb.10:20). His divinity was not limited, for in such a case He would cease to be God. Without this limitation, however, God would have remained at an epistemic distance of such magnitude that a normal person-to-person relationship would have been impossible (Deut. 18:15–19).

Whereas there exists a real ontological difference between God and man, God's personal interaction with the man—the person—would necessarily be on a different existential order than that which was known within the Trinity (uncreated). Within the Trinity the relationship is among equals and grounded in the eternal perfect moral character of each of the three persons in the Godhead. Whereas the created realm does not possess that same moral perfection, God's personal interaction with created personal beings must have a special *modus vivendi*, which takes into account the limitations of created person*ness*.

It is this *modus vivendi* that makes it possible for two persons of different ontological order to have a meaningful relationship in which the relationship is volitional and not determinative or coercive. Whereas man is made in the image of God, he has a mind. With this mind man is capable of intentionally loving both God (which includes obeying God) and other created moral beings. With the actualization of creation, two minds (that is, two kinds of minds) exist in reality—the mind of God and the mind of man. God's mind operates on the infinite level and man's operates on a finite level, yet there is meaningful intersection of the two. The *modus vivendi* called "creation-order" establishes the moral and physical parameters through which God is able to be involved dynamically and meaningfully in His creation. Man is thereby able to respond volitionally to this God in love (an important point noted by Hick). Whatever moral and physical parameters God establishes issue forth from the eternal, sovereign, all-wise, just and loving essence of God and would be binding on both God the person and on man in any relationship that would exist. The creation ordering would be just for all concerned and would make it possible for the person of man to be a real person in the same way that God is person. Furthermore, it would be the order was constructed in such a way that the providence of God assures the actualization of the counsels of God while at the same time giving man the power of moral choice.

## Two Minds

By definition, creation is different than Creator. Creation is not the mind of God but the expression of the mind of God. Neither is it the completeness of the mind of God but rather the product of the mind of God. Furthermore, creation reveals different levels of complexity and ability. Man, who is made in the image (shadow image) of God, appears to be the most complex and unique part of creation (Gen.1:26, 27). Part of what constitutes the image of God in man is that man is a moral being with a mind capable of moral judgment (a point made by

138 Foundations for a Creation-Order Theodicy

Leibniz). In this way, man is not only an expression of the mind of God but given a mind patterned after God's mind. This means that at least some of the same categories of thought in the mind of God are also in the mind of man. Because of this, the mind of man is capable of comprehending God's thoughts as those thoughts have been revealed by God to man (I Cor. 2:16). Although man's mind is inferior to God's mind, it nonetheless is capable of processing in a manner similar to the mind of God (Phil. 2:5).

The human mind must not be thought of as simply a repository for data. It has the function of rational cognition by which information is processed and utilized in various ways. Furthermore, man has a will that moves the mind to respond to information in either a positive or negative way. This is especially true of the information he receives from God. Man's mind is not controlled by some divinely created software that determines how the information will be appropriated; it has the capability of processing the information correctly.[7] If the mind were wired to respond to information in a predetermined fashion, it would be impossible for man not to love God. Instead, essential to being morally free is the liberty either to accept or reject information, and this extends to that which God has revealed. This is, in part, what it means to have a mind patterned after God's mind. God truly desired to have another mind outside Himself in the universe, a mind with which He could share in a personal way and establish a reciprocating loving relationship. Without libertarian freedom[8] (I actually prefer the term Thomas Flint calls *libertarian traditionalism*)[9] love is impossible, since by definition love is a volitional matter that requires judgment, either to love or not to love. Raw information without judgment is what one may have in a computerized machine. For example, one can control a rocket by programming it a certain way. In fact, one can even program it to function differently when it detects different conditions. This is not judgment or mind—it is control. One cannot command a machine only control it. It is possible, however, to give a command to a moral agent, realizing that ultimately the moral agent determines how he will respond to the command. A command implies the possibility of judgment in the hearer and carries with it the possibility that the command might be disobeyed. Consequently, as seen in the Bible, commands are often accompanied with resulting penalties if the command is disobeyed (example: Deut. 28–30). The moral ordering of creation was designed to account for the second mind in the universe so this that mind could operate as a true mind without overriding the creation plan of God.

While it is true that the mind of man and the mind of God function on different levels, there is an intersection at the existential level. God is able to give man instructions about his relationship to and responsibility for creation (Gen. 2:15–17 and 2:19 in the naming of the animals). The mind of man is able to comprehend the mind of God in revealed matters, but is free to either obey or disobey. It is also possible for God to give man moral instruction in such a way that the mind of God accurately communicates to the mind of man and man is morally responsible (Gen. 2:17). Failure to follow God's moral instruction can result in serious moral/physical consequences for man even as God promises (Gen. 3:1–19). When Adam is confronted with his disobedience, he does not offer a defense based on not understanding what God had said (Gen. 3:10–12). The essential properties of man are patterned after the essential properties of God, though they differ in degree because the essential properties of God are intrinsic to God while the essential properties of man are acquired by a divine creative act. It is the difference between a necessary being and a contingent being.

By this, the two minds work in conjunction with one another and are responsible for the shape of human history. Man's mind contributes to the content of history but always within limits of the ultimate plan of God. Regardless how far he may to go against God, man's actions can never go too far for two reasons. First, he is limited in what he can do by virtue of the moral ordering itself. Man's choices are limited and he cannot live against the way the universe is. Second, he is limited by intrinsic limitations—he is finite in all respects. However, as is seen in Genesis 11:1–9, even in a fallen state, (which includes man's mind) man's mind is capable of some rather amazing feats. It also reveals how the providence of God limits in certain ways man's plans. These parameters establish how the will of God and the will of man function together within the matrix of God's creation-order.

This creation-order determines the parameters by which man exercises the legitimate use of his power of moral choice.[10] In order for the two minds to interact within a context of community, freedom must exist for both parties. If man is to love God, then he must be free to respond to the person of God. As Hick notes, love cannot be coerced as this would not be love. Jesus taught that the two great commandments concern love—love for God and man—and on these two laws hang everything else. (Matt. 22:37–40). It is clear that man is to love God. This requires true freedom of judgment and subsequently responsibility for that judgment. Furthermore, it is important to point out that loving God is a command given to fallen man. Whatever happened to the mind in the fall, does not mean that the mind ceased to be a mind.

Something is learned of the relationship between the mind of God and the mind of man by considering the Incarnation. Here one sees what was truly intended for man. For example, Jesus (God-man) prays to the Father not my will, but your will be done (Matt. 26:39, 42). Here one sees how the two minds were intended to work together—the human voluntarily (freely) submitting to the divine in matters where the divine has made His mind clear. Unless this is just a piece of theater where words are spoken for the audience and nothing more, this must be taken seriously as representative of the optimum relationship between the divine and human mind—the divine and human will. Jesus, the man, submitted to the creation-order while here on earth. He exhibited that, while there is a difference between the divine mind and the human mind, there need be no conflict.

## Moral Ordering of Contingent Reality

God's creation-order includes a moral ordering that establishes the moral parameters for proper human activity. This moral ordering is given in the form of commands accompanied by consequences for both obedience and disobedience. It includes such ordering agencies as the family and civil government. Each moral agent is held accountable for his choices relative to the moral commands and compliance with the agencies of moral ordering. Each choice becomes a part of human history, thereby determining to some degree the way history looks. This is evident in Genesis 2:17 with its clearly stated consequence for a choice made by moral agents. Here the word is that if you eat you will die. No follow-up statement says, "But do not worry, I will bring a greater good from your evil, or it will really not make any difference." No, choices have real consequences. History would have been different had Adam obeyed God. Because he disobeyed, history followed that trajectory and unfolded shaped by the subsequent good and bad choices of men. Because man continued to have the power of moral choice after the fall, God progressively revealed the particulars of such moral ordering found in the Ten Commandments (Ex. 20).

This moral ordering to which man is accountable is based on God's perfect character. If also formed consistently within the limits and possibilities of man's power of moral choice. The moral ordering does not address matters outside man's realm of choice. It addresses only those areas or matters that God has extended to man as real possibilities. Moreover, moral choices involve real personal consequences for the individual, which in turn help shape that person's history and to varying degrees, the history of humanity. For example, Hitler's choices had a profound impact on the way history looks. The latitude that makes human freedom a reality often results in gratuitous evil.

As profound as such consequences are, man's choices are limited both in kind and effect. In the beginning, God established a creation-order designed as being not only compatible with His larger plan for humanity, but also as a means whereby the end is achieved. By this, God gives his moral creatures the potential of having some input into the way things work out in history, but never to the extent that God's ultimate plan for humanity is distorted or destroyed. For example, one must believe that if Abraham had been able to find ten righteous in Sodom that God would have spared the city (Gen.18: 23–33). Hezekiah prayed and received an addition fifteen years to his life (II Kgs. 20: 6). It seems that Hezekiah would have died had he not prayed, but because he prayer he lived another fifteen years. Here is a difference of fifteen years in the history of the world which would have been different if he had not prayed. There appears to be some latitude in what God can do in relationship to His answer to prayers and how His providential hand guides matters.

The command regarding the tree of knowledge of good and evil (Gen. 2:17) demonstrates that man was given the power of moral choice and that the direction of human history would be determined by the choice made. Yet, why does man choose to act contrary to the command of God if the mind of man is patterned after the mind of God. Surely, the will itself could not be evil, for as Augustine, Aquinas and Leibniz agree, the will itself is good because it comes from God. The will does, however, have the capability of turning in an inappropriate way to do what is against the divine moral command. It seems that Leibniz is correct when he concludes that the answer must be found in that which is independent of man's will. This led him to argue that the weakness is in the "ideal" nature of man. He writes, "We must consider that there is an *original imperfection in the creature* before sin, because the creature is limited in his essence; whence ensues that it cannot know all, and that it can deceive itself and commit other errors."[11] The nature of man, although it is morally good (in fact the best a created moral being could be), is limited by the fact it is created (finite), which means man is finite in every respect, including knowledge. Therefore, it is impossible for man, as a creature, to know everything. The limited-ness (man as a finite creature) of man's "ideal" nature (his nature was good because it came from God) proves to be the opportunity for evil. It is not a moral defect or deficiency, but rather an ontological limited-ness necessary to man's finiteness.

Adam, in his attempt to overcome his limitedness, choose to not love God, and disobeyed God in an attempt to be like God (unlimited). God had warned that should that happen, death would come upon creation. For this flows (either directly or indirectly) all suffering and pain in this word. This is the result of man's choice to not love God and to act in self interest, created order (including man) was corrupted and in some sense distanced from God. Therefore, God is not morally responsible for the limitation, for all created beings, of necessity, have this limitation, as anything created could not be limitless in all or any respects, for such an attribute belongs only to God who is uncreated. Nonetheless, man's power of moral choice equipped him to live properly within the moral order God designed for humanity. Any deviation was due to man's creaturely freedom and a misuse of the freedom he had been given. The consequences of man's rebellion although it was very severe did not go beyond the bounds of God's knowledge, nor did it in any way change the counsels of God.

## The Natural Ordering of Contingent Reality

It seems there can be little doubt that there is an ordering of the physical operation of what has been created. The facts of the universe with its regularity and predictability are learned early on in school science classes. In practical terms, this physical ordering is binding upon all who wish to live safely in the universe or who wish to harness the powers of nature for human use. For example, anyone desiring to build an airplane must abide by the laws of physics. Such an ordering limits what man can do or at least the way in which he does it. This includes the principle of cause and effect. The physical ordering, however, is not ultimately what maintains the universe in its orderly fashion. It is simply the framework within which God works in the space/time context.

The Bible teaches that Christ holds all things together (Col.1:17; Heb. 1:3) and He is faithful to His creation (I Pet. 4:19). As such there is a certain observable regularity within created order (Gen. 8:22). Therefore, what is witnessed by man as regularity in the universe is the result of Christ's faithfulness to natural order. Science can observe such things but may not know why things work this way and not another way. However, scientists can know how nature works or what nature does. While this is not the main point here, it does seem best to drop the notion of Laws of Nature (which is an 18th century notion) and simply understand that created order has regularity and predictability because of the power and promise of God (Gen. 8:22). This would be consistent with the fact of miracles.[12] So when speaking of the creation-order, this does not present a picture of a deistic God.[13] Miracles are part of the creation-order within which the providence of God works. Just as God can intervene within the moral order. He can intervene in the physical order as long as in doing so He neither contradicts His own character nor inflicts moral harm to an innocent moral agent

By Him all things consist as He upholds all things by the word of His power. This is not the idea of some deist God who simply establishes rules and lets things run by themselves. Instead, this is a view where God is dynamically involved, but His involvement is according to the moral and physical ordering of created-order. In this way, His actions within space/time are dependable and the relationship between man and God is maximized. The creation-order sets the limits and provides stability as it also determines the nature of the conditions under which God interacts meaningfully with man and by which man is accountable to God. Furthermore, the only limitation on God's actions within the time-space context are in those areas where He has given a specific promise that conditions will be one way and not another (Gen. 9:11). Although not explicitly spelled out in Scripture, this would include both the principle of cause and effect and the of law non-contradiction.

### Covenant Restrictions

In addition to the moral and physical ordering of creation, God has also limited Himself by certain covenants, which also form part of the creation-order. For example, in Genesis 3 there is a promise to humanity about redemption (Gen. 3:15). In Genesis 9, His covenant with Noah guarantees that the earth would never again be covered by a flood of water (Gen. 9:11). Such covenant proclamations were initiated by God and without provocation as God is sovereign. Once a covenant of this nature is made, God must abide by the terms of the covenant He voluntarily established. There are other such covenants, such as the covenant with Abraham in Genesis 17 assuring the descendants of Abraham a land as well as kings and greatness. Furthermore, in Jeremiah 31 a new covenant binds God to certain activities in relationship to the redeemed. These covenants support the point that beyond the particular creative ordering of the universe, God has also committed to certain covenants He has made with humanity or special groups within humanity. These covenants limit God the person to certain actions, not because He has lost power to do otherwise, but precisely because He is the immutable God, He keeps His self-restricting word, which is primarily for man's benefit.

## Sovereignty and Prayer

The infinite God created a rational/moral being in His image and placed him in a physical context called earth with the intent of having a relationship with man in the created context (Gen. 3:8). God created man in His image for this purpose and established the creation-order to provide a framework within which this relationship would unfold. In addition to what has already been said, the creation-order established other boundaries within which God's interaction with man takes place. In this way, man can know what is expected of him and what he should expect from God. These boundaries are not contrary to God (essence), nor do they make Him (person) less than God.

Often the simple definition of omnipotence is that God can do anything, which is only true if the statement is qualified. There are things that God cannot do, namely things that are logically impossible, but this seems rather self-evident. Beyond this, there are things that God cannot do within the space/time context, which are not a matter of logical concerns but of self-limiting concerns applying to something other than God (namely creation). To stand in the circle of uncreated reality—God—and say God can do anything in here that is logically possible is a correct statement. To stand, however, in the circle of created reality—creation—and make the same statement is simply not so. Part of the limitation involves the fact that man lives in a material environment and God's existence is a non-material. These are different existent orders but not contrary orders as God created the material. Almost everything we know about God is related in some way to the material state of affairs (including space and time). Therefore, God's acts are most often reported within a space/time index. His acts are spoken of as past or future. This is right because the act either has, is or will take place within a material context. This is part of the creation-order vocabulary and must be understood as speaking about God's involvement with a material context.

The events surrounding the serious illness of Hezekiah recorded in II Kings 20: 1–11 provide an instructive lens through which to appreciate the reality of God working in space/time. First, it should be pointed out that prayer is one aspect of the creation-order as established by God's sovereign choice. God has worked into His interaction with man the principle of prayer by which God will, under certain circumstances, respond to the request of man. Prayer was constructed so it did not eliminate God's sovereignty but provided a vehicle for man truly to petition God to act in space/time based upon the prayer within the limits set by the creation-order. Prayer is more than matching one's request with the predetermined will of God in heaven. This text shows also illustrates the reality of God responding to a prayer of one of His own and changing the direction of things for that person. Upon hearing from the prophet Isaiah that he will die, Hezekiah prays to God to grant him more days on earth. God stops Isaiah, who had left before the prayer was offered and tells him to return and tell Hezekiah that he will not die in the next day or so. In fact, God says that He will give Hezekiah fifteen more years. The change comes because of Hezekiah's prayer. God says, "I have heard your prayer, I have seen your tears; surely I will heal you" (II Kg. 20:5b). The prophet was right when he first brought the message from God. At that point in space/time the king was going to die, so the message was true. It was true in relation to the point on the space/time continuum when it was spoken. Had the king not prayed, he would have died within the next few days. Hezekiah, however, did pray and God answered. When Isaiah returned to the king and told him he was going to live, this was true at that moment of time. Here is a clear example of prayer changing matters in history but only within the limits of the creation-order as determined by the wise and just God. Such limits give God the freedom to answer a prayer of man and at the same time not abrogate His counsel. Furthermore, His providence works in conjunction with the answer to prayer to insure the proper ending of all things.

## Persuasion and Human Freedom

Persuasion is another part of the creation-order whereby one can influence the mind of another without violating his power of moral choice. God can effectively persuade man without compromising the principle of individual freedom. Persuasion never violates the person even though God may use extreme means to persuade some men. An example of this is the persuasive act of God in the life of Saul of Tarsus (Acts 9:1–4). In the matter of salvation, all men are persuaded sufficiently to repent and trust Christ (Jn.16:7–11). However, in many cases this persuasive work of God may be resisted (Acts 7:51; Heb. 3: 7–11, 15; 4:6, 7). The vehicle of persuasion is one way by which God is able to influence men while respecting the freedom of His moral agents.

Sometimes God persuades through signs. Think of Moses who had a command from God to lead His people out of Egypt. Moses was resistant. God persuades Moses with the miracle of turning a stick into a serpent (Ex. 3–4). Gideon is another example. When Gideon is told by the Angel of the Lord to deliver Israel from the hand of Midianites, he questions the task. The miracle of the sacrifice being consumed and the fleece convince him to do as commanded. During His earthly ministry,

Jesus responds to those who question His words to believe because of His works (Jn. 10:38). These examples illustrate the principle of persuasion whereby God is able to move men to choose or do the right thing under the circumstances without violating their freedom of choice. Not everyone who was the object of God's persuasive acts were in fact persuaded to the right choice. Consider the Exodus generation. They resisted God's Spirit (Heb. 3:7–11) so after ten times God decided to no more try to persuade them (Num. 14:20–24).

## MIDDLE KNOWLEDGE AND THE BEST OF ALL POSSIBLE WORLDS

In addition to the ideas of creation-order all ready mentioned, two other issues related to the creation-order theodicy require explanation: the concept of middle knowledge, and this is the best of all possible worlds. Middle knowledge is a way of understanding God's omniscience which recognizes God's sovereignty and the integrity of man's power of moral choice. Affirming that this is the best of all possible worlds assures the theist that what is could not be improved upon, thereby lessening the need for some greater-good premise.

### Middle Knowledge

An important (and somewhat controversial) element of the creation-order theodicy is the view that God's omniscience includes middle knowledge, a view introduced by Spanish Jesuit theologian and philosopher, Luis de Molina (1535–1600). According to this, God's omniscience encompasses three types of knowledge: natural knowledge, free knowledge and middle knowledge. According to Thomas Flint, natural knowledge refers to the necessary truths—those truths innate to God. It is God's natural knowledge that "provides God with knowledge of which worlds are possible."[14] Out of God's natural knowledge of all the possible worlds, He actualized one world—the world that is. His knowledge of the world that is actual constitutes God's free knowledge. God knows everything about this world. This knowledge results from God acting freely in a particular way actualizing this world and, therefore, such knowledge is comprised of contingent truths. God's middle knowledge is that knowledge which is neither natural (necessary and eternal) nor dependent upon God's free creative acts. Middle knowledge is the knowledge God has regarding all the nondetermined acts of his moral agents in all possible circumstances. Flint names this "counterfactuals of creaturely freedom."[15] Further, Flint explains, "Molina's answer is that knowledge of counterfactuals of creaturely freedom is part neither of God's natural knowledge nor of his free knowledge, but instead is part of a third category of knowledge which lies between the other two."[16]

This third category involving counterfactuals[17] of creaturely freedom is what Molina termed middle knowledge. That is, God knows all possible contingents (hypotheticals) stemming from the free choices of his moral beings. Because of His middle knowledge, God knew all the possible worlds and from the possible worlds chose to actualize the best world. The perspective supported here is that God's middle knowledge was what made it possible for Him to see conceptually all the free choices of His moral creatures and then actualize the best of those possible worlds. At this place, I am not defending middle knowledge, I am accepting it as a legitimate understanding of God's omniscience. I realize, however, that if middle knowledge is found to be unsatisfactorily either theologically or philosophically, there would need to be some slight adjustments made to my proposed Creation-Order theodicy. However, I am not sure it would defeat the theodicy and furthermore, I think there are good and sufficient reasons for accepting middle knowledge.

## Best of all Possible Worlds

It would appear that the concept of the best of all possible worlds is more understandable if God actually has middle knowledge. It seems, however, a case could be made for the best of all possible worlds without appealing to middle knowledge. Middle knowledge seems more straightforward because God knows that a possible world is best because He knows it in some true sense before He actualizes it. If God has middle knowledge, then He truly knows each world before He actualizes one. Under such conditions, God knows all true counterfactuals which would be true knowledge prior to actualization of any world. As William Craig says:

> Considerations pertinent to divine providence and predestination require that God possess His knowledge of true counterfactuals logically prior to His decree to actualize some world. As for the means of such middle knowledge, God does not derive His knowledge from any predetermination or comprehension of the will, but rather possesses innately an immediate intuition of all truth simply in virtue of His being God.[18]

This understanding of middle knowledge appears to escape the objection related to counterfactuals.

Each arrangement of different possibilities constitutes what is referred to as a book of a world or world book (not to be confused with the encyclopedia). As each book has its own story, so each world has its own set of events. The creation-order package is applied equally to each feasible world. God's middle knowledge gives Him knowledge of all the nondetermined choices of his moral agents and subsequent effects that constitute a different world. For example, God knows what will happen if Bruce marries Nancy and what will happen should Bruce not marry Nancy. The first state of affairs can be called $W$ and the second state of affairs named $W'$. There are many other aspects to both $W$ and $W'$. The point is, they would be two different worlds. If God actualizes $W$ then that would be the world in which Bruce freely chooses to marry Nancy. If $W'$ is actualized then the world would be the one in which Bruce freely chooses not to marry Nancy. In either world, his choice was free. Each world has nondetermined choices including the prayers and answers to prayer and in fact, everything that makes up a possible world permitted within the creation-order package. This means not only the good choices, but the bad/evil choices and any subsequent pleasure or suffering. According to middle knowledge, before any of the worlds existed in actuality, God knew them in every detail and it is from these possible worlds that God actualized the best.

In this way, there is harmony between divine sovereignty and true human power of moral choice without any appeal to mystery in order to solve contradiction. Each person is free (in the sense earlier discussed) in all nondetermined choices to choose from the possibilities present as he wills in every world in which he exists. So, if in one world Paul prays and is healed and in another world Paul chooses not to pray and is not healed, in each world he was free to exercise his power of moral choice to pray or not to pray. If God actualizes the world in which Paul chooses not to pray and consequently is not healed, Paul is responsible for his state of health (just as Hezekiah). However, once God actualizes a world, all the free choices of man are set. That is the way the world will play out, but it is simply the playing out of individual choices. As Craig points out, "It is up to God whether we find ourselves in a world in which we are predestined, but it is up to us whether we are predestined in the world in which we find ourselves."[19] Because God's middle knowledge is comprehensive, one can be assured that God selects the best world for actualization.

The matter of this being the best of all possible worlds is not without its adversaries. Few object to the notion of possible worlds as philosophically acceptable, but the idea that there is a best of the possible worlds is another matter. Many theodicists question whether or not one can claim this to be the best of all possible worlds. The two main points of concern center on the fact there is no way to know what a best world would look like or that the concept itself is incoherent. Swinburne believes "it follows that the objection from the existence of God is not that he did not create the 'best of all possible worlds', for to do that is not logically possible: there is no best of all possible worlds."[20] Bruce R. Reichenbach concludes that "there could be no best possible world, since for any world which we would name there would always be another which was more optimific. Again, the notion of best possible world proves to be meaningless."[21] Alvin Plantinga argues that "no matter how marvelous a world is—containing no matter how many persons enjoying unalloyed bliss—isn't it possible that there be even a better world containing even more persons enjoying even more unalloyed bliss?"[22] Agreeing with Plantinga, Peterson writes, "We now know that it is simply not true that God, if he exists, could have actualized any possible world. Another error in the argument is that it seems to presuppose that there *is* 'a best of all possible worlds,' a concept that is incoherent."[23] There is general agreement among those rejecting the idea of a best world that the notion is either logically impossible or definitionally impossible.

Those who think it is impossible on grounds of definition argue that God could have always made a better world. Of course this is predicated upon what some think constitutes a better world. Plantinga and others maintain that if there are a number of possible worlds, no matter which world is picked, there is always a better world or it is possible there is a better world. According to this argument, another happy person added to a world would make it a better world. That is, where W stands for a world with a number of persons as in this present world and W + 1 represents a world with that number of people plus one. W+1 is better than W because there is one more person who can enjoy blissfulness. But this seems to confuse the notion of 'best'. Best when used in this discussion clearly refers to that which has the highest possible moral order intrinsically under the circumstances. Best is not a quantitative, but qualitative notion. Number has nothing to do with the idea of best in a moral sense. One does not increase the moral value of a group by simply adding more moral people to the group. This would be a confusion of categories. Therefore, just adding more moral people does not increase the moral character of the group in terms of ontological categories. Furthermore, there is no guarantee that the person added would experience some recognizable felicity. Getting one more person to experience felicity might require forty people who commit horrible crimes. It would be hard to argue that based on numbers alone this world would be a better world just because it contains one more person experiencing felicity.

Although many have dismissed any idea of a best world as philosophically unacceptable, others think it has possibilities. David Blumenfeld indicates in his discussion of Leibniz's notion that this is the best of all possible worlds (*BPW*). When Leibniz is understood it follows that his position entails an "implicit proof of the consistency of the concept of the *BPW*."[24] Blumenfeld suggests that it is possible to hold to this possibility without denying God's freedom.[25] Leibniz, however, believed that the character of God requires God to do His best, but not that God has no choice in the matter. Blumenfeld summarizes Leibniz's position as: "Being omnipotent, God could have created any possible world he pleased; but, being all-good, he would certainly have chosen to create the very best world."[26] Another advocate of the best of possible worlds, David Schrader claims that the proposition that an all-powerful and all-good God will prevent evil is not necessarily so. He suggests, "If God is good He will surely create the best of all possible worlds."[27] In a helpful article, R.W. K. Paterson defines what he understands by the notion that God is perfectly good. "I shall take this to mean that God chooses to create the best world that is logically capable of being created, 'the best of all possible worlds'."[28] C. Mason Myers maintains that, "[o]n the other hand a deity having omnipotence, omniscience, and omnibenevolence as necessary attributes must of *necessity* create a world of maximum possible goodness if he is to create at all," which for Myers is the "best of all possible worlds."[29] What is in view here when speaking about a best world is its moral integrity, not the felicity of the inhabitants of such a world. As Philip Quinn points out, "If an omnipotent and superlatively good moral agent had to choose between less than complete felicity and surpassable moral goodness when actualizing a possible world, he would choose less than complete felicity."[30] It seems reasonable both on philosophical as well as theological terms that this is the best of all possible worlds, when world is understood as the complete book from creation to the Kingdom.

When examining the justification for the claim that this is the best of all possible worlds, it is imperative to understand what world signifies. The word "world" primarily refers to the realm of humanity and its culture (See Jn. 3:16; II Tim. 4:10; I Jn. 2:15). Therefore, it includes humanity as a whole from the point of creation to the full realization of the Kingdom of God on this earth throughout everlasting. World does not refer to any particular periodic arrangement under which man lives. Broadly speaking, world is a term given to the created order to which mankind belongs. It is as Leibniz confesses. "I call 'World' the whole succession and the whole agglomeration of all existent things . . . . For they must needs be reckoned all together as one world or, if you will, as one Universe."[31] Biblically, it appears there are different stages or states of affairs (ages) as a part of this world's history, but there is only one world that exists substantively. There have been accidental changes to the world (such as what happened in the fall of mankind), but this does not constitute another world nor does the Kingdom to come (or heaven) constitute another world. There is real continuity from creation to the Kingdom (or whatever one understands the final form this world will assume). Those who will populate the Kingdom belong to this world and not another as brought into being, as recorded in Genesis 1. Christ came to redeem this world and not another. Therefore, when affirming that this is the best of all possible worlds, we are not looking at some particular state of affairs at any one point but the whole. For example, surely one can think of things being a little better than what they are at the particular moment, but this is not what is meant when it is affirmed that this is the best of all possible worlds. Moreover, to call heaven or the Kingdom of God another world seems philosophically unacceptable as a possible world because it would break continuity with this world.

Further, when arguing that God has created the material world (I would take this to include angels) it is important to make a distinction between speaking of the world in a material sense and using the word "world" to refer to human culture-history. The statement that God created this world means only the material aspect (heaven and earth). The statement that God actualized this world, refers to the culture-history of humanity. To say that God created the culture-history of this world would mean that He determined the history of humanity. In turn, this requires denying creaturely freedom making God responsible for evil. The distinction seems obvious. If God created the history of the cosmos, then there really is no discussion at all, as the history of the cosmos would simply be a piece of theater with players following a predetermined script.

Furthermore the word "possible" carries two important notions. The first is that there are some worlds that are simply not possible. Here the word implies limitations on what worlds could actually exist. One world that is impossible or unfeasible is a world where all free men obey and love God. In a second way, possible signals the fact there are limitations on anything that is created. In this way the term "possible" means that this world is the best it can be given the fact that it is created. In that it is created, it cannot have the moral perfection as experienced by God. So, there are some limitations to what "possible" can include when applied to the quality of that which is created. To say that this is the best of all possible worlds entails that there are some worlds not possible and that, of the possible worlds, there are limits to what can be expected of that world which is actualized.

With this foundation, there are at least two reasons why this is the best of all possible worlds. The first reason is found in Genesis 1:31 where God surveyed all that He had created pronounced it "very good." Granted the text does not say explicitly that it was the best, only that it was very good. Grammatically, however, the word can mean moral goodness, in which case it is a statement affirming something of the intrinsic moral goodness of creation in comparative terms. The only standard to which it can be compared is God. In this sense, it cannot be best in any absolute sense because only God is best. (It has already been argued that creation cannot be substantively the same as the Creator). The fact, however, that the text provides the reader with this particular information is instructive in and of itself. God wanted humanity to know that regardless how things would appear at some time later, when it came from the word of God, creation was very good. The evaluative statement is one made from the character of God whose judgment is perfect.

When God evaluates His creation, He does so as the omniscient, morally good One. His omniscience insures that He knows all things about creation. As the morally perfect One, He cannot lie or deceive. Further, the only point of reference from which to make the pronouncement is His own perfect character. When God pronounces something very good, "very" and "good" are the measurement of the One, who is absolutely good. It is common understanding that the character of the one making an evaluative statement conveys something to the evaluative statement itself. For example, consider two people making a similar claim about different soups. Suppose that on a very cold day a street person who has not eaten for a day is given some poorly made hot soup and upon eating it exclaims that it is very good. Also suppose a connoisseur of fine soups tastes soup made in his kitchen and upon tasting it pronounces it very good. Surely one would not assume that the two soups are of equal quality. So it is with God. If God says that something is very good, it is measured against His perfect character which can only mean that it is the best. The statement is not about what creation would become or anything else, it is a statement about the substantive quality and moral ordering of what has been made. Moreover, if God does not do His best, then what is created lacks some logically possible perfection. Accepting Augustine and Aquinas on the point that evil is the lack in that which is good, follows that if creation lacks some perfection possible to creation, then creation is in some sense evil from the beginning. This would mean that God is responsible for evil and that the concept of "very good" loses all normal meaning, for now something that lacks what it could have is called very good.

There is a tacit assumption behind most denials that this is the best of all possible worlds. That is, the redeemed state is better than the initial state of creation. The argument here is that God is morally justified in allowing evil because through the redemption that is in Christ, redeemed man is elevated to a better state than possible through creation. (This will be recognized as a form of the G-G argument). To assume, however, that the state of the redeemed is a *greater* good state than the state of man at the point of creation raises at least two concerns. The first (which says that the end is better than the beginning) is to claim that God did not do His best at creation, in which case He is not the all-good God He claims to be. The second concern involves the omnipotence of God. If the Kingdom is a better state than initial creation and if the Kingdom comes about because of sin and Christ's subsequent redemption, then sin is necessary to the best state. According to this line of thought, God is morally justified in requiring evil since from it He brings into being by redemption a better state for humanity (of course not all humanity!). This requires that evil is necessary to the best world which, if it does not make God the author of evil, does make Him dependent on evil. Moreover, it seems questionable to affirm that the end of things, when measured against original creation, is either better or worse. Possibly one could argue that it will be different, but intrinsically better is another matter altogether. When measured against what sin has done, this reasoning holds the end for the redeemed is better than the original state making the fall necessary. It seems theologically inappropriate to argue that the consequent justifies the antecedent in any case, but especially when the antecedent is evil.

If this world is not the best of all possible worlds, then one of the following must be true: (1) God chose not to do His best, which seems to question His goodness; (2) God did not know which world would be best, which questions His omniscience; (3) God knew which world would be the best and wanted to actualize it but lacked the power to do so. This, of course, would question His power. All three possibilities seem unacceptable, leaving the only one possibility—this is the best of all possible worlds. To argue that there is no way to establish what a best world would look like fails to understand properly the notion of best in the context of this world and reveals a commitment to the statement on evidential grounds alone. Given the options, this must be the best of all possible worlds. After all, if God is able to bring about a greater good out of evil as G-G theodicies maintain, it would seem a small thing for God to bring the best world out of nothing

Some may, however, reply that the best world would be where all God's free moral agents love and obey God. Surely a world where all people do no evil would undoubtedly be a better world, supposing it were a possible world. Whereas this is not the world that is, it can only be concluded that this is not a possible world if moral agents are to have the power of moral choice in nondeterming circumstances (an example of a nondetermined circumstance would be Mary's conception). Alvin Plantinga has argued that this would be an impossible world based on what he calls transworld depravity which seems to have similarities to Calvin's total depravity. His concept, however, is different from total depravity. Plantinga writes, "What is important about the idea of transworld depravity is that if a person suffers from it, then it wasn't within God's power to actualize any world in which he produces moral good but no moral evil."[32] Plantinga tries to show that if transworld depravity were to be an actual state of affairs, then all possible worlds would contain both moral good and moral evil. His point is that it would be impossible under transworld depravity conditions for God to create a world in which moral evil is absent. He writes:

> How is transworld depravity relevant to this? Obviously it is possible that there be persons who suffer from transworld depravity. More generally, it is possible that everybody suffers from it. And if this possibility were actual then God, though omnipotent, could not have created any of the possible worlds containing just the persons who do in fact exist, and containing moral good but no moral evil.[33]

Barry Gan notes that what Plantinga is suggesting,, is that "it is possible that any human being, once created, will in some way do evil and that therefore it may not be possible for God to create a world containing human beings but no evil."[34] Furthermore, Craig suggests,

> Suppose, then, that God has so ordered the world that all persons who are actually lost are such persons. In such a case, anyone who actually is lost would have been lost in any world in which God had created him. It is possible, then, that although God, in order to bring this many persons to salvation, had to pay the price of seeing this many who are lost, nevertheless He has providentially ordered the world such that those who are lost are persons who would not have been saved in any world feasible for God in which they exist.[35]

If Craig is right on this point, God's choice of worlds would not determine who was lost. However, even if Craig is not right (I think it has promise), those who are lost in any world are lost because of their choice, not God's determination. The only thing God determines is the means of salvation.

As Leibniz suggests, any created being is limited in all respects. Only God, who is unlimited in all respects can be perfect. The limitation in man is not a moral defect, nor is it the causal agent for turning away from God. It is the condition which makes turning away from God possible. If there is to be something other than God, it will have to exist as a created being. Created beings with the power of moral choice are better than created beings without this possibility, as Augustine argues. The best possible world is one in which man has power of moral choice (libertarian traditionalism) even though this means limitation in the exercise of that power. This limitation means that a world where all free creatures always to what is right and love God is impossible. If it is possible, it would be the world we have.

The best possible world should not be measured primarily on that of human felicity of some kind, but on the Kingdom of God itself— namely what man was created for initially. What ever achieves the best in this sense is what world God actualizes. The best world would be a world in which there is an optimal relationship between good and evil as defined by the Kingdom of God. William Craig has offered an interested and promising suggestion. He writes,

> On the analogy of transworld depravity, we may accordingly speak of *transworld damnation,* which is possessed by any person who freely does not respond to God's grace and so is lost in every world feasible for God in which that person exists (this notion can, of course, be more accurately restated in terms of individual essences and instantiations thereof).[36]

Craig posits that, based upon middle knowledge, God "has actualized a world containing an optimal balance between save and unsaved, and those who are unsaved suffer from transworld damnation."[37] If Craig is right on this point, this argument can be used to explain how this can be the best of all possible worlds. It seems to this author that this position has real promise both theologically and philosophically, and allows for the existence of gratuitous evil as well as this being the best of all possible worlds. One might argue that this is the best of all possible worlds because it contains an optimal relationship between good and evil. If this is true, then there is not a good reason to reject this as the best of all possible worlds and sufficient reason to claim that it is.

## SUMMARY

This chapter has outlined what need to be true in order for the Creation-Order theodicy to have viability. The principles of created-order show how God in His sovereignty has established the rules His interaction with man (the second actual mind) and in what way man is responsible to God. Furthermore, these principles explain how God*ness* can manifest itself in the realm of material, which must be different from how it is manifest in the realm of non-material. This, in turn, provides a framework by which the attributes of God are understood and applied to contingent reality. It also suggests how God's providence is worked out within the context of created order—the only place or time there is need for providence. All of this provides for the latitude in history where man can make real choices with real consequences, often resulting in gratuitous evil without counting against God morally or His creative purposes substantively.

Admittedly, some of these ideas are debatable; however, they can be defended against objections. Furthermore, because creation-order allows for gratuitous evil, it avoids the weakness of G-G theodicies. It is important to the Creation-Order theodicy that this be the best of all possible worlds since this theodicy argues for gratuitous evil. If this is the best of all possible worlds, then the amount of gratuitous evil is at a minimal level, all other matters being considered.

## NOTES

1. This does not mean that the person necessarily lives as if God exists, only that he thinks it is more likely that God exists than He does not exist.

2. Unfortunately, many grievous acts have been committed against humanity in the name of God. However, hardly is this an argument against the existence of God. It says more about the wickedness of men's hearts than it does about the existence of God. Neither can one argue that because people do good things in the name of God that this is justification for believing that God is real. Many people do good things in the name of Santa Claus, but that does not mean that he exists.

3. Remember, most atheists are not saying that there could be no evil/suffering in this world made by God, but that the fact there is so much evil and that it involves often the innocent. Furthermore, evil/suffering is so unequally distributed. This is what the atheist believes is conclusive evidence against God's existence.

4. This is not to say that people would not be justified in believing in God in the absence of a theodicy, but that the argument from evil would be unsolved as an objection to God's existence.

5. There may be other forms of theism that are involved, but all that is being defended here is trinitarian theism.

6. Certainly there are objective acts which are called evil acts, and in this sense people may think of evil as something of substance. This, however, is not what evil is fundamentally. It is only how a condition is manifested, and its manifestation causes human pain in an objective measurable way.

7. This does not mean that man always processes correctly, only that it is possible. Furthermore, the fall has certainly impacted how man processes some information.

8. I am not attempting to determine the degree or extent of freedom in terms of antecedent causes. It seems that Christians could differ at this point and still be in agreement with the notion of libertarian freedom as defined here.

9. Thomas Flint, *Divine Providence: The Molinist Account* (Ithaca, NY: Cornell University, 1998), 34. He gives parameters to his understanding of libertarian traditionalism when he writes, "It seems more accurate to think of our free actions as invariably reactive—as responses to divine initiatives. Our movements may not be determined by the natural and supernatural influences to which we are subject, but the presence and power of such influences can hardly be gainsaid."

10. It will be assumed at this point that animals do not have the power of moral choice, although it is clear that they do make choices. The point would be that they do not make conscious moral choices based upon some objective moral criteria.

11. Leibniz, *Theodicy*, 135.

12. Concerning miracles. God is free to touch any piece of reality and cause things to happen that are beyond the normal regular flow. It seems that only two things would apply: (1) When God does such, He cannot act unjustly or capriciously. (2) He cannot directly violate anything He has promised to be a certain way always. For example, God cannot miraculously destroy the world by a flood at this point in time.

13. Consider the cursing of the fig tree where one sees some interruption in the normal flow of things. Of course a fig tree withering is not unusual, but as the disciples report, what caught their attention was that it happened so soon. Jesus was able to touch just a piece of reality and speed up the decaying process. If a law was broken, then all things under that law would have changed, as any law of nature is by definition universal. So, all things under the rule of decay should have withered. The only areas that seem off limits for God to touch are those things such as He has promised in Genesis nine. For example, He cannot destroy the world by flood and summer and winter will continue as will seed time and harvest.

14. Thomas P. Flint, *Divine Providence: The Molinist Account* (Ithaca, NY: Cornell University Press, 1998), 38.

15. Ibid., 40.
16. Ibid., 41.
17. A counterfactual is that which is of the hypothetic category. If this, then this. Jesus said, "If the mighty works which were done in you [Capernaum] had been done in Sodom, it would have remained until this day" (Mt. 11:23). The issue of debate involves the relationship between God's foreknowing the future and the certainty of the future. That is, is there a causal relationship between God's knowledge of the future and the actual shape of the future as it relates to the choices of His moral creatures? If, as some argue, God's foreknowledge necessarily determines the future, then free will is destroyed. But, if God's foreknowledge of the future does not determine the future, how can He know it since God can only know that which is true?

The concern with God knowing anything that does not come to pass is that it seems to contradict the axiom that one can only know that which is true. The question is whether or not God can foreknow something and it not come to pass? This is referred to as knowledge of the counterfactual of freedom. It seems that there are four possibilities at present: (1) God foreknows all future actual events but not necessarily in a causal way for all events; (2) God knows all future events in a determinative way; (3) God does not foreknow certain future events (choices of his moral creatures) that do come to pass; (4) God knows all future events (possible and actual).

If (1) is true, then there must be some explanation as to how God foreknows such things. If (2) is right, then there is no human free will. If (3) is right, then, as already seen, certain theological problems arise. If (4) is right, it would serve (1) while escaping the problems of (3). (4) would be the position of middle knowledge.

The challenge of middle knowledge, however, is that of demonstrating it is possible for God to know counterfactuals of freedom. If God knows all actual and possible events (choices of His moral creatures), then whatever is not actualized would not be true when measured against the history of this world. But, there could be a world in which it would have been otherwise. Had it been another world, it would have happened exactly as God had known it to be. If this is correct, then there is no difficulty in God knowing what would have been the case had it been actualized. Of course, God cannot know that it is the case if it is not, but that is another issue.

18. A. J. Vanderjagt Gen ed., *Brill's Studies in Intellectual History*, vol. 7 *The Problem of Divine Foreknowledge and Future Contingents From Aristotle to Surarez*, by William Lane Craig (Leiden: E. J. Brill, 1988), 233.
19. William Lane Craig, *Faith and Philosophy*, "'No Other Name': A Middle Knowledge Perspective On The Exclusivity of Salvation Through Christ" (vol. 6, no. 20 (179) 172–188.
20. Swinburne, *Providence and the Problem of Evil*, 8.
21. Bruce R. Reichenbach, *Evil and a Good God* (New York: Fordham University Press, 1982), 128.

22. Alvin Plantinga, "The Free Will Defense," in *Philosophy of Religion*, ed. Melville Y. Stewart (Sudbury, MA: Jones and Bartlett Publishers, 1996), 386.

23. Peterson, *God and Evil*, 49.

24. David Blumenfeld, "Is The Best Possible World Possible?" *The Philosophical Review* 84 (April 1975), 165.

25. Ibid., 169, Blumenfeld argues on Leibniz's behalf saying: "It is, strictly speaking, possible that God should choose less than the best, though it is *certain* that he will not. Leibniz's motives for holding this view are clear: he wishes to preserve God's freedom and avoid the charge that this world is the only one that is (really) possible. How God's choice of the best can be contingent, given that he is by definition all-good, is a serious and well-known problem. But for our present purposes it is enough to note that Leibniz thought he had shown that it was certain that God would be determined by considerations of perfection: the more perfect a possible world, the greater it attractiveness to his will. So, it seems, if a given possible world were the most perfect, that would be a sufficient condition for God's choosing it."

26. Ibid., 163.

27. David Schrader, "Evil and The Best of Possible Worlds" *Sophia* 27 (July 1988): 27. It is not necessary to accept Schrader's total argument in order to use his notion of the best of possible worlds.

28. R.W. K. Paterson, "Evil, Omniscience and Omnipotence," *Religious Studies* 15 (March 1979): 2.

29. C. Mason Myers, "Free Will and the Problem of Evil," *Religious Studies* 23 (1987): 29.

30. Philip L. Quinn, "God, Moral Perfection and Possible Worlds" in Michael Peterson, ed. *The Problem of Evil* (Notre Dame: Notre Dame Press, 1992), 301.

31. Leibniz, *Theodicy*, 128.

32. Alvin Plantinga, "The Free Will Defense," in *Philosophy of Religion,* ed. Melville Stewart (Sudbury, MA: Jones and Bartlett Publishers, 1996), 397.

33. Ibid.

34. Barry L. Gan, "Plantinga's Transworld Depravity: It's Got Possibilities" *International Journal for Philosophy of Religion* 13 (1982): 169.

35. Craig, "No Other Name," 184.

36. Ibid.

37. Ibid.

# Chapter 6

# Creation-Order Theodicy

It is now possible to formulate the Creation-Order (C-O) theodicy. This theodicy recognizes the reality of gratuitous evil while maintaining that God is morally justified in permitting such. Admitting to gratuitous evil in this way, seriously weakens the argument from evil and lays a proper foundation for speaking to those who are suffering. Rejecting the premise of G-G theodicies does not deny there are never any cases where God brings good from evil intent (or at least it appears that good has come from the evil). The objection here is that the evil is allowed for that purpose.[1] Moreover, if the basic tenets of the C-O theodicy are right, then the atheist's argument is seriously undercut and the power of emotional skepticism often experienced by believers overridden. In the case of the C-O theodicy, the believer does not solace himself with the thought of some eventual good springing from his suffering, but rather he looks directly to the mercy and comfort of God Himself to sustain and encourage him in times of suffering (II Cor. 1:3–4; 12:9). One difficulty of G-G theodicies when carried to their logical conclusion is that the very God who is to help in time of need is also the God who wills the suffering in the first place. In this case, God becomes at best like the boy scout who pushes the old lady into traffic so that he can save her and at worst something like a witch doctor (you can never be sure what you will get from him). If it serves God's purposes to allow some terrible evil in your life, you should rejoice because His purposes are being served at your expense. It is suggested that the C-O theodicy would avoid this tension.

## THE CREATION-ORDER THEODICY

Evidential and rational arguments for God's existence form the theodic prolegomena of the C-O theodicy much in the method of Aquinas. The argument from evil necessarily assumes some evidence for God's existence but that the evidence from evil overpowers it. Therefore, the C-O theodicy begins with a cursory presentation of the evidence for God's existence in order to establish that there is more to the debate than the evidence from evil. All the evidence must be weighed. Whereas many sources adequately present theistic arguments, nothing more beyond what was done in Chapter Five will be offered here. The C-O theodicy, as presented here, begins by certifying the divine prerequisites under which God does His creative work.

## Uncreated and Created Reality Connection

God, who is neither chaotic in nature nor in act, necessarily creates in an orderly fashion and establishes the principles of creation-order. This order is necessary to the harmonious physical and moral function of creation[2] and His personal interaction with creation.[3] It appears that in order for there to be a stable created environment in which God and creation interact in a purposeful way, only two possibilities exists. Either God determines *everything*, thus assuring the order of creation based on divine predetermination, or God provides for the suitable function of creation by establishing certain moral (internal) and physical (external) ordering consonant with man's power of moral choice. Determining all things necessarily eliminates man being made in God's image (God is not a determined being). However, since man is the crowning act of God's creation, to eliminate man (as man) from creation would mean that God has not done His best in what He created. In fact, even most G-G theodices argue that it is better to have a man with power of choice than a being without the power of choice, even if it means man goes against his Creator God. As Augustine noted, "A runaway horse is better than a stone."

God's choice to create entails, at least part, that creation is compatible with His being. This means creating man as a rationally functioning personal being capable of authentic love and moral judgment. As a rationally functioning moral personal being, man enjoys creaturely freedom in order that he might authentically (freely) choose to love God (among other things). Loving God is the highest function of a created being to which all men are called (Matt. 22:37–40). The creation of man in God's image, however, requires a certain creation-order design whereby the two minds can intersect and interact as two legitimately constituted and functioning minds. Whereas God would place man over the other creatures on earth (Gen. 1:26–31), man would function as God's vassal. The finite mind (man) governs over the circle of created reality on behalf of the infinite mind (God). The purpose of the creation-order design is to establish boundaries and guiding principles for both God and man, through which the vassal can actually govern earth but in such a way as not to confound the rule of the Sovereign. The genius of the created-order design is that it gives man power of moral choice in a way that is authentic. This authentic power of moral choice makes it possible for man authentically to love and obey God. It also leaves the opportunity for man significantly to disobey God. This possibility of disobeying God means that such disobedience will have real consequences. The consequences of this disobedience often results in gratuitous evil. The created-order does not provide a means for God to filter out the bad choices from which He cannot bring about a greater good. Instead, the creation-order design allows for gratuitous evil as a corollary to the authenticity of the power of moral choice. However, the created-order design is crafted so that real human choices bring real consequences without negating the counsels of God. Furthermore, the created-order design makes possible God's providential working in, and His personal care for, His created beings without sacrificing man's authentic power of moral choice. At no time does gratuitous evil jeopardize the counsels of God or exceed the providential power of God.

## Could God Prevent All Horrific Evils?

Is it possible that God could prevent the most horrific evils and still honor the power of moral choice? If one asks this question from the perspective of God's power, the answer is yes. However, as we have seen, God's work within creation is not just about his power. When answering this question, the entirety of creation must be considered since everything is interconnected in some way. Granting that such is possible, other problems arise with the proposal.

Let's think through the question in terms of what the question entails. First, horrific evils are horrific because this is how they look in comparison to other evils. When one says that this or that evil is "horrific", he is saying that it is a worse evil than some other kind of evil. A conclusion drawn from comparison of evils is determined by the perspective of the one drawing the conclusion. For example, Hitler thought that the existence of an inferior race was a greater evil than exterminating them. While many disagree, the point is that what might be a horrific evil for one person might not be for another person. When asking God to prevent the worse of evils, it is necessary to determine whose standard of morality will be used to conclude which evils should be prevented. At this point it might be rather difficult to achieve any consensus.

Another problem arises when one thinks through the logic of the question. If a horrific evil is horrific because of how it compares to another evil, then logically this will mean that all evil should be prevented. Consider the following argument. Suppose we represent the evil in the world by X and the varying degrees of evil by X+1, X+2, X+3 and so forth, where the higher the number associated with X, the worse the evil. X+3 is a worse evil than X+1. For arguments sake, let's also assume that X+5 is the worse evil imaginable to man. Man requests that God prevent X+5. The request is for God to prevent the evil before it happens (this in itself poses a problem). This means it will never have been a part of the human experience. Assuming God prevents X+5, the worst evil in the human experience will be X+4. However, when the same logical procedure is applied to X+4 as was to X+5, the worst evil in the human experience is now X+3. Taken to its logical conclusion, the request would not stop until God has prevented all evil. Whereas people really do choose to do evil, but God intervenes so their choices cannot come to fruition, then it follows that there is no way for God to prevent the worst evils without seriously impinging on the authenticity of the power of moral freedom. In reality, the only choices that people would be permitted to make would be the choices resulting in good or, in other words, obedience to God. In attempting to fix one thing, this logic concludes with the very aspect of man that makes him unique being is destroyed, forming him into something other than a being made in the image of God. In the end, the possibility of God eliminating all horrific evil is not a real possibility regardless of how good it sounds in the sentence.

## The Created and Uncreated Reality Connection

When God sovereignly chose to create, He brought into existence a second circle of reality. Prior to creation, only one circle of reality existed—God (uncreated reality). Within this circle the perfect character of God meant a perfect relationship between the members of the Trinity. With the dawn of creation, however, a second circle of reality existed different from, but compatible with, the first circle of reality. At creation there were now two circles of reality—the *contingent* reality circle of creation (created and material reality) and the *necessary* reality circle of God (uncreated and immaterial reality). Contingent reality includes rational, personal man with a mind capable of authentic love, and moral judgment (among other things) because he has the power of moral choice. In creation, the human mind is patterned after the divine mind and functions similar to God's mind (Gen. 1:26) but necessarily (because of its created*ness*) at a diminished level since it is limited in knowledge and power (Is. 55:8–9). God's necessary knowledge is intrinsic (or innate) and His knowledge of contingent reality is comprehensive (omniscience), while man's knowledge is acquired and limited. Furthermore, man exists in a material context and God in an immaterial context. Although these two circles differ in certain respects, they are not contrary, for God created the material circle (including space and time) in such a way that it is compatible with what is immaterial. In this way God can occupy both without character distortion as the material does not squeeze out the immaterial. Moreover, He could be in, as well as act in, the space/time circle without conflict to His own being. (The particulars of the relationship between time and supra time are important but belong to another discussion.)

Making it possible for God legitimately to engage creation requires some self-imposed restraint (not change) in the way certain attributes of God are manifest in the material circle.[4] This intentional restraint does not diminish God*ness*, as can be seen in the Incarnation. Here, God becomes man without ceasing to be God and lives in the material circle without forfeiting His eternality. Moreover, Christ submitted to the will of men in the crucifixion because He submitted to the will of the Father that it should be so but did so without damage to His own sovereignty. In this event, one witnesses divine sovereignty, love, justice, mercy and human freedom all coming together without conflict. This was made possible by God's creation-order design. With the existence of creation, God's attributes express themselves under two conditions—within the circle of uncreated reality (unrestrained) and within the circle of created reality (restrained). While God is sovereign, His free choice (sovereignty) to give man the power of moral choice within the material circle does not limit Him in the uncreated circle but only restrains the manifestation of sovereignty (and other attributes) in the created circle. The creation-order design makes the interface possible between the circle of created reality and the circle of uncreated reality in such a way that both divine sovereignty and human freedom exist without impingement one or conflict. One sees a similar operation in the Incarnate Christ—divinity and humanity bridged in one person with two natures. Man is made in the image of God and, therefore, there is a compatibility between the nature of God and nature of man even though they are different. One might say that there is a sameness in function (or mode) but difference in predication. In the Incarnation, God becomes a man. The nature of God and the nature of man co-exist, unmingled in one *person*. There is no tension, no conflict. The nature of God and the true (sinless) nature of man existed without creating a dual person.

As there is order within the circle of uncreated reality, a similar order is also required within the circle of created reality if the two circles are to interact. Whereas in uncreated reality the order within the Trinity is established by the perfect nature of God, in created reality order must be prescribed as a creative act. Without established order, chaos would result both in the moral and physical realm, which would then render God's intention to interact meaningfully with man impossible (Amos 3:3; II Cor. 6:14). God, in His divine wisdom and grace, created just such an ordering that maximizes creation's potential while being compatible with His divine attributes. In this way, God is able to act in the material circle without abuse of or conflict with His God*ness*. Man is made capable of enjoying creaturely freedom making it possible for him to know God relationally and to love Him. This is part of the creation-order design.

One could argue that this is not the only logically possible created-order design. Nonetheless, given the infinite wisdom, goodness and power of God (Eph. 1:5; Rom. 11:33), it is difficult to maintain (at least consistently) that this is not the best of possible created-order designs. This includes both the moral and physical ordering of creation, which is to say that creation-order optimizes the function of creation and its interaction with the Creator as well as its conformity with the counsels of God. If this is correct, then once God establishes the created-order design, it is within this order that He works when interacting within the material circle. To do otherwise would abandon what is optimum. Although God clearly has the power and prerogative (theoretically) to act in any way consistent with His character, He submits that power and prerogative to the creation-order established by His wisdom and power. Looking at God acting in the circle of uncreated reality, the only limits are His own character. However, to speak of God acting within the circle of created reality one must recognize the parameters of His intentionally established creation-order design. Therefore, when addressing the expressed possibilities of God's sovereignty and power, one must be careful to consider which circle of reality is in view. God must abide by that to which He voluntarily commits Himself when first choosing to create. To violate His own creation-order design would mean going against Himself, something the faithful Creator will not do. Those who counter that this disallows miracles should refer to the discussion in Chapter Five where we noted that the creation-order design allows for God's intervention under certain circumstances in a way consistent with creation-order. However the intervention is viewed, we must not understand that it is caused by some unknown development that catches God by surprise.

Given God's omniscience, it is difficult to think of a situation in which God would be required to act contrary to his established creation-order to avert some unwanted state of affairs. Suggesting this implies that a state of affairs could develop which would threatened either man's existence or God's ultimate plan of which God has no knowledge. The only way such a state could develop is if God's knowledge is limited. However, as we have seen, God's knowledge is not limited as understood within the framework of middle knowledge. This creation is not an experiment by God to see how things will turn out. Experiments by their very nature indicate a lack of knowledge on the part of the one doing the experiment. The one who is experimenting does so because he is not sure how things work or turn out. That is not true of God as He knows all things. He therefore does not need to experiment. Whereas God is the faithful omniscient Creator who established the creation-order by His wisdom, goodness and power, it is difficult to explain why God would be required to abandon His own ordering either because of some unexpected event or because He has learned a better way to do things.

## The Principle of Cause and Effect

Among other things, creation-order determines that given certain actions, particular consequences follow. This is often referred to as the law of the harvest (Gal. 6:7) or in the physical realm as cause and effect. In some cases, it is possible for God to reverse the intent of certain evil intent but not the act itself. Joseph is an example of this. In this story the evil intent of the brothers is reversed, and God brings about something totally different. Nonetheless, Joseph really suffers as a result of their evil actions. It is only the intent, not the suffering, that is reversed through God's intervention, as stated by Joseph himself. In other cases, however, the evil intent is matched by evil consequences. One can think of many examples from history, such as the Holocaust. An example of this can also be found in the Bible. Luke 13:1–5 where the murderous intent of Herod results in terrible consequences for the worshipers. The point Jesus makes from this incident is instructive. Jesus does not indicate that the intent is reversed or that some good results from the evil. The worshipers died and no comfort is given that some greater good obtained. Instead, Jesus uses the event to teach us that we should be prepared to die at any point, since the evil intentions of others can spell death for their victims. God gives commands that govern how one treats others. When the neighbor is treated with love and respect, gratuitous evil is minimized. The moral commands are codified aspects of the creation-order by which man is instructed to live rightly in his material existence. Man can live out the morality given to man by God which is written both on the hearts of men and in the Bible.

## Moral Power of Choice and Social Justice

Each man is required to act righteously (Micah 6:8) as well as to defend others against evil (I Thess. 5:15). Precisely in this way God intends to minimize gratuitous evil. Given the corruption of man's heart and man's power of moral choice, gratuitous evil does exist. Furthermore, wherever and whenever man in general and the believer in particular fails to stand against evil (as in the case of the Holocaust or slavery in the United States), gratuitous evil can grow very large and ugly. In fact, such horrific gratuitous evil often reminds man of the wickedness of the human heart and through this he renews his resolve to stand against social and moral evil. This can be seen in the aftermath of the Trade Towers massacre. The C-O theodicy does not argue that the renewed effort against evil is the good that justifies the evil. However, it recognizes that sometimes some good may come from the evil, while maintaining that the evil was not necessary to the good.

The two planes striking the Trade Towers on September 11, 2001 offers an example of gratuitous evil flowing from evil choices leading to evil acts. It happened because a few people made certain decisions and it was within their power to carry out those plans. One can see the same thing in the case of those killed by the falling of the tower in Siloam and Pilate's hideous slaughter of those offering a sacrifice in worship (Lk. 13:1–5). According to Jesus, the lesson here is not that some good comes from the evil but rather that life is fragile and one never knows when death might unexpectedly take him. Therefore, all men should be prepared for life after death. These examples instruct the living in a very forceful way that today is the day of salvation—"except you repent you shall likewise perish." There are no guarantees in this life. In these examples, certain people make choices based upon their own evil desires. The intent is evil and the consequences are evil. The choices of those involved are freely made and intentionally evil.[5] Such choices and subsequent results stand as an example of potential evil within man and the power that man has to cause great harm or great good in this age his choices. Jesus is an example of one who used His human will to bring about a great good, while Herod illustrates the use of the power to bring about the great evil of the slaughtering of newborns (Matt. 2:16). It is the potential of the power of moral choice that makes possible both authentic good and evil including actual gratuitous evil.

God intends for man to exercise his power of choice to do what is right and stand against evil. The C-O theodicy argues that the very fact Christians are commanded to stand against evil is a strong indication that gratuitous evil exists. If all evil allowed by God necessarily becomes an evil that brings about a greater good, then the only evil present in the world would be God-allowed evil. Should the believer be successful in preventing this evil, he would also defeat the good that would have come from that evil. Whereas the good that is prevented is a necessary good, God must find another way for the good to obtain. Either the world would forever be minus that good or God would need to find another way to bring it to pass. Whatever alternative way God chooses could not be by means of a greater evil. If it is a lesser evil, then the question is why did God not use the lesser evil in the first place? If it is an evil of equal weight, why is it not defeated as in the first case? The Bible indicates that Christians should stand against all evil and defeat it where possible. If God wants evil stopped (either by some external deterrent or by personal choice), then it must not be necessary for some good to obtain. At times (probably more often than not) evil is not stopped, not because it was designed as the means to some good, but because men are evil and often disobedient to God's Word. It is this evil that falls into the category of gratuitous. Out of this category of evil, God at times will accomplish some good. Most often this happens in spite of the evil not because of it. Furthermore, the good obtained under these circumstances is not a necessary good and could have been accomplished without the evil or by different circumstances. If the concept of creation-order is right, gratuitous evil does not count against God morally. In fact, it is just the opposite. It reflects His faithfulness to the order He has established for His creation—an order necessary for it to be the creation God intended (something more that a system of predetermined motion).

## Power of Moral Choice Necessary for Authentic Love

John Hick's point that human freedom is necessary for man to love God seems convincingly argued. The C-O theodicy maintains that, without controversy, man loving God is man's highest calling. Next to it comes man loving his neighbor (Matt. 22:37–40). It is impossible for any human response that is coerced or compelled in any manner to be defined as love. By definition, love is a free response. If it is not free, it is not love. However, the potential to love entails the possibility of the opposite. One who has the power of moral choice must be free to choose not to love God or his neighbor, as well as to love either or both. This fact is made clear in Genesis 4 where Abel freely chooses to love and obey God, while Cain freely chooses to disobey God (not loving God). As a consequence of the choice to disobey God, Cain also hated his brother and chose to do him bodily harm. Cain's choice was free (Gen. 4:7). Consequently, he was held accountable for it as seen in Genesis 4:11–14. It is possible to obey God without loving God, but if we love God we will obey Him. Jesus said that if we love Him we will keep His word (Jn. 14:23–24).

Hick's point is a most important one for understanding humanity and its relationship to God. It is possible for God to create man to always do what God wants Him to do. That is, man could have been created so that he could only do what is right. In this case, doing right would not be by choice but rather by a determinative creative act of God. However, it is impossible for God to determine that man will love Him. The only way to make love an authentic possibility for man would be to give man the power of choice. Authentic love is the highest function of mankind. It is bound up in the two great commandments (Matt. 22:37–40). Paul says that love is the fulfillment of the whole law because love does no evil to his neighbor (Rom. 13:10). To love requires the power of choice to either love or not to love, which arguably is a moral choice.

## Good When the Righteous Suffer for Righteousness Sake

The C-O theodicy does not deny that in some cases good does come out of evil, that is, not all evil is gratuitous. It does maintain that when the good obtains, it does not provide evidence that the good is the moral justification for God permitting the evil. If a good obtains, it may be the providential work of God reversing some evil intent. Surely, Peterson's notion of character building or Swinburne's the good-of-being-used (or any of the other many suggestions of what the good might be) may have merit in some instances of evil. There is no objection to the claim that in some cases this can be observed. The C-O theodicy only contends that the good obtained is not a necessary good and that the evil is not necessary to the good. It can be thought of as a providential good. Moreover, the C-O theodicy argues that there is no way to demonstrate that the good would not have obtained without the evil. Furthermore, only when the believer suffers for righteousness sake can there be any assurance that God is working it out for good.

The C-O theodicy maintains there are two distinct categories, broadly speaking, under which a Christian may experience suffering. One category of suffering is that which comes to the believer because of righteous living. The other category is when a Christian suffers because of the brokenness of this age. When suffering under the former category, the believer can be assured that God is at work to reverse evil intent against him and bring good to him either in this life or the age to come. This is the only condition, however, that God promises to work in this way on behalf of the sufferer. This appears to be the teaching of Scripture as seen in several texts on suffering. Matthew 5:11 records the Lord's teaching that those who suffer "for My sake" are blessed. In James 1:3, James tells believers that in "the testing of your faith" you can rejoice. Peter reminds believers that when they suffer, they can rejoice as it demonstrates the "genuineness of your faith." (I Pet. 1:7). In II Timothy 3:12, Paul says those who "desire to live godly" will suffer persecution, but the text says nothing about it being necessary in order for some good to obtain. Suffering is a fact when men live righteously, especially in an unrighteous community (Is. 59:14–15). Consider the following examples: Job suffered because of his righteousness (Job 1:10), Joseph because of his faithful proclamation of God's dreams to him (Gen. 37:19—"Look, this dreamer is coming"), Shadrach, Meshach, and Abed-Nego for not worshiping the golden image (Dan. 3:8–25), and Daniel for praying to God (Dan. 6:10–23). The causal agent for the suffering in each case may be different. But in each case, the target was a righteous person and the reason was his righteous living. In each case the peaceable fruit of righteousness prevails.

When Christians suffer for righteousness sake, God is at work to work things together for their ultimate good as reckoned in the terms of the economy of His Kingdom. Then, it is in spite of the evil, not because of the evil. Because Christians will suffer in this world (as our Lord did), the Spirit of God speaks to the matter of suffering and encourages the Christian by informing him that there is a blessedness for those who suffer accordingly. Romans 8 is a case in point. Here Paul speaks about suffering for righteousness sake. In the middle of the discussion, he encourages believers "that all things work together for good to those who love God, to those who are called according to His purpose" (Rom. 8:28). Later, he reminds Christians there is nothing that can separate them from the love of God which is in Christ Jesus our Lord (Rom. 8:35–39). In the cataloging different possibilities of suffering such, as famine or nakedness, the context of the text points to the fact that suffering results from living righteously. Hebrews 11:36–40 gives a similar account. The point is that the Christian should not compromise his faithfulness to the Lord just because it might result in some form of suffering. Instead, the Christian should live boldly for Christ, noting that nothing can separate him from the love of God. According to II Corinthians 1:3–7, Christians can also be assured that the Father of mercies and God of all comfort is present to encourage and comfort them when the "sufferings of Christ abound" in them (v. 5). While these verses speak of blessedness, things working out for good, and/or rejoicing in the midst of suffering, they are always in the context of suffering for righteousness. It seems inappropriate to apply these truths to situations where Christians suffer because of the brokenness of this world. This includes such things as cancer, heart attacks and a variety of other diseases. This is not to say there is no word from God concerning such suffering, only that the verses mentioned do not address suffering in this category.

## When the Righteous Suffer From the Brokenness of This Age

Many of God's people have suffered because they live in this fallen place where things are terribly out of joint. The broken phase of this world is rather overwhelming at times. Evil can be very ugly and damaging both on personal and national levels. The presence of such suffering is due to sinful choices, the wicked works of the god of this age, and the fallen*ness* in general. One gets a feel for the general fallen*ness* when reading Genesis 3:16–19. It is precisely this fallen*ness* that accounts for some (even much) suffering for both the believer and the unbeliever. God forewarned the first parents in the Garden that "in the day you eat of it you shall surely die" (Gen. 2:17). There are, however, many wonderful verses concerning God's help in time of need that serve to encourage the believer in difficult times (such as Psalm 23:4; Psalm 73:23–26; II Corinthians 12:9; or I Peter. 5:7). It is precisely the love and care of the Lord Himself on which the believer should rest and not the idea that some good will come from cancer or whatever form of suffering that might be involved. For the believer, there is help through trusting in God's grace and comfort in the midst of the suffering. While trusting in God, the believer does what he can to mitigate the effects of the suffering (Gen. 39:14 – 40:14) and looks forward to the day of redemption when all will be made new (Rev. 21:3–5).

According to the C-O theodicy, even when Christians suffer because of the brokenness of this present age, there is still opportunity for good in the Kingdom. This is not to say that the suffering comes in order for the good. Rather, in the flow of life when the suffering comes, the Christian can respond in such a way that his testimony in suffering points people to God. Christians, who live by God's grace in the midst of their suffering, are a testimony to God's mercy and comfort. By this, unbelievers may come to believe in God and a wayward Christian might return to the Lord. The person who suffers might also give a testimony thanking God for the suffering if he believed it plays some positive part in his spiritual life. In such cases, the testimony is legitimate, but it is not the basis for a theodicy. Furthermore, the only person who has a right to testify in such a way is the person who suffered. This is not something that can be used to comfort others who are suffering, for in other cases there is no assurance that this good or any good may obtain. However, other Christians can be encouraged by the testimony of the reality of God's mercy and comfort in the midst of suffering.

The point of the C-O theodicy is that a testimony is not the basis for a theodicy. Suffering does not always result in a believer's spiritual welfare, as much depends on how he responds to the suffering. Furthermore, just because some good comes from suffering one cannot argue that either the suffering was necessary to the good or that the good would not have obtained without the suffering. Furthermore, if the evil is allowed by God in order to bring about the good, then it appears counter to pray for the healing of that person. Because it maintains that gratuitous evil exists, the C-O theodicy would teach consistently that there is purpose in praying for such a person.

Many cases of suffering involve the unbeliever. In cases of intense devastating suffering, the unbeliever, left to himself, often shows tremendous resilience which speaks something of the wonder of humanity. Often, one does not understand how anyone without the Lord can face such suffering. The fact is, many do and move on with life. In some cases when faced with extreme difficulty the unbeliever is instructed in the fragility of life and his own mortality leading him to a repentance and turning to Christ. However, even should this happen, it should not be used as a theological explanation for why the evil was allowed. It is even possible under this scenario that the person himself would testify he is thankful for the suffering because it brought him to Christ. While this is a legitimate testimony for the individual, it is not a theodicy. One can think of many who have publicly so testified, and such a testimony should not be disallowed. To say, however, that God allowed that evil for this purpose is going beyond revelation and should not be a basis for a theological position.. There have been many who have suffered and as a result have become deeply embittered against God (Pharaoh is a case in point).

## Natural Evil

It appears that much of natural evil falls into the category of suffering because of the fallen*ness* of this present age. An example of natural evil is found in Luke 13:4, which reports that 18 persons were killed when the tower in Siloam fell on them. One can imagine different explanations for the tower falling (probably due to deterioration), but the text does not give such information. Since Jesus makes no reference it is assumed that it was not a moral lapse on the part of the engineers who designed the tower. The falling appears to have happened without warning or mischievous activity on the part of any particular person. The text states merely that it happened. Some people asked Jesus why such things should happen. He does not suggest that the evil is allowed in order that some good might obtain. Instead, he points out that things like this happen. The story provides instruction for all persons to be prepared to die at any time. The text does not even say that God allows it for this purpose, only that such things happen and this is one lesson to be learned from it. It is not necessary, however, to learn this lesson from only such events. The course of life is sufficient to establish the fact that death can come unpredictably at any moment. Furthermore, the Bible teaches the same lesson. While one may see such truth reinforced by the events of life, the events of life are not necessary to know the truth.

Of course, all natural evils do not fall neatly into this category. God causes some natural to bring judgment on a person or persons. In such incidences as famine and earthquake[6] in the Old Testament God offers a word to explain why such things are happening, so it is not left up to the imagination of men to determine the purpose of the event. One must be very careful today in crediting such natural evils as God's judgment. (This is not to say they are not, only that there would be no way to know unless there was a word from God). Some made this mistake following the September 11th massacre at the Trade Towers. They immediately proclaimed that it was a judgment of God on America for her sins (particular sins were even mentioned). However, it seems the evidence from the event warrants no such conclusion. Later, there were those who felt constrained to change their pronouncements because they realized there was simply no way to determine if this was the case. (Of course, pressure from supporters may have also contributed to the retraction).

Moreover, Satan causes some natural evils (Job 2:18–19) as well as the evil choices of men. It seems difficult to argue that the presence of such evils is based on some good that would obtain. Consider the case where a contractor uses inferior materials to build a public building and later it collapses, killing many people. On its face, this is a natural disaster. There is no guarantee that a building will collapse if inferior materials are used, although it could be the cause. Consider another case where a famine occurs because politicians embezzle money earmarked for land conservation, leaving the land without proper management. It would be difficult to argue that hundreds of deaths in a collapsed building were worth it so that stricter inspections would be imposed. Sure, such an incident might save lives in the future, but hardly is the death of innocents necessary to make a building safer. One would also be hard pressed to make the case that God allows thousands to die or suffer from malnutrition (usually children) if it leads to the politicians being brought to justice (or any other good one might think up). Such a good would hardly justify such a horrific evil. Furthermore, once the lesson is learned, the purpose for the evil would be served and the evil would disappear. Clearly this is not the case.

The C-O theodicy explains such evils simply as the outworking of evil choices with horrific consequences within created-order. They are not allowed by God in any active sense but in a passive sense, as this is the way things work within the structure of the created-order design. Death and disease are enemies of God, as can be seen in the Lord's response when on earth: He weeps at the tomb of Lazarus (Jn. 11:35) and raises the widow of Nain's son without any appeal from the crowd (Lk. 7:14). The heart of God is grieved when the innocent are harmed. He does not countenance it in any way by bringing some good from it and then say, "See that suffering was worth the good." It is not that God is powerless according to His power to do something, but that He has established the creation-order within which He must interact with His creation. In some cases, according to the good pleasure of God, divine protection may be given, but it is not promised nor should it necessarily be expected. If it comes, then praise belongs to God as it is for His purposes. What can be expected is that in all situations He never leaves nor forsakes His own (Heb. 13:5–6).

Suppose that God intervened and prevented every horrific evil, which would not bring about some greater good. Under such circumstances, choices would not be choices because the appropriated consequences would not follow. This, however, is precisely what the G-G theodices require. If the only evil allowed by God is that which brings about a good, then He must prevent all other evils. At what point should He not intervene, and for whom should He intervene and on what basis? The fact is there is no way to answer this question because the G-G theodices are built on an faulty assumption. The sad fact is that in this present age there is much suffering and a large measure of it is gratuitous, which seems to be exactly what one would expect in a place alienated from God. The Christian can have hope the day to come when righteousness will rule in this world and can know the mercy and comfort of God until that time.

## The Best of All Possible Worlds

Gratitous evil was present in all worlds possible. Before there was anything but God, all possible worlds existed as ideas in the mind of God. God's natural knowledge (eternal knowledge) informed Him on what worlds were possible and what worlds were not possible. All worlds possible were structured according to the same creation-order design as were as certain events, such as the Cross (Rev. 13:8). (Remember, in Chapter Five we saw that a world where all moral creatures always do right is not a possible world). In all worlds, man is limited in what choices he will have as well as what would be possible for him ontologically. In all possible worlds man has the power of moral choice. God, informed by middle knowledge, saw all counterfactuals of creaturely freedom and, consequently, all possible worlds as they unfold based upon the choices of men within the prescribed limits. Each world includes (but, is not limited to) men's choices, men's prayers, God's responses to prayers, His interventions, His persuasive acts among men, and certain predetermined events which are part of all possible worlds—everything that pertains to the creation-order design. In each world, men freely choose each act and freely respond to all persuasive measures of God. In any possible world, what each man does, he does freely, which is to say he is not determined regarding any moral choice. That is not to say that there are no influences in his life, both natural and supernatural, only that his choice is his choice. God, in His knowledge knows all things of this world (Is. 46:9–11) for this is the world He actualized.

From all possible worlds, God selects the best of all possible worlds to be the world that He will actualize. Once that world is actualized, things will be as they are in that world and they cannot be otherwise. While creation-order establishes how God interacts with any and all possible worlds, the only possible world now is the one God has actualized. The choice to actualize this world is from God's wisdom and goodness and, therefore, it is the best of all possible worlds. Should anyone object that in another world things would be different for him, the fact is what is true for him today is what he chose freely in this world. Because he might have chosen freely but differently in another world is of no consequence. The best of all possible worlds was not selected on the basis of the state of affairs of one or two individuals but on the world as a whole. The issue here is that man's moral choice is his own, regardless of what world he is in.

From the possible worlds, God actualizes the world where there is an optimum relationship between good and evil. In terms of salvation, this world is the best world with an optimum balance between those who are saved and those who are lost. This would be in contradistinction to those who say that man's felicity is God's intent and governing principle. However, man's true felicity is dependent on righteousness and peace. Therefore, even if one argues that felicity is God's intended good for man, good must always be understood in terms of the Kingdom of God. In the end, we know that his world is the best of all possible worlds because God pronounced it "very good" (Gen. 1:31).

## C-O Theodicy In Review

The C-O theodicy begins by describing the two circles of reality and how creation-order design makes possible an interface between the two. God determines the principles and boundaries governing the relationship between Himself and His creation. This is what I have called the creation-order, which includes the function and boundaries of both natural and moral ordering. Creation-order enables the possibility that the infinite and the finite mind have a meaningful interaction. The infinite personal being is compatible with the finite personal to such a degree that the finite can properly act on behalf of God within created reality. God's creation-order is based upon His perfect wisdom, wholly good character and omniscience, and provides the parameters within which and by which He interacts with the world He has actualized. It determines in what ways God will limit the expression of His own attributes within created order, which appears to be necessary for man to be true man. It is necessary in order for man to function as a true rational being in a way that man's choices will have real consequences that will influence, to some degree, the shape of human history where men are neither robots nor totally autonomous. The creation-order provides the framework within which man can exercise his God-given power of moral choice while assuring the end will be as God purposed.

Within the structure of the creation-order, man can choose good or evil, even where much of the evil turns out to be gratuitous. This is illustrated early in the book of Genesis when Cain kills Abel. There was no greater-good from this horrible act. Cain was punished, Adam and Eve undoubtedly grieved. There is no indication that Seth was more righteous than Abel. Cain killing Abel was gratuitous evil, but it did not count against the character of God nor did it defeat the plan of God. God's providence works amidst all the evil in this world. Sometimes His providence brings good from the suffering and other times His work of providence is corrective. Admitting that gratuitous evil exists in this world and arguing that it does not count against God, severely weakens the atheist's argument from evil. The most the atheist can argue is that he does not like the structure of the creation-order.

God's omniscience is understood as including middle knowledge by which He has actualized the best of all possible worlds. Once this world is actualized all things remain as they were in its state of potentiality. Based upon His middle knowledge, God selects from all the possible worlds the best possible world. This is a complete world, one that includes all human choices, prayers, answers to prayers, good and bad events, as well as God's promises, commands, interventions (including miracles), and all other matters that make up a possible world. Furthermore, the world encompasses everything from the moment of creation to the final Kingdom state. When it is affirmed that this is the best of all possible worlds it means that what God created from the beginning was the best it could possibly be. This is not saying that this world is flawless existentially. Under the circumstances, this world is the best both morally and aesthetically in terms of ordering and design. For God to create anything, it would be His best (by choice and not necessity).

In this world, God uses some evil to bring about good. Some evil is gratuitous. The amount of gratuitous evil is at an irreducible minimum in relation to the good, because God knows all the worlds (not actual, but potential worlds—middle knowledge—assuring that the best would be actualized). God decided if He were to create a world (which of necessity is contingent, and, therefore, not morally perfect in the same sense God is) at all (and it seems that it is better to exist than not exist), He selected the one with the least amount of evil as a whole, the least amount of gratuitous evil in particular and the greatest amount of good. There was an optimum balance between the good and evil in general and, in particular, an optimum balance between the saved and the unsaved. Each category dependent on man's power of moral choice.

As history reveals, man used his power of moral choice to disobey God and brought sin and death into this world. Man rebelled against his limitedness and chose to disobey God in the hope that He could become like God. Working within the boundaries of creation-order, God provided redemption and the assurance of the Kingdom of God on this earth. When God enacted the plan of redemption, He did not create a new man from dust. He worked providentially through the normal procreative process to bring to fruition this redemptive plan. Furthermore, just as it was human choice that brought sin into the world, even so human choice is involved in man being reconciled to God and delivered from sin and its consequences. God placed two trees in human history and gave commandments concerning both. The fruit of the tree in the

Garden came with the command, "Eat and die." The fruit of the tree on Calvary comes with the command, "Eat and live."

These are examples of God working the plan of redemption within the boundaries of creation-order. Furthermore, because sin brought about accidental changes in man and separated him from God, God sent His Spirit to persuaded men of their need of Him (Gen. 6:3; Jn. 16:8–11). God determined the consequences of the disobedience and the consequences of obedience, all of which was a part of creation-order. Moreover, the world that was actualized included the entire world (book), that is from creation to the Kingdom.

When taken as a whole, this is the best of all possible worlds even though it contains evil in general and horrific evil in particular. Of this evil, some is moral and some is natural/physical, but it all flows from the fact that because of sin, creation is not like it was intended to be. When believers suffer for righteousness sake, they can know that God is at work for the good of His Kingdom, and they can be encouraged as God administers mercy and comfort for living. When believers suffer because they live in a fallen world, they look to the grace and comfort of God to encourage and strengthen them. Sometimes God delivers from and sometimes God delivers in the circumstance. In all cases His grace is sufficient. Because of those who obey God's law, evil and suffering are often prevented so that the events of this world are not as bad as they might be (II Thess. 2:6–7). In addition, there is the common grace of God by which God provides in a general way for His creation (Matt. 5:45). All of this is part of God's creation-order which is suggested here as a more adequate way to understand God's relationship to created reality in general and evil in particular.

While this may give the appearance that God has no control, such is not the case. One can see God's control of matters in several ways. First, the direction of human history is shaped in some fashion by God limiting human choices as part of creation-order. There are some things that man is not permitted to do from the beginning. Second, God can providentially intervene as He did in Noah's day or as He did at the Tower of Babel. These are cases involving divine intervention where God's intervention is in the name of justice or the welfare of humanity and does not violate anything He has promised. His providential work assures that gratuitous evil never defeats His plan. Third, God has established the creation-order in such a way that human history passes through predetermined points, moving towards a determined end (Is. 46:10). There are some events determined by God and, as such, they form outer boundaries to the possibilities and therefore the direction of human history. Fourth, God can exercise persuasive power to convince men to choose a right course. Consider the salvation of Saul of Tarsus (Acts 9:3–6) or King Nebuchadnezzar (Dan. 4:28–37). Fifth, God's answers to prayers are limited in such a way as to direct history. For example, Hezekiah did not get sixteen extra years, only fifteen, and Sodom would have been spared had there been ten righteous living in it. Sixth, God works through His people to do that which is consistent with His Kingdom. This is why there are commands for things man is not to do and things he is to do. God's Spirit works through believers to restrain the evil in the world (II Thess. 2:7–8). This is not to say that believers have always acted in this restraining way. There is no doubt, however, that much evil has been restrained by the forces of righteousness, either by believers or unbelievers acting from a Hebrew-Christian world view.

## APPLYING THE C-O THEODICY

One of the most difficult tasks in ministering to people is comforting them in time of suffering, particularly when the suffering appears to be senseless (for example, a little girl kidnaped, raped and strangled to death). In such times, it will not do to say what is not true or speak of that for which there is no biblical foundation just because it sounds good. Nor will it do to romanticize the suffering and death because the little girl was a Christian. To comfort the suffering by saying that God will bring some good out of the evil may be well intended but is without warrant. Maybe God will bring some good from the evil, but which man can promise it? Those suffering have the right to ask about the particulars related to them. If the suffering is for good, then who is it that receives the good? For example, if it was my daughter who was raped and strangled to death, was the good for her or for me as a grieving parent? If it is for the one who suffers directly, what about those who suffer indirectly? What about Jacob and the suffering he experienced because of what was done to Joseph. Jacob's testimony is that his days had been few and evil (Gen. 47:9).

God is always faithful in the difficulty, but this is an entirely different issue. To argue that suffering is necessary to experience the grace of God seems beyond the warrant of Scripture. (Of course we can experience His grace in our suffering). What Scripture says about God's grace in suffering takes suffering as a given, not a necessity. Whereas grace is not an essential attribute of God, it is not necessary that man experience it in order to know the fullness of God. Those who promise the good must also be prepared to answer the other questions as well. It is not difficult to find many examples where a believer has suffered intensely and has become bitter, not better. The C-O theodicy attempts to avoid just such difficulties by rejecting the greater-good premise as a universal principle for understanding the presence of evil in this world.

Some Christians may think that a theodicy is not necessary because it is only theoretical. They long for something practical. They are right on that count. They err in thinking that there is no relationship between the theory and practice. In fact, any theory without practical application is of little value to humanity. Certainly, people who are diagnosed with cancer are not interested in some long explanation on cancer research, how cancer develops, and what it looks like under the microscope. They want something that will restore health to the body. The truth is, however, those who are going to prescribe a course of treatment for the cancer must have some understanding of the pathology of cancer if the treatment is to be successful. People with cancer go to an oncologist because he knows about cancer as a disease. So it is with suffering. A person's theodic framework guides him in answering the tough questions of those who are suffering and provides some comfort. The value of the answers will be determined by the comprehensiveness of the understanding of evil itself and how it relates to God and His creation. Healing for the sufferer must be grounded in the truth—the way things are in reality. This is the purpose of a theodicy.

All too often, the suffering of the Christian has been minimized (or at least romaticized) with the mentality that one should not grieve. God is going to bring something good from the suffering (or so-and-so is better off in heaven). I am not saying that this cannot bring some comfort, but it does not explain why the evil was allowed in the first place. Those who are consistent with the greater-good approach are in the end required to confess that the particular evil was God's will (a position many take). At this point it becomes problematic to lead a person confidently to look to God, because if God is responsible for the suffering then it must be His will that I suffer. So why ask Him for some relief? When confronted with the logical conclusion of this position regarding the will of God, many respond by saying that it is the permissive will of God, not His sovereign will that accounts for this. If this is true, then how do we escape some disturbing conclusions. First, is it God's sovereign will that man not murder man? It seems the answer is yes. If it is then argued that God's permissive will allows murder, which will is stronger? The sovereign will or the permissive will of God? Since murder occurs it must be that the permissive will is stronger than the sovereign will. If His permissive will is stronger than His sovereign will, how can one be assured that the sovereign will prevails in the end?

Furthermore, if it has all been allowed for my good (or some other God-ordained good) then I should rejoice that it has come my way. Does it not sound a little strange in light of God's love to say that I should rejoice that my three-year-old was raped and murdered? In such cases, Christians who try to live with this explanation often spend much of their time trying to find the good instead of looking to God's comfort and mercy. The consolation is not in God but in the good that obtains from the suffering. This seems not only futile but biblically wrong-headed. Moreover, when the good is not forthcoming, Christians often become bitter with God or life, and their spiritual life declines miserably. If one argues that this happened because they chose not to trust God, then where is the good?

I remember a young lady in a class I was teaching on evil. I presented the C-O theodicy. After the class she approached me crying as she told her story of a great tragedy in her Christian family's life ten years earlier. The family had tried to console themselves with the idea that God allowed a terrible thing in order to bring about some good (this is what they had been told). After several years of watching for the good to appear, in the absence of any discernable good, some of her family became bitter towards God. In the absence of any discernable good, there was only disappointment. God had willfully allowed a great evil in their lives without any compensation. And the argument that it would all come later, did not square with the facts. They were believers going to heaven before the incident happened. All the family experienced was prolonged difficulty. When the young lady realized that had what happened was an example of gratuitous evil and not God's will, she was overwhelmed with the release. She could look to God for grace, strength and mercy for living in the less than pleasurable circumstances in which she and her family now found themselves. (Similar stories abound, many of which I know of personally from some thirty years serving as pastor.) The C-O theodicy points people to God and not some possible good. To trust in His grace, mercy and love to minister to them in their distress and to know His comfort.

According to the C-O theodicy, when a Christian suffers, he should determine the reason suffering has come. Is it because he is living righteously, in sin, or is it because he is living in a fallen place? If it is the first, then he should look to God and His mercy for help and comfort, knowing that the evil intent will not prosper against him since it will be tempered by the providential hand of the loving, omnipotent heavenly Father—nothing can separate him from God. If it is the second, then the Christian should confess his sin and purpose in his heart to forsake the sin by the power of God working in him (I Jn. 1:9;

Rom. 6:11–13). Should it be the third, he should look to God for strength and grace, while being comforted knowing that in the next phase of this world, suffering will be abolished (Rev. 21:4). If good comes from any evil, then he can thank God and maximize that good. In all cases he can know that this world is guided by a creation-order designed and sustained by an all-wise, all-good and all-powerful God— this is the best of all *possible* worlds. It is better to have this world than not have this world. God is in control (not in the sense that He determines everything but because He knows all things and is providentially involved) and His Kingdom will come. What He began in Genesis 1 will be completed in spite of the evil that has made its way into this creation. One day, redeemed persons will enjoy what God intended for Adam and Eve, and it will be enjoyed forever.

Lastly, I would like to submit a brief discussion regarding suffering in general. Today, there is a growing belief that the goal of science is to remove all suffering at all costs. Americans have come to demand the absence of suffering at any cost. Consequently, moral boundaries are being pushed to the limits, and beyond, in the name of science's quest for eliminating suffering from the human experience. This goal rests on two erroneous assumptions. The first is the cause of suffering and disease. Science sees these as only a biological/chemical issue when in fact they are a spiritual issue. Death and disease came into the world by sin. The second is that suffering is without redemptive value. If one believes that the elimination of suffering is an absolute in itself, then any means will be acceptable to that end. Consequently, even basic morality can be set aside in the interest of eliminating suffering. While it is legitimate to fight against the fall, it is not to be done outside basic moral boundaries. Surely, no one wants to suffer. To eliminate as much suffering as morally possible is desirable. But one must not assume that suffering has no value. This is not a greater-good idea. Suffering that cannot be eliminated does not mean that the sufferer has no profit from his suffering.

There are several important things to be learned from suffering. While things can be learned otherwise, suffering makes the point more personal and hence effective. Suffering is an undeniable and unerasable reality because on this side of final redemption sin will produce death. Even Jesus suffered and, remember, that the servant is not greater than his Lord. Suffering instructs us in our own mortality (Job 1:20–22). Suffering can teach us to depend on God and His grace (Ps. 73:1–2, 21–26; II Cor. 12:9; Ps. 23:4). Suffering also helps us to see the value of God's Word (Ps. 119:50,67,71). Suffering puts us in touch with God's mercy and comfort (II Cor. 1:2–4) and offers an opportunity to experience God's grace and strength (II Cor. 12:9–10). In addition, suffering has value in building character (Rom. 5:1–5; Ja. 1:2–4). Such benefits certainly do not provide moral justification for God allowing the suffering; however, when suffering comes it can benefit to the sufferer regardless of the intent (if there is one) of the one perpetrating the evil. This is because of the design of the creation-order.

## CONCLUSION

C-O theodicy undoubtedly has its weaknesses. However, I believe that it offers a paradigm shift, which is useful for answering the argument from evil. Instead of making the good that obtains from evil the grounds for God being morally justified in permitting evil, this theodicy focuses on the arrangement necessary for finite beings and the Infinite Being to have a meaningful relationship. In this, the C-O theodicy attempts to avoid what I perceive to be a fatal weakness of the greater-good premise, namely the denial of gratuitous evil. On the practical side, it directs the sufferer's attention to God and His grace in the suffering rather than to the good that might obtain. I believe the Creation-Order theodicy offers not only a better response to the argument from evil, it also provides a stronger theological framework within which one can minister effectively to the needs and questions of those who suffer, especially those with a Christian world view.

## NOTES

1. This does not include suffering which may result from justice carried out either by God or man. That type of suffering is not in view in the discussion of evil.

2. This would include notions bound up in what is included in the anthropic principle. The word "harmonious" is not intended to communicate the idea of perfect, only orderly operation.

3. It appears from such texts as Job 39:26–30 that God is dynamically involved in the daily function of creation in general and texts like Genesis 3:8 that God personally interacts with man.

4. I say "certain attributes", since it appears that not all are involved in the same way. For example, it appears that there was no restraint on the love of God or the knowledge of God.

5. When I say "freely made" I am not suggesting that there are no influences acting upon them either mediately or immediately. That is not the type of libertarian freedom (power of moral choice) argued in this book.

However, each freely choose how to respond to other antecedent influences even though they may have had no choice concerning which influences would be a part of their history. Ultimately, they are accountable for their choices and, hence, morally responsible.

6. When I say that this is a natural evil, I am not suggesting that God was not involved, only that it was an evil within the order of nature.

# Selected Bibliography

Ackermann, Robert. "An Alternative Free Will Defence." *Religious Studies* 18 (1982): 365–72.

Adams, Marilyn M. "Redemptive Suffering: A Christian Solution to the Problem." In *The Problem of Evil*. Edited by Michael Peterson. Notre Dame: University of Notre Dame, 1992.

_____. "Problems of Evil: More Advice to Christian Philosophers." 5 (Apr 1988):121–41.

Adams, Robert M. Adams. "Must God Create the Best?" In *The Problem of Evil*. Edited by Michael Peterson. Notre Dame: University of Notre Dame Press, 1992.

Ahern, M. B. *The Problem of Evil*. New York: Schocken Books, 1971.

Allen, Diogenes. "Suffering at the Hands of Nature." *Theology Today* 37 (Jul 1980): 183–91.

Alston, William. "The Inductive Argument from Evil and the Human Cognitive Condition." In *The Evidential Argument from Evil*. Edited by Daniel Howard-Snyder. Bloomington: Indiana University Press, 1996.

Aquinas. *Summa Theologiae*. English Dominican Translation (1911) [CD-ROM] Albany, OR: Ages Software, 1998.

Augustine. *The Problem of Free Choice*. Trans. Dom Mark Pontifex in *Ancient Christian Writers*. Westminster, MD: The Newman Press, 1955.

Basinger, David. *The Case for Freewill Theism*. Downers Grove: InterVarsity Press, 1996.

_____. "Middle Knowledge and Human Freedom: Some Clarifications." *Faith and Philosophy* 4 (Jul 1987): 330–42.

Berkhof, Louis. *The History of Christian Doctrine*. Grand Rapids: Baker Book House, 1996.

Blumenfeld, David. "Is the Best Possible World Possible?" *The Philosophical Review* 84 (Ap 1975):163–77.

Boethius. *The Consolations of Philosophy*. Translated by S. J. Tester. Cambridge: Harvard University Press, 1973.

Bourke, Vernon. *Augustine's Love of Wisdom*. West Lafayette, IN: Purdue University Press, 1992.

Boyd, Gregory. *Satan and the Problem of Evil*. Downers Grove: InterVarsity Press, 2001.

Broadie, Alexander. "St. Thomas Aquinas." In *The Oxford Companion to Philosophy,* 1995.

Brown, Colin. *Christianity & Western Thought*. Vol. 1. *From the Ancient World to the Age of Enlightenment*. Downers Grove: InterVarsity Press, 1990.

Brown, Robert. "Divine Omniscience, Immutability, Aseity and Human Will." *Religious Studies* 27 (1991):285–95.

Burgess-Jackson, Keith. "Free Will, Omnipotence, and the Problem of Evil." *American Journal of Theology & Philosophy* 9 (Sept 1988): 175–85.

Bush, L. Russ. *A Handbook for Christian Philosophy*. Grand Rapids: Zondervan Publishing House, 1991.

Cahn, Steven and David Shatz, eds. *Contemporary Philosophy of Religion*. New York: Oxford University Press, 1982.

Carson, D. A. *How Long, O Lord?* Downers Grove: InterVarsity Press, 1996.

Chisholm, Roderick M. "The Defeat of Good and Evil." In *The Problem of Evil*. Edited by Marilyn McCord Adams and Robert Merrihew Adams. New York: Oxford University Press, 1990.

Christlieb, Terry. "Which Theisms Face an Evidential Problem of Evil?" 9 (Jan 1992): 45–64.

Chryssides, George D. "Evil and the Problem of God." *Religious Studies* 23 (1987): 467–75.

Chrzan, Keith. "God and Gratuitous Evil." *Religious Studies* 27 (1991): 99–103

____. "Necessary Gratuitous Evil: An Oxymoron Revisited." *Faith and Philosophy* 11 (1994): 134–7.

____. "When Is a Gratuitous Evil Really Gratuitous?" *International Journal for Philosophy of Religion* 24 (Mr 1988): 87–91.

Copleston, Frederick. *A History of Philosophy*. Vol. 2. *Mediaevel Philosophy: Augustine to Scotus*. Westminster: The Newman Press, 1962.

____. *History of Philosophy*. Vol. 4. *Descartes to Leibniz*. Westminster: The Newman Press, 1974.

Couturat, Louis. "On Leibniz's Metaphysics." In *Leibniz: A Collection of Critical Essays*. Edited by Harry G. Frankfurt. Notre Dame: University of Notre Dame, 1976.

D'Arcy, Martin C. *St Thomas Aquinas*. Westminster: The Newman Press, 1955.

Davies, Brian. *The Thought of Thomas Aquinas.* Oxford: Clarendon Press,1992.

Davis, Stephen. Editor. *Encountering Evil: Live Options in Theodicy.* Atlanta: John Knox Press, 1981.

_____ . "Critique." In *Encountering Evil.* Edited by Stephen T. Davis. Atlanta: John Knox Press, 1981.

_____. "Defense of the Free Will Defense." *Religious Studies* 8 (D 1972): 335–44.

_____. "Divine Omniscience and Human Freedom." *Religious Studies* 15 (Sep 1979): 303–16.

_____. "The Problem of Evil in Recent Philosophy." *Review and Expositor* 82 (Fall 1985): 535–48.

Davis, Wayne. "Counterfactuals," in *The Cambridge Dictionary of Philosophy,* 1995.

Dilley, Frank. "Is the Free Will Defence Irrelevant?" *Religious Studies* 18 (1982): 355–64.

Draper, Paul. "Pain and Pleasure: An Evidential Problem for Theists." In *The Evidential Argument from Evil.* Edited by Daniel Howard-Snyder. Bloomington: Indiana University Press, 1996.

Erlandson, Douglas and Charles Sayward. "Is Heaven a Possible World? *International Journal for Philosophy of Religion* 12 (1981): 55–58.

Erickson, Millard. *Christian Theology.* Vol. 1. Grand Rapids: Baker Book House, 1983.

_____. *God the Father Almighty.* Grand Rapids: Baker Books, 1998.

Feinberg, John S. *Deceived By God?* Wheaton: Crossway Books, 1997.

_____. *The Many Faces of Evil: Theological Systems and the Problem of Evil.* 2nd ed. Grand Rapids: Zondervan, 1994.

Flemming, Arthur. "Omnibenevolence and Evil." *Ethics* 96 (Jan 1986): 261–81.

Flint, Thomas P. *Divine Providence: The Molinist Account.* Ithaca: Cornell University Press, 1998.

Friedman, R. Z. "Evil and Moral Agency." *International Journal for Philosophy of Religion* 24 (1988): 3–20.

Gale, Richard M. "Some Difficulties in Theistic Treatments of Evil." In *The Evidential Argument from Evil.* Edited by Daniel Howard-Snyder. Bloomington: Indiana University Press, 1996.

Gan, Barry L. "Plantinga's Transworld Depravity: It's Got Possibilities." *International Journal for Philosophy of Religion* 13 (1982): 169–78.

Geach, Peter T. "Providence and Evil." *Theology* 81 (Ja 1978): 55–56.

____. *Providence and Evil.* Cambridge: Cambridge University Press, 1977.

Geisler, Norman. *Thomas Aquinas: An Evangelical Appraisal.* Grand Rapids: Baker Book House, 1991.

Geisler, Norman and Winfried Corduan. *Philosophy of Religion.* 2nd ed. Grand Rapids: Baker Book House, 1988.

Geivett, R. Douglas. *Evil and the Evidence for God.* Philadelphia: Temple University Press, 1993.

Griffin, David Ray. *God, Power, and Evil: A Process Theodicy.* Philadelphia: Westminster Press, 1976.

Gilson, Etienne. *The Christian Philosophy of Saint Augustine.* Translated by L. E. M. Lynch. New York: Vintage Books, 1967.

____. *The Christian Philosophy of St. Thomas Aquinas.* Translated by L. K. Shook. New York: Random House, 1956.

Hasker, William. *God, Time, and Knowledge.* Ithaca, NY: Cornell University Press, 1998.

____. "Chrzan on Necessary Gratuitous Evil." *Faith and Philosophy* 12 (Jul 1995): 423–25.

____. "Must God Do His Best?" *International Journal for Philosophy of Religion* 16 (1984): 213–24.

____. "The Necessity of Gratuitous Evil." *Faith and Philosophy* 9 (Jan 1992): 23–44.

____. "Middle Knowledge." In *The Cambridge Dictionary of Philosophy,* 1995

Henry, Carl F. *Christian Personal Ethics.* Grand Rapids: William B. Eerdmans Publishing Co, 1957; Grand Rapids: Baker Book House, 1977.

Hick, John. "An Irenaean Theodicy." In *Encountering Evil.* Edited by Stephen T. Davis. Atlanta: John Knox Press, 1981.

____. *Death and Eternal Life.* New York: Harper & Row Publishers, 1976.

____. *Evil and the God of Love.* Rev. Ed. San Francisco: Harper & Row, 1978.

Howard-Snyder, Daniel. "The Argument from Inscrutable Evil." In *The Evidential Argument from Evil.* Edited by Daniel Howard-Snyder. Bloomington: Indiana University Press, 1996.

____. Introduction to *The Evidential Argument from Evil.* Edited by Daniel Howard-Snyder. Bloomington: Indiana University Press, 1996.

Hume, David. "Evil and the God of Religion." In *The Problem of Evil.* Edited by Michael Peterson. Notre Dame: University of Notre Dame, 1992.

Hunt, David P. "Middle Knowledge and the Soteriological Problem of Evil." *Religious Studies* 27 (1991): 3–26.

Jones, William T. *A History of Western Philosophy,* 2<sup>nd</sup> ed. Vol. 2. *The Medieval Mind.* New York: Harcourt, Brace & World, 1969.

Kane, G. Stanley. "The Concept of Divine Goodness and the Problem of Evil." *Religious Studies* 11 (Mar 1975): 49–71.

_____. "Evil and Privatio." *International Journal for Philosophy of Religion* 11 (Spring 1980): 43–58.

_____."The Failure of Soul-Making Theodicy." *International Journal for Philosophy of Religion* 6 (1975): 1–22.

La Croix, Richard. "Swinburne on Omnipotence." *International Journal for Philosophy of Religion* 6 (Winter 1975): 251–55.

Legenhausen, G. "Notes Towards An Ashàrite Theodicy." *Religious Studies* 24 (1988): 257–66.

Leibniz, Gottfried Wilhelm *Theodicy.* Translated by E. M. Huggard from C. J. Gerhardt's Edition of the Collected Philosophical Works, 1878–90. LaSalle: Open Court, 1985.

Lewis, C. S. *The Problem of Pain.* New York: Macmillan, 1962. Reprint, New York: Simon & Schuster, 1996.

Loemker, Leroy. "Leibniz and the Herborn Encyclopedists." In *The Philosophy of Leibniz and the Modern World.* Edited by Ivor Leclerc. Nashville: Vanderbilt University Press, 1973.

Lowry, Richard. "The Dark Side of the Soul: Human Nature and the Problem of Evil In Jewish and Christian Traditions." *Journal of Ecumenical Studies* 35 (Winter 1998): 88–100.

Mackie, John L. "Evil and Omnipotence." In *Philosophy of Religion.* Edited by Melville Y. Stewart. Sudbury, MA: Jones and Bartlett Publishers, 1996.

Madden, Edward and Peter Hare. *Evil and the Concept of God.* Springfield: Charles Thomas Publishers, 1968.

Mavrodes, George, "A Response to John Hick." *Faith and Philosophy* 14 (Jul 1997): 289–301.

_____. "Keith Yandell and the Problem of Evil." *Philosophy of Religion* 20 (1986): 45–48.

McCloskey, H. J. *God and Evil.* The Hague, Netherlands: Martinus Nijhoff, 1974.

_____. "Problem of Evil." *Journal of Bible and Religion* 30 (Jul 1962): 187–97.

Myers, C. Mason. "Free will and the Problem of Evil." *Religious Studies* 23 (1987): 289–94.

Middleton, J. Richard. "Why the 'Greater Good' Isn't a Defense." 9 *Koinonia* (1997): 81–113.

Miller, Ed. *Questions That Matter.* 3rd Ed. New York: McGraw-Hill, 1992.

Nash, Ronald. *The Concept of God.* Grand Rapids: Zondervan Publishing House, 1983.

_____. *Faith & Reason.* Grand Rapids: Zondervan Publishing House, 1988.

Newport, John. "Life's Ultimate Questions." Dallas: Word Publishing. 1989.

O'Connell, Robert J. *Images of Conversion in St. Augustine's Confessions.* New York: Fordham University Press, 1996.

O'Connor, David. *God and Inscrutable Evil.* New York: Rowman & Littlefield Publishers, 1998.

_____. "Hasker on Gratuitous Evil." *Faith and Philosophy* 12 (Jul 1995): 380–92.

_____. "Swinburne on Natural Evil From Natural Processes." *International Journal for Philosophy of Religion* 30 (1991): 77–87.

Patterson, Ronald W. K. "Evil, Omniscience and Omnipotence." *Religious Studies* 15 (Mr 1979): 1–23.

Pelikan, Jaroslav. *The Christian Tradition.* Vol. 1 *The Emergence of the Catholic Tradition (100–600).* Chicago: University of Chicago Press, 1975.

Peterson, Michael. *Evil and the Christian God.* Grand Rapids: Baker Book House, 1982

_____. *God and Evil.* Boulder, CO: Westview Press, 1998.

_____. "God and Evil: Problems of Consistency and Gratuity." *Journal of Value Inquiry* 13 (1979): 305–13.

_____. ed. *The Problem of Evil.* Notre Dame: University of Notre Dame Press, 1992.

Peterson, Michael, William Hasker, Bruce Reichenbach, and David Basinger, eds. *Philosophy of Religion.* New York: Oxford University Press, 1996.

Peterson, Michael and others. eds. *Reason and Religious Belief.* 2nd ed. New York: Oxford Press, 1998.

Pike, Nelson. "Divine Omniscience and Voluntary Action." In *Contemporary Philosophy of Religion.* Edited by Steven M. Cahn and David Shatz New York: Oxford University Press, 1982.

_____. "Hume on Evil." In *The Problem of Evil.* Edited by Marilyn McCord Adams and Robert Merrihew Adams. New York: Oxford University Press, 1990.

Pinnock, Clark, Richard Rice, John Sanders, William Hasker, and Davie Basinger, eds. *The Openness of God.* Downers Grove: InterVarsity Press, 1994.

Plantinga, Alvin. *God, Freedom and Evil.* Reprint. Grand Rapids: William B. Eerdmans Publishing Company, 1996.

____. *God and Other Minds.* Ithaca: NY: Cornell University Press, 1990.

____. "The Free Will Defense." In *Philosophy of Religion.* Edited by Melville Y. Stewart. Sudbury, MA: Jones and Bartlett Publishers, 1996.

____. "God, Evil, and the Metaphysics of Evil." In *The Problem of Evil.* Edited by Marilyn McCord Adams and Robert Merrihew Adams. New York: Oxford University Press, 1990.

Plantinga, Cornelius, Jr. *Not The Way It's Suppose to Be.* Grand Rapids: William B. Eerdmans Publishing Company, 1995.

Purtill, Richard L. "Flew and the Free Will Defence." *Religious Studies* 13 (Dec 1977): 477–83.

Quinn, Philip L. "Philosophy of Religion." In *The Cambridge Dictionary of Philosophy,* 1995.

Reichenbach, Bruce. *Evil and A Good God.* New York: Fordham University Press, 1982.

Rescher, Nicholas. "Logical Difficulties in Leibniz's Metaphysics." In *The Philosophy of Leibniz and the Modern World.* Edited by Ivor Leclerc. Nashville: Vanderbilt University Press, 1973.

____. *The Philosophy of Leibniz.* Englewood Cliffs, NJ: Prentice-Hall, 1967.

Richman, Robert. "The Argument from Evil." *Religious Studies* 4 (1969): 203–211.

Runzo, Joseph. "Omniscience and Freedom for Evil." *International Journal for Philosophy of Religion* 12 (1981): 131–48.

Russell, Bertrand. *A Critical Exposition of the Philosophy of Leibniz.* London: George Allen & Unwin, 1967.

Russell, Bruce. "Defenseless." In *The Evidential Argument from Evil.* Edited by Daniel Howard-Snyder. Bloomington: Indiana University Press, 1996.

____. "The Persistence Problem of Evil." *Faith and Philosophy* 10 (1993): 121–39.

Rowe, William. "The Evidential Argument from Evil: A Second Look." In *The Evidential Argument from Evil.* Edited by Daniel Howard-Snyder. Bloomington: Indiana University Press, 1996.

____. "Evil and the Theistic Hypothesis: A Response to Wykstra." In *The Problem of Evil.* Edited by Marilyn McCord Adams and Robert Merrihew Adams. New York: Oxford University Press, 1990.

_____. "The Problem of Evil and Some Varieties of Atheism." In *The Evidential Argument from Evil*. Edited by Daniel Howard-Snyder. Bloomington: Indiana University Press, 1996.

Schilling, S. Paul. "Evil and Freedom Revisited." *Quarterly Review* 11 (Winter 1991): 4–17.

Schlesinger, George. *Religion and Scientific Method*. Dordrecht-Holland: D. Reidel Publishing Company, 1982.

Schrader, David E. "Evil and the Best of Possible Worlds." *Sophia* 27 (Jul 1988): 24–37.

Schwarz, Hans. *Evil: A Historical and Theological Perspective*. Translated by Mark Worthing, Minneapolis: Fortress Press, 1995.

Sontag, Frederick. "Critique." In *Encountering Evil*. Edited by Stephen T. Davis. Atlanta: John Knox Press, 1981.

Surin, Kenneth. *Theology and the Problem of Evil*. New York: Basil Blackwell, 1986.

_____. "The Impassibility of God and the Problem of Evil." *The Scottish Journal of Theology* 35 (1982): 97–115.

_____. "Problem of Evil." In *The Blackwell Encyclopedia of Modern Christian Thought*, 1993.

Stump, Eleonore. "Aquinas on the Suffering of Job." In *The Evidential Argument from Evil*. Edited by Daniel Howard-Snyder. Bloomington: Indiana University Press, 1996.

_____."Biblical Commentary and Philosophy." In *The Cambridge Companion to Aquinas*. Edited by Norman Kretzmann and Eleonore Stump. Cambridge: Cambridge University Press, 1993.

_____. "Knowledge, Freedom, and the Problem of Evil." In *The Problem of Evil*. Edited by Michael Peterson. Notre Dame: University of Notre Dame Pres, 1992.

_____. "The Problem of Evil." *Faith and Philosophy* 2 (Oct 1985): 392–423.

Swinburne, Richard. *The Coherence of Theism*. Oxford: Clarendon Press, 1977.

_____. *The Existence of God*. Revised ed. Oxford: Clarendon Press, 1991.

_____. *Providence and the Problem of Evil*. Oxford: Clarendon Press, 1998.

_____. *Responsibility and Atonement*. Oxford: Clarendon Press. 1989.

_____. "Some Major Strands of Theodicy." In *The Evidential Argument from Evil*. Edited by Daniel Howard-Snyder. Bloomington: Indiana University Press, 1996.

Tomberlin, James and Frank McGuiness. "God, Evil, and the Free Will Defence." *Religious Studies* 13 (Dec 1977): 455–75.

Trau, Jane Mary. "Fallacies in the Argument from Gratuitous Suffering." *The New Scholasticism* 60 (Aut 1986): 485–89.

_____. "The Positive Value of Evil." *Philosophy of Religion* 24 (1988): 21–33.

Van Inwagen. "The Problem of Evil, the Problem of Air, and the Problem of Silence." In *The Evidential Argument from Evil*. Edited by Daniel Howard-Snyder. Bloomington: Indiana University Press, 1996.

Walls, Jerry. "Will God Change His Mind? Eternal Hell and the Ninevites." In *Through No Fault of Their Own*? Edited by William V. Crockett and James G. Sigountos. Grand Rapids: Baker Book House, 1991.

Wetzel, James. "Can Theodicy Be Avoided? The Claim of Unredeemed Evil." *Religious Studies* 25 (Mr 1989):121–39.

Whitney, Barry. *What Are They Saying About God and Evil?* New York: Paulist Press, 1989.

_____. *Theodicy: An Annotated Bibliography on the Problem of Evil.* Bowling Green, OH: Bowling Green State University Philosophy, Documentation Center, 1998.

Wykstra, Stephen J. "The Humean Obstacle to Evidential Arguments from Suffering: On Avoiding the Evils of 'Appearance'." In *The Problem of Evil*. Edited by Marilyn McCord Adams and Robert Merrihew Adams. New York: Oxford University Press, 1990.

_____. "Rowe's Noseeum Arguments from Evil." In *The Evidential Argument from Evil*. Edited by Daniel Howard-Snyder. Bloomington: Indiana University Press, 1996.

Yandell, Keith. "Gratuitous Evil and Divine Existence." *Religious Studies* 25 (Mr 1989): 15–30.

Vanderjagt, A. J. ed., *Brill's Studies in Intellectual History*. Vol. 7. *The Problem of Divine Foreknowledge and Future Contingents From Aristotle to Suartez*, by William Lane Craig. Leiden: E. J. Brill, 1988.

Zacharias, Ravi. *Cries of the Heart*. Nashville: Word Publishing, 1998.

# Index

# About the Author

Bruce A. Little has a Ph.D. from Southeastern Baptist Theological Seminary where he is associate professor of Philosophy of Religion. Prior to teaching at Southeastern, he served as pastor to congregations in New England, Pennsylvania and North Carolina. For the past nine years, he has lectured on various topics from a Christian worldview perspective at universities in Ukraine. In addition, he has authored several books with professors from the Tavricheskiy National University in Simferopol, Ukraine, the latest is titled, *The Importance of Religious Values for Cultural Development.* A native of New England, he now lives in Wake Forest, North Carolina with his wife Nancy.